Amusement Parks, Movies,
and American Modernity

ELECTRIC DREAMLAND

LAUREN RABINOVITZ

COLUMBIA UNIVERSITY PRESS NEW YORK

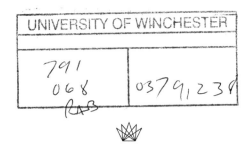

COLUMBIA UNIVERSITY PRESS
PUBLISHERS SINCE 1893
NEW YORK   CHICHESTER, WEST SUSSEX

cup.columbia.edu

Cover design by Julia Kushnirsky

Library of Congress Cataloging-in-Publication Data
Rabinovitz, Lauren, 1950–
Electric dreamland : amusement parks, movies, and American modernity / Lauren Rabinovitz.
p. cm. — (Film and culture)
Includes bibliographical references and index.
ISBN 978-0-231-15660-8 (cloth : alk. paper) — ISBN 978-0-231-15661-5 (pbk. : alk. paper) —
ISBN 978-0-231-52721-7 (ebook)
1. Amusement parks—United States—History—20th century. 2. Motion pictures—Social aspects—
United States—History—20th century. 3. United States—Social life and customs—20th century.
I. Title.
GV1853.2.R34   2012
791.06'8730904—dc23   2012011284

References to Internet Web sites (URLs) were accurate at the time of writing.
Neither the author nor Columbia University Press is responsible for URLs
that may have expired or changed since the manuscript was prepared.

In memory of my sister, Jill Santivasi . . .
my childhood companion at amusement parks and movies

With love to Greg Easley . . .
my partner in amusement parks, movies, and life

CONTENTS

LIST OF ILLUSTRATIONS

ACKNOWLEDGMENTS

ALTHOUGH THE FOUNDATION FOR THIS BOOK WAS LAID IN MY previous book, the shape of this story did not take hold until I began to do research in the late 1990s for a digital humanities project on turn-of-the-century amusement parks. The ideas for that project originated in a cross-country drive with my partner, Greg Easley. But the means to expand those ideas came from a National Endowment for the Humanities Educational Development Grant. The University of Iowa provided additional funding on numerous occasions, including the University of Iowa Faculty Scholar Award, the May Brodbeck Humanities Fellowship, and the College of Liberal Arts and Sciences Collegiate Fellow Award. At the University of Iowa I have received advice, support, and important feedback from both colleagues and students. Deans Linda Maxson and Raul Curto were especially helpful. I am also indebted to colleagues in the Departments of American Studies and Cinema and Comparative Literature: Bluford Adams, Rick Altman, Paula Amad, Susan Birrell, the late Ken Cmiel, Corey Creekmur, Kim Marra, Kathleen Newman, Horace Porter, John Raeburn, Laura Rigal, Harry Stecopoulos, Deborah Whaley, and Nick Yablon. I received encouragement from two research centers at the university, the Obermann Center for Advanced Studies and the Project on the Rhetoric of Inquiry. Over the decade in which I researched this book, I was aided by a number of research assistants, especially Sarah Toton and Abe Geil.

As the various chapters took shape, I benefited from insights and feedback from several peers. Sharon Wood pointed me toward the papers of Nan Aspinwall Gable at the University of Nebraska State Historical Society. Dick Abel and Jennifer Bean shared ideas and feedback over a period of years and offered continuous support; Jennifer also accompanied me to the Boardwalk Amusement Park in Santa Cruz. Shelley Stamp and Charlie Keil edited an earlier version of chapter 5. Alison Griffiths, Paula Amad, Peter Bloom, and especially Jeff Ruoff were my conversation partners in a seminar that helped to frame chapter 3. As I revised and crafted the final manuscript, JoAnn Castagna provided daily feedback that helped inspire and encourage me in the project's completion.

At Columbia University Press Jennifer Crewe and Anastasia Graf helped to shepherd this book through its final stages, and series editor John Belton championed my scholarship when I most needed his support.

I owe even more to those amusement park aficionados and collectors outside the academy for sharing with me their postcard collections and knowledge about early amusement parks: thanks to Rick Davis, John Bowker, and Ralph Decker. I am especially grateful to Jim Futrell, who generously gave me his time, allowed me complete access to his private collection, and arranged an out-of-season tour for me at Kennywood Amusement Park.

I originally tried out portions of this book at various scholarly conferences, and portions of chapters 2, 3, and 4 first appeared in draft form in my essays "'Bells and Whistles': The Sound of Meaning in Train Travel Film Rides," in *The Sounds of Early Cinema*, ed. Richard Abel and Rick Altman (Bloomington: Indiana University Press, 2001), 167–182; "More Than the Movies: A History of Somatic Visual Culture Through Hale's Tours, IMAX, and Motion Simulation Rides," in *Memory Bytes: History, Technology, and Digital Culture*, ed. Lauren Rabinovitz and Abraham Geil (Durham, NC: Duke University Press, 2004), 99–125; and "The Coney Island Comedies: Bodies and Slapstick at the Amusement Park and the Movies," in *American Cinema's Transitional Era: Audiences, Institutions, Practices*, ed. Charlie Keil and Shelley Stamp (Berkeley: University of California Press, 2004), 171–190.

While authors frequently cite their families for being supportive, I am very thankful to my family for serving double duty on this endeavor. Not only did they support me, listen to my ideas, and give me the time and space I needed to complete the book, but they were often pressed into accompanying me to various amusement parks. My mother, Jeanette Rabinovitz, continuously supported my research goals. Mara, Tyler, and John Santivasi accompanied me to old and new amusement parks in Colorado, California, and Minnesota. (So I didn't have to twist their arms to ride the rides with me.) They were always affable, even when I sometimes pressed them into repeat trips on the same rides and amusements or when I took notes in the middle of an amusement park.

On that score Greg Easley contributed more to this book than anyone else. From the outset he listened to my ideas, suffered through my regular analyses—often while we were in the middle of a thrill ride or a movie—and helped me to sharpen many claims. The exigencies of this book's preparation took me from Iowa to Florida, California, Colorado, Georgia, Washington, D.C., Nebraska, Nevada, New York, Pennsylvania, Minnesota, and even to London, and Greg was with me through most of these travels. He rode motion-simulation rides with me in California, Las Vegas, Minneapolis, and Orlando as I tried to understand the "thrill" of *Hale's Tours and Scenes of the World*, experienced the "London Eye" Ferris Wheel and panoramas at the Victoria and Albert Museum and Gettysburg National Military Park with me as I tried to reconnect to experiences of turn-of-the-century entertainment, and partnered with me on countless other roller coasters, carousels, and antique dark rides. We traveled together to historic period amusement parks (including Lakeside in Denver, the Boardwalk in Santa Cruz, and Arnold's Park in Lake Okoboji, Iowa), and he was my most reliable sounding board during my archival endeavors. For these journeys, and for everything else, I am grateful.

ELECTRIC DREAMLAND

Introduction

ARTIFICIAL DISTRACTIONS

What more ludicrous and what more sad than the spectacle of vast hordes of people rushing to the oceanside, to escape the city's din and crowds and nervous strain, and, once within sight and sound of the waves, courting worse din, denser crowds, and an infinitely more devastating nervous strain inside an enclosure whence the ocean cannot possibly be seen? Is it thus they seek rest, by a madly exaggerated homeopathy? Is it thus they cure Babylon, not with more Babylon, but with Babel gone daft?

—Rollin Lynde Hartt, Congregationalist minister, 1907

The urban worker escapes the mechanical routine of his daily job only to find an equally mechanical substitute for life and growth and experience in his amusements. . . . The movies, the White Ways, and the Coney Islands, which almost every American city boasts in some form or other, are means of giving jaded and throttled people the sensations of living without the direct experience of life—a sort of spiritual masturbation.

—Lewis Mumford, "The City," 1922

AT THE TURN OF THE LAST CENTURY, AMERICA GOT SERIOUS about amusement. Nightclubs, restaurants, vaudeville, melodrama theaters, dime museums, penny arcades, and all kinds of commercial entertainments flourished: "artificial distraction for an artificial life," lamented the minister Rollin Lynde Hartt about these new amusements taking over cities and towns.[1] In his consternation about a new public culture dedicated to the consumption of enjoyment rather than moral and aesthetic uplift, this social critic flags the start of what is today considered popular culture. Among the litany of amusements that preoccupied both the public and the preacher, two stand out for the novelty of their technological bases as well as for the attention—both welcome and unwelcome—that they attracted: the amusement park and motion pictures.[2] Amusement parks and movies appeared simultaneously—between 1894 and 1896—and succeeded rapidly, often in relationship to each other. Over the subsequent fifteen years they separately and together became wildly popular across the country.

More than other types of available contemporary commercial leisure, amusement parks and movies represented new kinds of energized relaxation that also functioned to calm fears about new technologies and living conditions of an industrialized society. Together, they helped to define a modern national collective identity regardless of where their subjects actually lived in the United States or who they were. During an era in which there were numerous efforts to define a sense of national belonging through popular or vernacular expressions and rituals (e.g., Fourth of July parades, "The Pledge of Allegiance" adopted in 1893), amusement parks and movies combined industrialized experiences with a sense of a new national corporate culture steeped in manufacturing. They represented uniquely *modern mechanized* responses to turn-of-the-century American culture. More than burlesque, cheap theater, or dance halls, amusement parks and movies taught Americans to revel in a modern sensibility that was about adapting to new technologies, to hyperstimulation analogous to the nervous energies of industrial cities, to mechanical rhythms and uniformity, and to this perceptual condition as itself American.

THE RISE OF AMUSEMENT PARKS
AND MOTION PICTURES

After the 1893 Chicago World's Columbian Exposition's midway demonstrated the popularity of an entertainment zone couched in exotic foreign shows and the technological utopianism of its massive Ferris wheel, entrepreneurial showmen tried to mimic the midway's style and success. Chutes Park—organized around a mechanized toboggan waterslide—opened one block away (at 61st Street and Drexel Boulevard) from the exposition grounds almost as soon as the world's fair closed. It was a short-lived attempt to capitalize on the success of the fair's midway by making amusement a continuous affair. Famed showman Paul Boynton, the owner of Chutes, left Chicago after only one season to open a second water and animal park at Brooklyn's Coney Island, a district that had housed everything from luxury hotels and ballrooms to gambling dens, a racetrack, and saloons. Two years later, George Tilyou opened another enclosed park charging admission—Steeplechase Park—next door to Boynton's Sea Lion Park. In 1903 Boynton sold Sea Lion Park to Frederic Thompson and Elmer "Skip" Dundy, and they reopened it as Luna Park (fig. 1.1), a full-scale amusement park featuring fanciful architecture, mechanical rides, shows, animals, and restaurants. In its first season Luna Park achieved forty-five thousand admissions in a single day.[3] One year later, a third park styled after Luna (Dreamland) opened to equal success. By 1909 the combined daily attendance of Coney Island's three parks reached half a million, and these parks served as models for amusement parks opening across the nation.[4]

Around the country existing parks metamorphosed from picnic grounds, gardens, and zoos to enclosed amusement parks that mimicked Coney Island's new parks. From New England to the Rocky Mountains to the Pacific Coast, parks added mechanical attractions, live theater, moving pictures, and pyrotechnical displays. For example, Lake Compounce in Bristol, Connecticut, had a long history as a picnic grounds. In 1895 it began adding attractions, and by 1911 it was a full-fledged amusement park. Palisades Park in Fort Lee, New Jersey, started as a bucolic nature preserve in 1898 but began to compete with Coney Island in 1907. Even in the country's heartland, Riverside Park in Hutchinson, Kansas, had housed a zoo since 1888 but in 1902 became an amusement park. Denver's Elitch Pleasure Gardens began as a zoological garden in 1890 and, over the next twenty years, added numerous mechanical rides, as well as a pyrotechnical show and motion pictures. As far away from Coney Island as the regionally isolated copper mining town of Butte, Montana, Columbia Gardens—which had been a children's playground and garden since 1899—added a zoo, mechanical rides, a dance pavilion, and motion pictures as soon as amusement parks and movies established themselves as popular entertainments. In California the seaside resorts of Ocean Park (Santa Monica) and the Boardwalk (Santa Cruz) both added mechanical attractions early in the century.

Where there were no such parks, new ones were built. Chicago added five amusement parks to compete with Chutes, and by the time that Chutes

went out of business in 1907, half a million people, roughly one quarter of Chicago's citizens, visited the area's amusement parks on an average summer weekend in 1908.[5] In other midwestern industrial cities like Columbus, Ohio, Oletangy Park boasted a regular Sunday attendance of a quarter of its population.[6] Booming railroad towns like El Paso, Texas, could count on half of the town at their amusement parks on a summer holiday.[7]

Amusement parks were especially plentiful and popular in outlying suburbs of fast-growing industrial cities, where attendance on a special holiday could reach as high as 70 percent of the metropolitan population.[8] As the El Paso example demonstrates, these parks were not just restricted to the Northeast and Midwest industrial belts. Electrified amusement parks sprang up in all regions of the country. By 1912 there were as many as two thousand amusement parks nationwide.[9] Americans flocked to them for mechanical rides, electrical illuminations, live entertainment, crowd experiences, and recreation.

Electric amusement parks were not the only new carnivals of noise, light, and motion sweeping the nation. Movies "began" in the United States on April 23, 1896, when they were shown in Koster and Bial's Music Hall in New

York City. (The first actual public screening of motion pictures occurred in Paris in December of 1895.) More than twenty-five U.S. cities introduced motion pictures in the summer of 1896. (Summer was a good time to introduce movies because so many vaudeville acts went on vacation, and so many theaters closed completely during the heat.) Cinema's growth depended on the development of the equipment necessary to make and show movies. It owed an equally important debt to magic lantern shows, illustrated lectures, stereopticons, kinetoscopes, panoramas, and other commercial entertainment that all set the stage for movies, their topics and stories, and the ways they depicted subjects in motion.[10] As one Chicago newspaper reviewer said in 1896, "[Moving pictures are] a combination of *electrical forces* reproducing scenes from life with a distinctiveness and accuracy of detail that is almost startling, bringing out on the canvas screen on the stage not only the outlines but the details of color, motion, changeable expression."[11] At their outset movies represented themselves as both by-products and conveyors of electrification that employed a variety of projection machines—biographs, kinodromes, vitascopes. Like amusement parks, they represented new technologically driven arenas for the consumption of pleasure in a modern industrial age.

In many parts of the country the first motion pictures appeared as parts of shows run by itinerant lecturers and camera operators who traveled from town to town.[12] Some showmen used a combination camera-printer-projector to film local scenes and people, develop and print the results, and project the movie to the town's residents the next night.[13] Thus, early cinema was always a combination of mass-reproduced culture (certain images) and unique local events (special material, accompanying lectures, and the exhibitor's own arrangement and presentation of the show).

In 1898 the novelty began to wear off. Movies might have become a passing fad were it not for the Spanish-American War. U.S. intervention in Cuba and the Philippines provided new subjects that played to sold-out cheering, whistling, handkerchief-waving audiences. These shows combined views of actual American battleships and troops (*Soldiers at Play*, [Selig Polyscope Company, 1898]), reenactments of naval battles (*The Battle of Manila Bay* [Vitagraph, 1898]), and patriotic scenes of flag waving, the U.S. cavalry, or Uncle Sam (*Raising Old Glory over Morro Castle* [Edison, 1899]).[14] Charles Musser suggests their key role in consolidating nationalist identity in a new imperial era: "Much has been written about the yellow journalism and jingoistic press of Hearst and Pulitzer, but cinema complemented these efforts in a way that made them much more powerful and effective. Moving pictures projected a sense of national glory and outrage. . . . Cinema had found a role beyond narrow amusement, and this sudden prominence coincided with a new era of overseas expansion and military intervention."[15] These movies proved they were a new cultural force in their combination of journalism and patriotism.

Moving pictures flourished in vaudeville houses (located in commercial strips, as well as in amusement parks), and the films themselves began the transition from documentary subjects to more story-oriented films. The earliest movies were often scenes from everyday life (*actualités*) that made it possible for producers to keep up a steady supply of fresh subjects since a portable camera could film any view anywhere. Among early popular subjects were trick films (movies that included "magic tricks" created by stop motion or superimposition techniques), theatrical acts, play excerpts, vaudeville and stage stars, comically acted jokes, scenes from the male world of prizefighting or bodybuilding, and girls performing risqué dances.[16]

Then, in 1905—separate from motion pictures playing as "acts" in vaudeville houses—small storefront theaters began to show programs of movies. It is a commonplace that Harry Davis's *Nickelodeon*, which opened in Pittsburgh in June 1905, gave rise to the spread of such storefront theaters and also inspired the term *nickelodeon* for venues that charged a nickel or a dime for continuous programs of movies, illustrated songs, and live acts.[17] Many nickelodeons made audience participation and crowd conviviality part of "the show" through added sing-alongs and amateur shows. Indeed, the live entertainment at many nickelodeons played specifically to local immigrant audiences and often provided opportunities for local amateurs to sing or dance for small sums of money.[18] Film scholar Miriam Hansen explains, "The cinema . . . provided a space apart and a space in between. It was a site for the imaginative negotiation of the gaps between family, school, and workplace, between traditional standards of sexual behavior and modern dreams of romance and sexual expression, between freedom and anxiety."[19] With cheap prices, easy accessibility on commercial strips or at amusement parks, and continuous schedules that allowed passersby to drop in throughout the day and evening, small theaters flourished.[20]

By the end of 1906 the number of nickel theaters had climbed from a dozen or so in a few cities like New York, Philadelphia, Chicago, and Pittsburgh to hundreds. Chicago had more than 300 theaters by 1908 and 407 by 1909.[21] By 1908 Manhattan had somewhere between three hundred and four hundred.[22] In the vicinity of Brooklyn's Coney Island alone, since nickelodeons became a regular feature both inside and adjacent to amusement parks, there were somewhere between one hundred and three hundred nickel theaters. Even smaller cities like Indianapolis (twenty-one nickelodeons) or Grand Rapids, Michigan (fifteen nickelodeons), still boasted rapid growth and numerous cheap movie theaters to serve their populations.[23] Conservative estimates say there were five thousand nickelodeons nationally while others have estimated the figure upward to ten thousand.[24] By 1908 at least fourteen million people weekly watched movies at nickelodeons.[25]

Nickel theaters were typically plain, long dark rooms (fig. 1.2). Interiors were undecorated boxes with only a muslin screen at one end of the room or a cloth behind a small stage. A piano and drum set might be below the screen and off to the side for musical and sound effects accompaniment. Rows of wooden or camp chairs seated two hundred to as many as five hundred, depending on the theater.[26] Visitors and journalists alike, however, frequently reported on crowds standing (illegally) in the aisles and back of the room throughout the program. Because city authorities were concerned about both fire and public health safety, they often regulated not only the number of patrons in a small space but also the number of exits. They also often required some lighting, fans, and separated lead-lined projection booths to avoid fire spreading should the highly flammable nitrate film stock explode.

The exterior of the theater might be as simple as an unadorned storefront with the theater's name printed in block letters or as fancy as electrical illumination allowed. Typically, a ticket-seller booth sat adjacent to the front or side of the entrance, and posters advertising the program might be pasted onto the front walls or on sidewalk billboards. Most theaters employed "barkers" to cajole potential passersby while gramophones or phonographs blared out popular music to attract attention.

The movies made it possible for immigrants and migrants, as well as rural and urban Americans conscious of their rapidly changing society, to participate in shows that were both a national ritual of performance and singular, one-time events. Hansen likens the experience to the "short-term and excessive stimulation" already newly available in the emergent consumer culture—from advertising and department store window displays to "consumption-oriented spectacles—from the World Fairs and Pan American Expositions, through the Panoramas and Dioramas, to amusement parks like Coney Island."[27] The "show" may have been variable with each

1.2. NICKELODEON INTERIOR, UNKNOWN LOCATION, C. 1906. PHOTOGRAPH. AUTHOR'S PRIVATE COLLECTION. ⓢ

performance and immediate in its perceptual insistence on the here and now. But the contours of the program were repeated in more or less the same fashion everywhere and were governed by the participants' knowledge that they were seeing the same images as moviegoers in Chicago, Sioux City, New York City, or New Orleans.

THE ROLE OF THE RAILROADS

By 1910 *every* municipality with a population of more than twenty thousand had both amusement parks and motion picture theaters. Industrial towns whose populations were between ten thousand and twenty thousand also tended to have nickelodeons and at least one amusement park.[28] These electric parks were so plentiful that a *Billboard* magazine reporter apologized for Pittsburgh in 1909: "We regret that we are, possibly the only city in the country of any consequence, that will go through the coming summer season with only three amusement parks."[29] Even towns with fewer than ten thousand people had nickelodeons and an amusement park so long as they had an interurban railroad or trolley line. If a town had a railroad line, the line was likely to terminate at an amusement park.

The rise of amusement parks may be directly attributed to the scores of new traction companies, or privately owned electric streetcar and interurban railroads, that constructed these amusement parks at the end of their routes near their train sheds and turnarounds. David E. Nye even labeled the new parks "appendages" of the streetcar lines.[30] (Like all the other amusement parks around the country, Coney Island's Dreamland, Luna, and Steeplechase depended on cheap rail transportation for their successes.) By 1911, 75 percent of all parks were owned or controlled by the rail companies whose passenger cars traveled to them.[31] The rail or traction companies already had electric service and plenty of cheap land at their barns located on the outskirts of towns. Now they only needed to "break even" on park revenues so long as the parks promoted train ridership, especially during those hours when people were not filling the cars to go to and from work. In many cases, like Youngstown's Idora Park, the trolley line that ran to and from an amusement park became the most profitable route for the local traction company.[32]

While most working-class urban dwellers did not need to depend on rail transportation for access to the numerous neighborhood nickelodeons available within walking distance of work and home, they practiced a split type of leisure mobility that was unique to the larger cities. As Michael Aronson notes in describing Pittsburgh's industrial workers and the affordable commercial entertainment that they enjoyed, workers could either take a ten-cent trolley ride to an amusement park on the outskirts of town or walk to a nearby motion picture theater where admission was a nickel or a dime.[33] But their experience is not entirely characteristic of the nationwide relationships among motion pictures, amusement parks, and railroads.

For one thing, rural and small town citizens were more likely to see movies at venues (including amusement parks) accessible only by railway. In many instances, from Philadelphia to Waterloo, Iowa, it was even an amusement park's nickelodeon that was the first motion picture theater in the community, thus drawing the movie theater itself into destination railway travel. In Wilmington, North Carolina, for example, the Wrightsville Beach ocean-side hotel casino (owned by the trolley company) regularly began to show movies in 1903, using the motion pictures themselves as a lure for the nine-mile trolley ride from the city.[34] It is important to recognize that, despite the fact that big city nickelodeons were not necessarily railway destinations, motion picture theaters in other parts of the country required that their patrons, like those who attended amusement parks, maintained a purpose of serving the traction company.

In addition to carrying patrons to leisure-time amusements, the regional rail networks served another underlying function for transforming entertainment as well as market economics in this period. Robert Rydell and Rob Kroes put it succinctly: "The transcontinental railroad became the central node in a complex communication network that facilitated the expansion and export of American business and American mass culture industries."[35] They demonstrate how circuses, theater companies, and wild west shows made use of the new form of transportation. In other words the rail networks not only brought audiences to site-specific entertainment but also conveyed various types of entertainment to regional and outlying audiences, thus creating a national mass culture across regional lines. David Mayer has argued for how these rail networks provided the nerve system for traveling theatrical companies that carried sensational, affordable melodramas and variety shows to opera houses across the country: "Because of the transportation network of railroad companies, the principal theatrical economy was widely dispersed, away from New York and, to some degree, from East Coast metropolises. The overall reception and consequent earnings of a drama—and, indeed, the physical conformation of many popular pieces—were strongly determined by considerations of the road."[36] Some of these theatrical companies—as well as wild west show and circus performers—indeed traveled to venues at many amusement parks. It was no longer necessary to live in well-established, large metropolitan areas to enjoy the same commercial entertainments that were available in those cities since the entertainment itself traveled all across the country.

While the definition of these shows as itinerant or traveling types of amusement differentiated them from amusement parks or motion picture theaters themselves as importantly fixed, they had a basic political economy similar to movies and amusement parks. (Movies may have begun often enough as the product of an itinerant showman or traveling cameraman-exhibitor or lecturer, but they soon assumed a regularized structure as the products of theaters whose primary purpose was film exhibition.) Nickelodeons could thrive in medium-sized cities, small towns, and suburban pleasure resorts only because the rails provided easy access to the product they needed. Movie exchanges in major cities acted as wholesalers and twice weekly supplied the theaters with new movies via regional railroad deliveries. Richard Abel's study of early cinema in three different regions—eastern Massachusetts and Rhode Island, northern Ohio, and the upper Midwest—shows that movies could help to "Americanize" Americans across different regional, ethnic, and class lines when there were regional rail networks to carry movies to stops along those routes.[37]

So, the overall picture of American commercial amusement in this period intertwines many of its forms while being grounded in a dependency on the railroads. The rails allowed entertainment to flow *to* the hinterlands as well as the hinterland people to flow to the market cities and towns that organized their regions. The railroads carried people from whistle-stops along the routes to nearby industrial cities, farm towns, and booming suburbs that housed both nickelodeons and amusement parks. Audiences themselves now traveled for their entertainment, and the new trolley or electric park was a bellwether of this transformation. The rail services that carried workers to their industrial employment and provided cars for transporting farmers' goods also enabled laborers to travel cheaply and regularly to recreation destinations. (Thus, this study excludes from its focus those commercial itinerant modes like traveling carnivals, wild west shows, circuses, and combination theater companies.)[38] Despite a scholarly tradition that regards both nickelodeons and amusement parks as big-city phenomena, these fixed sites for entertainment or "artificial distractions" belong to both cities and the hinterland because they bridged the distance between the two and helped to transform Americans across regional, class, and racial lines into mobile tourists with new tourist sensibilities.

Of course, being a railroad passenger encouraged new ways of seeing and relationships to the world at large. Viewing the passing landscape as a passenger removed from tactile, contemplative immersion remade spectator experiences into a new set of detached subject-object relationships to the world-at-large as spectacle.[39] Both cinema and amusement parks were steeped in this sensorial reorientation, extended it from the railway journey to their structural organization, and made it the subject of their pleasures and thrills, a complex phenomenon that is unraveled across the chapters of this book. What is important at the outset, though, is the recognition that this new experience cannot be equated with urban industrial life alone. Amusement parks and movie theaters, in fact, brought urban modernity as a new perceptual experience to the population across the country.

THE MODERNITY ISSUE

Modernity itself has assumed many meanings in many different contexts. While it generally denotes "the modern era," the term can mean a range of historical time frames. Often, it has indicated the entirety of Western civilization from the Enlightenment to the present. More specifically, scholars have also used the term to describe a historical period in Western Europe and the United States in the late nineteenth and early twentieth centuries that gave rise to societies organized around industrialization, urbanization, and mass communication and transportation. In this regard modernity may also mean the conditions that resulted from the Second Industrial Revolution and the specific economic, political, and social applications of attendant new technologies. Tom Gunning explains: "[Modernity] was also, however, equally characterized by the transformation in daily life wrought by the growth of capitalism and advances in technology: the growth of urban traffic, the distribution of mass-produced goods, and successive new technologies of transportation and communication."[40] In this application modernity is not so much a historical period but a change in experience.

The thrust of industrialized modernity, therefore, is an argument for how labor and production associated with manufacturing, transporting, and selling goods of all kinds moved from the self-enclosed system of the "agrarian farm" to the factory and store, thus turning men and women into wage laborers and women into consumers for their families' needs. The household became transformed into a site of consumption rather than of production, and labor itself became a process measured in hours and minutes rather than by the results of what it produced. Indeed, when laborers weren't "laboring," they were understood to be at leisure. Thus, both cinema and amusement parks were "inventions" of a process of accommodation to this new world marked by the dichotomy of commercialized labor and leisure.[41]

A central component of experiencing modernity occurred as a reaction that has been characterized as a "shock" or jolt. The phrase "shocks of modernity" has become a cliché for describing the perceptual and physical assaults on the entire body that were a condition of life in this new world. The "shocks of modernity" consisted of radical reorientations to speed and distance, as well as to the assaults on one's senses from the noise, congestion, and visual bombardments in the modern city. The phrase's widespread use in cultural discourse originates with German cultural theorist Walter Benjamin describing Baudelaire's modern Paris in the latter half of the nineteenth century.[42] Benjamin drew his inspiration from sociologist Georg Simmel's 1905 work on the anxiety associated with urban crowd experiences. He built on Simmel's concerns about mob psychology and nervous overstimulation in modern city life and extended them to a variety of new spectacles (e.g., expositions, shopping arcades, and movies) for how these new institutions transformed modern social consciousness, modified the organization of mass society, and radically reframed what counts as modern knowledge.[43] Uneasiness about new lived experiences required new reassurances, and movies and amusement parks served their audiences by adjusting them to new features of city life, its modernization, consumerism, and alienation.

Benjamin's assessment of modernist perceptual experience as a "shock" metaphorically adopts a sensation associated with "the feel" of electricity itself, and electrification was perhaps the most prominent feature of modernity in this period. Beginning in the late 1870s, both outdoor and indoor electrical illumination grew. When Thomas Edison built an electrical generating plant in New York City in 1882, he launched the fastest growing industry of the next several decades. Between 1890 and 1910 most major manufacturers converted to electrical power, and more than two hundred American cities got electric trolleys and street lighting.[44] Although only 8 percent of America's wealthier households used electricity in 1907, that figure climbed steadily in urban areas for the first three decades of the twentieth century.[45] Nye summarizes this phenomenon: "Electric lighting dominated public spaces and changed the culture in ways that went far beyond the functional. American cities became the most intensively lighted in the world, not least because of the spread of electric advertising. . . . The illuminated skyline became a source of civic pride. Even small cities aspired to emulate New York City's 'Great White Way.'. . . Nightlife expanded as hundreds of brightly lighted amusement parks emerged as early as the 1890s, followed by stadiums and other outdoor venues."[46]

It wasn't just New York City and Coney Island that spectacularized electrical illumination, although Coney Island's entrance to Luna Park certainly accomplished such an effect (fig. 1.3). Amusement parks across the country, like Kansas City's Electric Park, lit up the nighttime skyline with thousands of electrical bulbs (fig. 1.4). They dramatized the codependency between modern experience and electrical illumination. What is important here, though, for the story of turn-of-the-century modernity is how urban electrical illumination taught urbanites and ruralites alike to love electricity.

URBAN VS. RURAL: ARBITRARY DISTINCTION

The transformation in transportation and urban electrical improvements affected much more than a shifting balance and populace fluctuation between metropolitan centers and rural regions. The efficient, faster,

© 1.3. ENTRANCE TO LUNA AT NIGHT. CONEY ISLAND, N.Y., C. 1907. POSTCARD. AUTHOR'S PRIVATE COLLECTION. ©

routinized distribution of agricultural products to urban consumers and delivery of industrial workers en masse to the factories also sustained a new mobility for consuming recreation and enjoyment. The notion that the industrial urban stood in stark contrast and separation to the rural agrarian is a myth borne of the transformation itself.[47]

In the United States, which continued its vital role as a producer and exporter of raw materials, modernity for many meant mechanizing agricultural production, industrializing food, and the new transportation technologies that made food distribution more efficient, as railways and refrigerated rail cars enabled market towns to grow not just as manufacturing centers but as distribution centers and hubs for their rural regions. Although the 1910 census showed for the first time that more people lived in cities than in rural areas, modernity's effects encompassed new economic and technological relationships for both city and farm. The tentacles of industrial modernity required and reached out to the rural areas that fed the cities. Unlike the European capitals that served as hermeneutic models for Benjamin, the United States enjoyed a different geographic configuration in relationship to the onset of modernity and its shocks.

Night Scene, Electric Park, Kansas City, Mo.

1.4. NIGHT SCENE, ELECTRIC PARK, KANSAS CITY, MO., 1913. POSTCARD. AUTHOR'S PRIVATE COLLECTION.

Even areas still associated with the western frontier—such as Cheyenne, Wyoming, and Boise, Idaho—were important railroad hubs for their regional economies and, as such, became regional entertainment centers as well. Farmers and ranchers were not isolated on their land and in their neighborhoods, dependent on only their immediate neighbors for community and such neighborhood institutions as churches and schools. They increasingly exercised regular contact and communication with the nearby railroad town and with its motion picture theaters and amusement parks.

Scores of newly electrified cities across the country became important regular destinations for the rural populations of their surrounding counties. As one contemporary reporter noted about the Midwest: "Chicago, with its wealth of tributary territory and with its varied systems of excellent transportation . . . quickly bring[s] the ruralite from the real country into that artificial sylvan retreat [the amusement park] so welcome to the city dweller and diverting to the country man."[48] While cities acquired electrical illumination and their households purchased an increasing array of electrical appliances over the next two decades, ruralites learned about electricity and its associations with modernity even more from their travels to town and visits to illuminated amusement parks or movies. As film scholar Lucy Fischer has observed, rural citizens came to the city for entertainment precisely because their homes lagged far behind in electrification, and the nearest city represented opportunity for relishing the electrical modern and overcoming the biggest thing that differentiated them from urbanites.[49] So, while the effects of new congestion, rising immigration, and poverty that were the outcome of the rapid growth of railroad hub cities in all regions fostered a new differentiation between urban and rural, everyone's work and leisure became organized more in relationship to the nearest city. For example, in a state still regarded as predominantly rural, Iowa claimed that only 25.6 percent of its population lived in cities in 1900, although there were at least fourteen cities in the state with populations exceeding ten thousand (Des Moines [sixty-two thousand], Dubuque [thirty-six thousand], Waterloo [thirteen thousand], Sioux City [thirty-three thousand], Council Bluffs [twenty-six thousand], Davenport [thirty-five thousand], Clinton [twenty-three thousand], Burlington [twenty-three thousand], Cedar Rapids [twenty-six thousand], Fort Dodge [twelve thousand], Keokuk [fifteen thousand], Marshalltown [twelve thousand], Muscatine [fourteen thousand], and Ottumwa [eighteen thousand]).[50] These cities are spread out across the state, and each had railway service that served surrounding rural counties. All but three reported amusement parks, and they all had nickelodeons. Thus, Iowans across a substantial portion of the state's geography had access to the new amusements. The Iowa example is but one instance of how turn-of-the-century boom towns and their railroad depots served as hubs for their entire rural neighborhood, a development that occurred in all regions of the United States. As Carolyn de la Peña confirms when describing similar growth in the South, "Many Southerners came to equate proximity to urbanity with success, current or pending; life on the farm could appear retrograde in comparison though in actuality little differentiated the quality of life in city and hinterland."[51]

Putting to rest the notion that there existed a "culture gap" between the urban and rural in this period is important for understanding how cinema and amusement parks accomplished the construction of a national identity in the years immediately preceding World War I. The "city slicker" and "the rube" may have been slang terms frequently used as badges of derision for separating the urbanite and the ruralite, and movies and amusement parks certainly took advantage of these caricatures and the tensions they represent. But, being blinded by them and seeing movies and amusement parks as purely urban phenomena is part of the baggage that obstructs any understanding of how a new national identity was forged.

Both culture historians taking up commercial leisure and film historians have had to contend with scholarly bias for designating urban turn-of-the-century amusements as exclusively the province of urban audiences. So, for example, historian John Kasson hailed Coney Island as a "laboratory for mass culture" for working-class, immigrant audiences from New York City boroughs.[52] His 1978 study is an important landmark for understanding the amusement park's singular role in New York's urban and social history, as well as in the rise of American modernity. But there were many such "laboratories for mass culture" across the country, and one has to be mindful that Coney Island and New York City pose limits as models for national patterns. While historian David Nasaw acknowledges the amusement park phenomenon as a national one, he depends largely on sources about a handful of northeastern parks and on nostalgic volumes about a small number of others in large cities like Cleveland and Chicago.[53] Cinema historians have begun to address this dilemma, and recent debates about how historical emphasis on New York City and Chicago has skewed thinking about movies as a purely urban phenomenon have given rise to new studies about early movie audiences.[54] Gregory Waller's work on Lexington, Kentucky, Kathryn Fuller's examination of small-town rural movie audiences, and Richard Abel's study of movies in regional hubs prove that cinema should not be understood solely as an experience *in* the metropolis.[55]

The concept of "metropolitanism" itself, or defining cinema and amusement parks as inherently like and in relationship to urban experience, is helpful for explaining how they work. But in characterizing both the amusements and their spectators' psychological and perceptual state in this way, one should not reduce the meaning of metropolitanism to a social history of moviegoing and park attendance as themselves inherently restricted to metropolitan areas. As a chronicler of Coney Island claimed, "Coney's new urbanism of Fantastic Technology generates spinoffs all across the U.S.A., even on sites that do not nearly approach a condition of urban density. Outposts of Manhattanism, they serve as advertisements for the metropolitan condition itself. . . . Their effect is stunning: rural Americans who have never been to cities visit the parks. The first high-rise building they ever see is a burning block [the *Fire and Flames* show at the amusement park]."[56]

Rather, metropolitanism helps to explain a process by which ruralites came to participate in and to understand "the metropolitan condition"

without actually living in cities. Indeed, they represent the first generation schooled by the movies to identify with and to know modernity through what today would be labeled virtual participation in it.

AMUSEMENT PLAYGROUNDS: THE SOCIOLOGICAL
SIGNIFICANCE OF SENSATION

An argument for the national spread and dissemination of a mechanical modern experience of movies and amusement parks is also not cause for wiping out all markers of social difference. Indeed, American racism and its intensification in this period, as well as the xenophobia that resulted from the country's new status as a colonizing empire, loom large in the story of both institutions and frame the issues, analyses, and conclusions throughout this book. To borrow and to extend Abel's characterization of the nationalizing effects of movies prior to World War I, the argument herein is about the achievement to "foster a more or less homogeneous *American* mass public . . . [that] serve[s] to reinforce an ethnically and culturally heterogeneous society."[57]

According to many culture critics of the period, the most damning aspect of parks and movies was their function as sites for encouraging reckless behavior, intermingling of classes and ethnic groups, and loosening of sexual propriety (especially among women). Among those who complained publicly, social workers Jane Addams, Louise De Koven Bowen, Sherman Kingsley, and Belle Lindner Israels chided amusement parks and nickelodeons equally for allowing more casual codes of social conduct among "the other half" (immigrants, migrants, working classes, farmers).[58] Addams took to task both motion picture houses and amusement parks: "The whole apparatus for supplying pleasure is wretchedly inadequate and full of danger to whomsoever may approach it."[59] According to Chicago reformer Louise de Koven Bowen, "The boys and men in such crowds often speak to the girls and invite them to see the show and there is an unwritten code that such courtesy shall be paid for later by the girls."[60] Kingsley, another Chicago charity worker, went even further: "More young girls are ruined through acquaintances they form at the small parks than through any other agency."[61] Amusement parks and motion picture theaters relaxed codes of proper conduct among heterogeneous groups, encouraged an independent female sexuality, and thus represented radical affronts to Victorian society.[62]

In writing about a synergistic relationship between amusement parks and motion pictures at the turn of the century, social critics understood that the two shaped each other as a national phenomenon that needed to be regulated in order to maintain the social hierarchy and middle-class standards and values they hoped to preserve. They regularly discussed amusement parks and moving pictures together, sometimes grouping them in with a larger category of amusements that could at different times include dance halls, burlesque, cheap theaters, dime museums, roller skating rinks, and baseball. Rollin Lynde Hartt summed up everything that could be said about the intertwined nature and function of amusement parks and movies: "To be gulled, to know you are gulled, and to know that the people who gull you know you know they're gulling you—ah! the bliss! Here at the park a mimic railway carriage, with biograph pictures at its farther end, takes you spinning along the funicular 'up Mt. Vesuvius'; likewise a make-believe airship transports you to realms beyond the stars. . . . Still subtler mysteries of optics permit your fellow mortals to be innocuously burned alive before your eyes, or turned into skeletons, or waited upon by spooks."[63]

Hartt reinforces a basic key to understanding the phenomenon: movie audiences were also simultaneously parkgoers. In other words the reception of movies may only be understood within the context in which movies were one spectacle among many, and this contextual condition united citizens across regional, class, and racial lines. Thus, while a new technologized intermedial environment allowed for a nationally shared experience, specific interpretations or reactions to the experiences of the amusement park and motion pictures yet depended on social position.

The overarching issue was that movies and amusement parks were a technologically driven playground for audiovisual special effects and virtual realities, and their significance was their sociological impact when they substituted sham spectacle for natural beauty and sensation for aesthetic contemplation. When culture critic Lewis Mumford several years later decried these amusements for providing "the sensations of living without the direct experience of life," he got at the heart of a new widespread cultural phenomenon fundamental to amusement parks and movies as new forms of entertainment at the turn of the last century.

While there had certainly been previous entertainment that asked audiences for empathy and immersion in fantasy, the experiences represented by amusement parks and movies seemingly trumpeted objectives of sheer sensationalism, unreflective mental and physical reaction, and joy in technologically induced "shocks" to the senses. One critic even referred to the proliferation of multimedia events that exhorted such sensationalism and unintellectual audience absorption as *spectatoritis*.[64] Pathologizing audience response into an imaginary malady of being too absorbed or wrapped up by amusement becomes one important means for a cultural elite wishing to preserve social hierarchies to distance itself from a nationwide, increasingly democratic popular culture.

ABOUT THE CHAPTERS

The case for how movies and amusement parks together and separately sold a new modern experience and what that experience meant is organized across four essays. The first two chapters occur "at the amusement park" and relay amusement park experiences, albeit taking note of how movies infiltrate amusement park spaces. The second two chapters occur "at the movies" and are ultimately about ways that new media represented amusement parks.

Chapter 2, "Urban Wonderlands: The 'Cracked Mirror' of Turn-of-the-Century Amusement Parks," lays out in detail what were the modern amusement parks sprouting and thriving across the country, what were their attractions, what happened at them and, ultimately, what happened to them. In examining their ebb and flow—their responsiveness to and as a harbinger of modern America—the chapter examines not only how amusement parks generated new ways of seeing and thinking but how ways of thinking affected racial, gendered, class, and national politics at the parks. Amusement parks included a substantial variety of activities—not only the mechanical thrill rides like roller coasters and Ferris wheels with which they have become most closely associated but also ballrooms, roller skating rinks, ethnological exhibits, restaurants and beer gardens, and band concerts and daredevil acts. The chapter describes the history, qualities, and many features of the parks themselves and then addresses the generally forgotten performance genres that were regular features of the parks, as well as significant influences on motion pictures: dancing girls, plantation shows and other living ethnological villages, disaster and pyrotechnical shows.

Chapter 3, "Thrill Ride Cinema: *Hale's Tours and Scenes of the World*," separately takes up another regular feature of amusement parks—movies. It looks, in particular, at a phenomenon that fused motion pictures and the amusement park mechanical ride in what later in the twentieth century became known as motion-simulation rides. The history and meaning of *Hale's Tours and Scenes of the World* and movie rides popular at amusement parks during this period express how movies and amusement parks together convincingly taught modern experience through virtual tourism (especially by railroad) and encouraged new attitudes about national identity and empire, technological utopianism, and epistemological experience.

Chapter 4, "The Miniature and the Giant: Postcards and Early Cinema," moves from the consideration of park experience that defines the first two chapters to how movies themselves represented amusement parks and spread information, knowledge, and enjoyment of them. While movies may be remembered as the most enduring new technology of mass visual communication of this period, they were not the only new visual communication technology. This chapter takes up a comparison between movies and picture postcards—also a new phenomenon of this period—for how they pictured amusement parks as the electrified sublime, as architectural monuments to modernity, and as containers for the human body (in all its different guises) in action.

Chapter 5, "Coney Island Comedies: Slapstick at Amusement Parks and the Movies," extends the work of chapter 4 to movies as they developed into longer formats. Chapter 4's comparison between movies and postcards stops when movies themselves coalesce as full-scale fictional narrative films, around 1908. Chapter 5 examines how slapstick comedy from 1909 until 1918 took up the amusement park as a subject time and time again. For many slapstick comedies the amusement park, as both an architectural backdrop and a motion-filled, mechanistic playground, was the perfect foil for physical, finely timed comic routines and themes of insult to Victorian mores and celebration of modernity. The chapter shows how the movies and amusement parks worked together to create a highly expressive comedy of social commentary.

Chapter 6, "Conclusion: The Fusion of Movies and Amusement Parks," looks forward to how Disneyland and the modern theme park look backward. It argues for how from its opening day Disneyland has combined movies and the amusement park to forge its identity. In so doing, Disney drew on the ways that movies and amusement parks worked together at the beginning of the century. In the postwar era a new generation of cinema and parks developed mutual strategies for themes of a posturban modernity and newly defined national unity and citizenship. They remade the lessons of early cinema and amusement parks.

Electric Dreamland demonstrates that long before Disney imagined the amusement park that became the model for today's technologically driven parks, electric or trolley parks taught Americans to adopt an urban

American sensibility by embracing new technologies that the parks had transformed from threatening to pleasurable. These pre–World War I venues worked both independently and together with motion pictures, encouraging a physical, visceral involvement in the experiences they offered. In this regard movies and electric parks were interlocked cultural phenomena: they offered a geographic space for dreaming about novelty and its shocks, technological transformations, and the national American identity that emerged in this process. This electric dreamland convinced Americans they could literally adapt themselves to the hyperstimulation, nervous energies, and mechanical rhythms associated with urban modernity. It invoked both a new modern perceptual response to contemporary life and a new set of behaviors for navigating the changes wrought by modernity's challenges to gender, race, class, and national identities.

Urban Wonderlands

THE "CRACKED MIRROR" OF TURN-OF-THE-CENTURY AMUSEMENT PARKS

Coney Island is only another name for topseyturveydom. There the true becomes the grotesque, the vision of a maniac. Else, why those nerve-racking entertainments, ends of the world, creations, hells, heavens, fantastic trips to ugly lands, panoramas of sheer madness, flights through the air in boats, through water in sleds, on the earth in toy trains! Unreality is as greedily craved by the mob as alcohol by the dipsomaniac; indeed the jumbled nightmares of a morphine eater are actually realized at Luna Park. . . . But nothing is real. . . . Everything is the reflection of a cracked mirror held in the hand of the clever showman.

—James Huneker, *New Cosmopolis*

Spectatoritis . . . depends upon crowds and crowd contagion. The crowd spirit is at work in almost every phase of the amusement [park] problem. Great masses of people, meeting in the highly suggestible state of crowd consciousness, are daily exposed to the professional entertainer, the expert crowd stimulator. . . . It is to the infection of these great crowds with *spectatoritis* and its deadening effects that we must trace responsibility for the toleration of low standards . . . throughout the nation.

—Richard Henry Edwards, *Christianity and Amusements*

Amusement parks helped to define a new concept of urban modernism—the celebration of motion and speed, the beauty of industrial technologies, and the experience of the crowd. Their modernity lay not in any specific style of architecture but in their sensory overstimulation—their bombardment and exaggeration of sight, sound, and kinesthesia. The amusement park made clear the importance of physical sensation in relationship to visual stimulation as a distinctly modern mode of perception. The estimated two thousand amusement parks across the United States between 1900 and 1915 thus offered a comprehensive reorganization of cultural knowledge that forwarded the importance of the range of sensory experiences in relationship to visual perception, accomplished this on a national scale over a continuing period of time, and contributed to an American modern industrial sensibility.

Of course, the best-known parks were those in New York City and Chicago. Brooklyn's Coney Island (Steeplechase [1897–1964], Luna Park [1903–1944], and Dreamland [1904–1911]) remains the paradigmatic example. But New Yorkers also frequented other area parks now generally forgotten: Palisades Park (1898–1971) across the Hudson River, Paradise Park (1895–1914) at Fort George in the Bronx, Golden City (1907–1934) at Canarsie Beach near present-day JFK Airport, Gala Park (1894–1921) at North Beach on what later became LaGuardia Airport, Steeplechase Park (1901–1928) at Rockaway Beach on Long Island, Midland Beach (1897–1920s) and Happyland (1906–1919) on Staten Island.

During this same period Chicago had six parks. Paul Boynton's Chutes Park (1894–1907) was the country's original, first amusement park. Sans Souci (1899–1929) on Chicago's south side appeared because Chicago City Railway Company constructed it at the end of its new streetcar line to encourage trolley business. White City (1905–1934) was the preeminent south side park near the old site of the 1893 Chicago World's Columbian Exposition. The short-lived Luna Park (c. 1907–1911) was near the Union Stockyards. Forest Park (1908–1923) was farther out past Chicago's west side. But the biggest, most enduring area park was Riverview (1904–1967) on Chicago's north side at Western and Belmont Avenues.

Riverview was the country's largest amusement park. Its advertisement proclaimed one important facet of the urban and suburban parks, "Riverview is as good a tonic as a visit to a summer resort and many of its visitors have decreed that it is an excellent place to spend one's vacation."[1] This statement was meaningful at a time when public health officials were alerting the population, particularly the working class, to the importance of outdoor life, relaxation, and exposure to fresh air for warding off cholera, tuberculosis, and other illnesses. In this regard amusement parks contained antidotes—beaches, picnic groves, gardens—to the excesses of urban stimulation.

But there were also parks named Coney Island or Luna Park in other American cities.[2] There were parks whose names conjured up the fantastic, designated the prosaic, or simply labeled themselves as locations for modern electrified sights. There were White City amusement parks not only in Chicago but in cities from coast to coast.[3] Other parks intimated they were romantic settings in nature: there were Forest Parks in Illinois, Missouri, Mississippi, Kansas, and Arkansas. There were Wildwoods in Minnesota, New Jersey, and Georgia. There were Riverviews and Riversides. There was a Willow Grove in Philadelphia, an Old Orchard Beach in Maine, a Saltair Beach in Utah, a Rock Cliff in South Carolina, a Rock Springs in West Virginia, a Pleasure Garden in Denver, and a Columbia Garden in Butte, Montana. There were Wonderlands, Dreamlands, Fairylands, and Joylands.[4] There were parks named after their geographic locations, their contractors, and their landowners.[5] There were parks quite generically called "Electric Park."[6]

Although only some parks were called White City, many actually *were* "white cities" since amusement parks, like other public and private recreational facilities, were racially segregated. At a time when amusement parks often unintentionally allowed for comingling of immigrants (many of whom were also considered nonwhite) and native-born Americans, many parks intentionally excluded African Americans. In the South, once segregation was nationally sanctioned by the U.S. Supreme Court's *Plessy v. Ferguson* decision in May of 1896, southern parks formally instituted "whites only" policies, and segregation affected how amusement parks developed and for whom across the country. For example, Glen Echo Park (1890s–1968) outside Washington, D.C., and Baltimore announced its exclusionary policy in 1901.[7] Other parks, like Lakewood Park (1910–1936) in Charlotte, North Carolina, and White City (c. 1908–?) in Norfolk, Virginia, ran separate late autumn seasons for African Americans after they closed their seasons for whites.[8] Since amusement parks have historically been celebrated as harbingers of melting pot culture, identifying amusement park racist policies and practices is necessary to reconsider whether parks truly served a social democratizing purpose.[9]

In the North, even though they made no official announcements and neither posted nor advertised exclusionary admission, amusement parks practiced de facto segregation. Historian David Nasaw attributes these new policies to "the almost universal proscriptions against interracial dancing, dining, and swimming in the early twentieth century, often enforced by the police, as well as the courts."[10] The *Cleveland Gazette* reported, immediately after *Plessy v. Ferguson*, that African Americans were now being excluded from the dance hall at Euclid Park Beach (1894–1969), and it subsequently reported in 1911 that African Americans were henceforth unwelcome at all area amusement parks.[11] In Youngstown, Ohio, an African American man sued Idora Park (1899–1984) when he was denied admission to the park's dance hall, and he ultimately lost the case when the courts ruled that a park dance hall was not "a place of public resort."[12] Certainly, segregationist practices intensified in this period in both northern and southern cities as southern rural, lower-class African Americans began to migrate in large numbers to cities like Washington, Baltimore, and Cleveland.

Many northern amusement parks thus increasingly adopted the practice of admitting African Americans only on special days, called Jim Crow Days or Colored Days. Cleveland's Luna Park (1905–1929) began an annual Jim Crow Day in 1910, Baltimore's River View Park (1898–1929) regularly had Jim Crow Days, and Chicago's White City (1905–1934) likewise advertised an annual day for African Americans.[13] But even on these days, bathing facilities—swimming pools, bathhouses, beaches—were off limits. A black Cleveland resident put it quite succinctly years later: "Everything worked at the park on those days except the swimming pool. The pool always 'happened' to be out of order on that day."[14]

But what cultural historians and amusement park history aficionados have largely overlooked is the number of "colored only" amusement parks (as they were called) that catered exclusively to African Americans in both the North and the South. There were a large number, especially in the South, that were from their outsets exclusively for African American populations.[15] Sometimes the African American parks were located adjacent to or down the beach from a white park; one case was Virginia's African American Bay Shore Park (1906–1947) (fig. 2.1) near Hampton and Norfolk, next to the "whites only" Buckroe Beach. Like their white counterparts, African American parks were also often at the end of city trolley lines and for the same reason. The Montgomery Traction Company built Washington Park (dates unknown) at the end of its segregated streetcar line through a black neighborhood to stimulate more fares. The Savannah Electric Company built the African American Lincoln Park at the end of its West End trolley route. Likewise, the Jacksonville Electric Company built the Florida city's African American Lincoln Park (dates unknown).

Occasionally, African American businessmen built and owned amusement parks. In Nashville, local wealthy undertaker Preston Taylor opened Greenwood Park (1905–1949) adjacent to his family's home at the end of the Fairfield Street trolley line. His park featured a swimming pool, rides, and a baseball park. At these parks amusements like swimming pools and exhibition baseball games were central since these were the very recreations to which African Americans were otherwise denied access. But, in general, African American parks—often scaled-down versions of neighboring or nearby "whites only" parks—still admitted an environment of crowd activities, hyperstimulation, and visual excess.

African American parks are important for understanding how amusement parks functioned as a national phenomenon because they ensured that African Americans were not excluded from the form of urban leisure that was being ushered in by modernity. African American parks made it possible for more African Americans to enjoy the same kinds of rides, shows, and concessions that their white counterparts did. So, although the pattern of amusement park admissions across the United States presents a variable set of segregationist practices that fit into a larger story of American racism, it is important that African Americans as a group also participated in this new form of leisure across the North and South. All parks were easily accessible by public transportation, were physically enclosed, were afford-able to their patrons, and were exciting.[16] The phenomenon of new modern-ist perception that was taught at the amusement parks thus truly happened on a national scale.

THE "CINEMATIC" ARCHITECTURE OF AMUSEMENT PARKS

A park's visual environment heralded visitors through its excess and veloc-ity of parts-in-motion. Park architecture was extravagant, large-scale, a diverse mix of fantastic, historic, and exotic styles painted in bold col-ors and dramatically illuminated with incandescent electric lighting. Fred-eric Thompson, planner of Coney Island's Luna Park, emphasized this to his fellow businessmen: "The very architecture must be in keeping with the spirit of carnival. It must be active, mobile, free, graceful, and attrac-tive. It must be arranged so that visitors will say 'What is this?' and 'Why is that?'"[17] Luna Park's central courtyard, for example, blended different col-ors, lights, and an eclectic mix of architectural styles in one space around a lagoon: it featured onion-domed towers topped by colorful waving ban-ners, walkways flanked by classical columns, bridges and stairways, and the exposed skeletal structures of the water toboggan's slide and other rides (fig. 2.2). The new cultural authority of the urban landscape was its invitation to knowledge through visual display, rapid movement, and sensory involvement, the same traits associated with cinema itself as a new medium.

These parks also brought together the legacy of several nineteenth-cen-tury institutions. Park managers capitalized on this cultural trust: to quote one, "If anything, the amusement park is the big-product of the Midway or amusement section of the Exposition or World's Fairs, and virtually the composite of the Exposition, Circus, County Fair, and Carnival."[18] Even one of the parks' biggest social critics (Rollin Lynde Hartt) agreed: "[The amusement park,] feebly imitating the exposition architecture and provid-ing a garish replica of its illumination, gave the Midway a dominant rank—indeed, permitted nothing but Midway. . . . The Middle Western street-fair, the Parisian *fete foraine*, the mardi gras, the fiesta, the penny vaudeville, the circus, the dime museum, and the jubilant terrors of Coney Island, were rifled of their magic. . . . Never was Midway so frantic, so extravagant, so upsetting, so innocuously bacchanalian!"[19]

As historians Robert Rydell and Rob Kroes put it, "The [1893] Chicago fair, with its park-like setting and popular Midway Plaisance . . . opened the eyes of several entrepreneurs to the possibility of making their fortunes from perpetuating the legacy of commercialized pleasures found at the fair."[20] While world's fairs or expositions or, more properly, their entertainment zones, may have been the catalyst for the modern amusement park, amusement parks also borrowed freely from a range of traditions and cheap entertainments.

Amusement parks were also descendants of European pleasure gardens, most notably Copenhagen's Tivoli Gardens and London's Vauxhall. For the price of an admission ticket, Vauxhall (opened sometime around 1660) afforded the middle and working classes entry to courtly flower gardens otherwise only accessible to the ruling classes, thereby opening up elite leisure to the bourgeoisie. Founded in 1843, Tivoli Gardens expanded on London's Vauxhall Gardens by offering a wider range of amusement—including cafes, theaters, a merry-go-round, and concerts. Pleasure gardens provided recreation for a burgeoning urban middle class at a time when nature was understood as an antidote to the business of commerce and amusement a pleasurable middle-class distraction from the social hierarchy of western European societies.

In the United States there was an abundance of nineteenth-century parks, groves, and gardens that both paralleled the European pleasure gardens and served as forerunners to the amusement park of the post–Civil War industrial revolution. For example, Cedar Point in Ohio began as a commercial bathing resort in 1880 and, little by little, added new attractions, including band concerts, a hotel, and a switchback railway before it became an amusement park with a midway of amusements in 1906.[21] Pennsylvania's Dorney Park began as a commercial extension of a private estate (Solomon Dorney's fish hatchery) in 1894 and became an amusement park only when a local railway company bought the land and transformed a botanical garden into a modern electrified park filled with mechanical rides and other attractions. Chicago's Riverview Park began as a private shooting club for wealthy German businessmen, then added a merry-go-round for members' children. Lake Compounce in Connecticut dates back to 1846 as a picnic grove. But, like so many other parks, when the trolley or interurban rail lines reached it in 1895, the rail company bought the land and transformed a romantic retreat into an industrialized amusement zone. Some charged admission fees, and some did not: the primary goal, however, was always to encourage ridership on the rail line, and the parks fulfilled an important economic function by serving as desirable destinations at the ends of traction company lines.

Parks were Erector Set worlds of mechanical thrill rides. Their dynamic landscapes featured a continual din of people and machinery in motion and electrically powered visual spectacle. Two mechanical attractions physically dominated the park landscape. The shoot-the-chutes waterslide swept passenger cars mechanically down an inclined track onto the surface of a large pool of water. As architect Rem Koolhaas describes the ride, "[It is] a toboggan that is hoisted mechanically to the top of a tower from which a diagonal slide descends toward a body of water. Anxiety as to whether the board will stay on top of the water or slip under the surface provides the suspense as the rider slides downward."[22] A steep incline, the speed of the descent, the bumpy ride, and the splashing waves made the Chutes the most exciting ride at the park (fig. 2.3).

The circle or aerial swing was a high steel tower whose radial arms each suspended a gondola or passenger carriage so that when the whole device was mechanically rotated at increasingly higher speeds, the cars spun outward and rotated (fig. 2.4). Circle swings were exciting because they were often the "fastest" thrill ride at the park (surpassed in later decades by roller

The Chutes, Tenth Avenue and Fulton St   San Francisco, Cal.
1068.

2.3. THE CHUTES, TENTH AVENUE AND FULTON ST., SAN FRANCISCO, CAL., 1910. POST-
CARD. AUTHOR'S PRIVATE COLLECTION.

Circle Swing in Mid Air,
Vinewood Park, Topeka, Kans,

2.4. CIRCLE SWING IN MID AIR, VINEWOOD PARK, TOPEKA, KANS., C. 1907. POSTCARD.
AUTHOR'S PRIVATE COLLECTION.

coasters' technological improvements that allowed for both greater speed and ease of braking).

These rides were simulations of danger; they provided a tenuous relationship between the perception of danger and the assurance of safety. Like all the park's other mechanical rides—scenic railways, velvet coasters, Ferris wheels, and ticklers—they ran on a routinized schedule of starting and stopping, offering to patrons a precise rhythm not unlike the rhythm of industrialized labor: they consisted of waiting, boarding, riding, and disembarking organized around the purchase, anticipation, experience, and relief of risk, danger, and pleasure. As John Kasson has observed, "Riders could enjoy their own momentary fright and disorientation because they knew it would turn to comic relief; they could engage in what appeared dangerous adventure because ultimately they believed in its safety."[23] These rides reversed the usual relations between the body and machinery in which the person controls and masters the machine: the person surrendered to the machine, which, in turn, liberated the body in some fashion from its normal limitations of placement and movement in daily life.

Most rides depended on railway apparatus, a technology that we now take for granted but was not understood in the same way one hundred years ago. Railway passengers felt ambivalent about train travel, and despite their thrill at being part of a projectile shot through space and time, they had an ever-present fear of potential disaster. Stories of streetcar and railway crashes and deaths regularly filled the front pages of the newspapers. Urban railroads, trolleys, and subways—the very transportation that brought the parkgoer to the gate—was at worst unsafe and, at best, dirty and uncertain.[24] The imagination of disaster, the fantasy of seeing technology go out of control, and the pleasure in the resulting terror were integral—whether the ride was a roller coaster, a scenic railway, or a miniature railroad.[25]

Thrill rides momentarily disoriented the rider, provided a novel perspective, amplified unfamiliar spatial relations, heightened cognitive sensations, and exaggerated the rider's physical self-awareness. By seemingly defying the forces of gravity and/or offering unaccustomed speed, they affirmed the instant as euphoric. As a 1901 magazine writer said, "[The amusement park's] specialty [is] to toss, tumble, flop, jerk, jounce, jolt, and jostle you by means of a variety of mechanical contrivances, until your digestion is where your reason ought to be, and your reason has gone no one knows whither. . . . If the same thing happened to you the next day on a trolley car, you would in all probability sue the company for a thousand dollars."[26] The amusement park addressed new perceptual orientations and anxieties about the modern technological world at large by ameliorating them at a very concrete level in the body of the subject.

THE BODILY THRILLS OF CINEMA
AT THE AMUSEMENT PARK

Movies figured prominently at vaudeville theaters, outdoor amphitheaters, or nickelodeons in over 75 percent of the nation's amusement parks. In many instances an amusement park movie theater was the first motion picture venue in that town or city and served as the means by which many patrons were introduced to the medium of the twentieth century. In the context of the amusement park, movies may be understood either as just another type of physical submission to a mechanized thrill or in contradistinction to the mechanically induced thrills of the circle swing or shoot-the-chutes since movies seemingly addressed vision as paramount among the senses—whereas thrill rides by their very definition were kinesthetic, that is, acting upon bodily motion for purportedly pleasurable effect.

Cinema at the amusement park, however, must be understood within a framework that admits both its intertextual definition among a range of amusement park attractions and its historically specific status as a "cinema of attractions." As a way to characterize early cinema, Tom Gunning's phrase "cinema of attractions" defines cinema prior to 1908 as exhibitionist, direct, visceral, and celebrating its ability to show something.[27] As a challenge to thinking about cinema as a mode of realistic representation and ultimately storytelling, "the cinema of attractions" binds the viewer to more than what is being depicted. Its magnetism is the capacity of the apparatus for summoning novel points of view, for extending the panoptic gaze, and for eliciting wonder at the apparatus felt as a sensation of delight and pleasure in the viewer's body. The cinema of attractions not only conquers space with the gaze but foregrounds the body itself as a site of sensory experience within a three-dimensionally contained space. In this instance moviegoing provides a spectatorship of sensory fascination, a *jouissance* instead of an out-of-body sense of panoptic projection into the screen space and mental absorption into an onscreen story.

In this regard movies may invoke a physical delirium of the senses just as much as a thrill ride. What separates the moving picture show from the thrill ride, however, is the way that movies excite the body "without the accompanying threat of breaching [the body's] integrity."[28] In contrast, as cultural analyst Tony Bennett points out, the thrill ride "addresses—indeed assaults—the body, suspending the physical laws that normally restrict its movement, breaking the social codes that normally regulate its conduct, inverting the usual relations between the body and machinery and generally inscribing the body in relations different from those in which it is caught and held in everyday life."[29] In the context of the amusement park space, then, *both* movies and thrill rides may have granted men and women mechanically induced thrills. But movies' "assault" on the senses was not so much an act of direct kinesthesia as a means for integrating or smoothing over the virtual space of visual observation and the physical space of bodily cognition.

Both thrill rides and movies did seek to reinscribe the body in new relations, but they did so at different points within a continuum available at the amusement park of imagined spatial and temporal freedom of speed, displacement, and the fantastic that freed individuals from Victorian comportment and sexually circumspect behavior. Only one component of what was available at an amusement park, thrill rides staked out one extreme of that continuum. Movies, perhaps closer to the other end of the continuum, acted on a promise similar to other amusement park attractions like the multimedia disaster shows; panoramas with stage shows and special effects (e.g., *A Trip to the Moon*); or rides through dark tunnels rife with dramatic dioramas (e.g., *Creation*, *Hell's Gate*, or *Canals of Venice*). Movies offered up spectacle while preserving haptic knowledge grounded in the body of the spectator, of being an observer in an architectonic space or environment of darkness that itself often admitted physical self-awareness and opportunities to transgress appropriate social behavior.

In one important instance movie exhibition even constituted a mechanical thrill ride in and of itself that blurs the distinction between the two. *Hale's Tours and Scenes of the World* consisted of theater railway cars that each seated seventy-two "passengers." The moving pictures that showed out the front end offered a filmed point of view from the front or rear of a moving train, emphasizing the commercial nature of railroad travel into scenic rural reaches of the United States and other countries. The goal was to create the illusion of movement into or away from a scene, accentuated by mechanical apparatuses and levers that vibrated, rocked, and tilted the car. While steam whistles tooted and wheels clattered, air was blown into the travelers' faces. Imitators and variants of *Hale's Tours* also offered "virtual" tours by auto, hot-air balloon, and steamboat. *Hale's Tours* and its imitators fused the amusement park thrill ride, ideological and technological ambivalence about rail travel, and the new medium of motion pictures into a cinema ride that for a time was the "jewel in the crown" of amusement parks' claims to modern perceptual experience and stimulation.

SOCIAL DISCOURSES OF THE AMUSEMENT PARK

The act of pleasurable and sexual looking so tacitly a structure of cinematic experience was likewise an implicit structure of the amusement park. The demarcation between being the surveyor and the surveyed was never clear at an amusement park. As one wandered from attraction to attraction (including movie theaters), one was never far from being an object of fascination for others. Historian Kathy Peiss describes the situation at Coney Island: "The patrons were whirled through space and knocked off balance, their hats blown off, skirts lifted, senses of humor tried. The patrons themselves became the show, proving interest and hilarity to each other. . . . Audience participation, the interaction of strangers, and voyeurism were incorporated."[30]

Park owners and film manufacturers understood this fact. George Tilyou, owner of Coney Island's Steeplechase Park, even incorporated "the-patrons-as-show" in his famous Blowhole Theater, a theater adjacent to a funhouse where people exiting the funhouse were surprised by jets of air blowing up their legs, a mischievous gag that led to jumps, outbursts, and skirts being lifted. Whether victims of brief humiliation, comic contortions, or erotic revelations, the surprised patrons who exited onto a stage in front of an audience acted out the same scenario of surprise and humiliation that fills countless early films. They shifted easily between being the object-in-motion on display and a member of the audience watching others assume their former place. Subjectivity at the amusement park—including in its theaters—never allowed for the fulfillment of voyeuristic desire without also subjugating oneself to others' voyeuristic gazes.

Learning with the body in this and all other amusement park instances served a particularly charged historical purpose. Mechanical rides, the Blowhole Theater, and the park as a whole liberated bodies from Victorian decorum, from rigid codes of social conduct and propriety, and from strict rules of sexual constraint. When the American painter John Sloan went to Coney Island in 1907, he observed, "Crowds watch the people coming down the . . . slide in Luna Park—lingerie displays bring a roar of natural 'vulgar' mirth."[31] A postcard of the Helter Skelter slide at Coney Island's Luna Park (fig. 2.5) hints at Sloan's description: it depicts three seated women shooting down the curvilinear slide and holding their arms out in front of them for balance while the forward motion gently lifts the bottom of their skirts, possibly providing the men, women, and children gathered at the end of the slide with a view of their ankles. While a static image—through its frozen implied motion—can only hint at the anti-Victorian conduct of the park-goer, numerous movies verify and animate Sloan's comment. *Bamboo Slide* (American Mutoscope and Biograph, 1903) offers a full frontal view of the same slide, with patrons whisking down the length of the slide and often crashing into a pileup of bodies at the end of the slide. A group of men gathered at the bottom alternate between watching the "show" on the slide and looking at the camera. Similarly, *Rube and Mandy at Coney Island* (Edison, 1903) and *Jack Fat and Jim Slim at Coney Island* (Vitagraph, 1910) depict male and female park patrons being flung forward like rag dolls at the end of slides where skirts are lifted, hats are knocked askew, and any sense of decorum is destroyed.

The rides also required intimate seating, often in pairs that led to close public contact between men and women. Peiss has already written convincingly about the parks' other opportunities for informal heterosocial relations and public intimacy at the roller rinks, bowling alleys, beaches, and ballrooms.[32] Similarly, film scholars have also established that the darkened rooms of the movie theaters presented new opportunities for sexual conduct and intimate contact.[33]

Across the country the parks thus fostered a new independent, unchaperoned, sexually relaxed courtship between relative strangers. Social worker Belle Israels's 1909 survey of working-class girls concluded that the parks were dangerous because they fed young girls' desire for entertainment and, in order to fulfill that desire, girls found young men to "treat" them to the park's concessions, all the while aware that the young men expected sexual "favors" in return.[34] O. Henry exploited this type of encounter in "Brick-dust Row," a 1907 short story in which a wealthy tenement landlord goes to Coney Island and meets a working-class girl whom he then "treats" to the park.[35] At the end of the day the gentleman expresses naive surprise at the girl's cynical understanding of "treating" and wonders aloud why his new girlfriend does not respectably entertain gentlemen at her home. In O. Henry's fashion the story ends with an ironic twist when the girl replies that she lives in a deplorable slum ("Brickdust Row") too disgusting for callers—it is, of course, the very tenement owned by her Coney Island suitor.

2.5. HELTER SKELTER SLIDE, LUNA PARK, CONEY ISLAND, N.Y., C. 1907. POSTCARD. AUTHOR'S PRIVATE COLLECTION.

Even the nation's most famous progressive reformer, Jane Addams, echoed O. Henry's social critique. She, too, held up the amusement parks for scrutiny: "'Looping the loop' amid shrieks of stimulated terror or dancing in disorderly saloon halls are perhaps the natural reactions to a day spent in noisy factories and in trolley cars whirling through the distracting street, but the city which permits them to be the acme of pleasure and recreation to its young people, commits a grievous mistake."[36] Addams's comment exemplifies an attitude shared among social reformers and culture critics that amusement parks represented a perversion of play.

Specific to the concerns of social workers like Addams and Israels was that young girls were consuming alcohol at the parks and losing reason and the ability to make sound judgments about proper sexual conduct and behavior. In 1915 a Young Men's Christian Association (YMCA) reformer campaigned against the parks: "Temptations of personal intimacy are especially aggravated here by the ease with which the innocent under multiplied and insistent suggestions can be reduced into intoxication and immorality in the space of a few hours, and the whole gamut of illicit relations foisted on them." He goes so far as to call the parks part of a plot of "the forces of evil" against young girls.[37] While not all progressive reformers claimed the parks were part of urban conspiracies against female virtue, they recognized that an atmosphere that encouraged loosening inhibitions combined with the consumption of alcohol led to promiscuity and female immorality.

If many temperance arguments were made on the basis that alcohol in the neighborhood saloon made workers and family men wastrels, abusive fathers and husbands, and unproductive citizens, historians have generally overlooked how fiercely reformers advocated temperance because alcohol served to women at amusement parks contributed to delinquency and female immorality. Since most parks did indeed serve beer, they found themselves central in state and national fights about temperance and the evils of alcohol. By 1906 the Iowa Street and Railway Interurban Railway Association, for example, specifically singled out amusement parks as "potent factors in the promotion of temperance," as well as a new state bill prohibiting liquor sales on Sundays.[38] But while park owners recognized that they were often in the "eye in the storm" of societal controversy, they also complained to each other that a "temperance park" (i.e., a park that did not serve alcohol) could not break even.[39]

This response, however, was not uniform among amusement parks. Palisades Park in northern New Jersey was financially successful and received public endorsements from New York area social workers when it banned alcohol and gambling and billed itself as a family park. Olympic Park in Newark likewise advertised itself as a family park: "Representatives of the rowdy element will not be tolerated. Games of chance and buncombe of any and every sort are tabooed. Only clean and wholesome amusements are permitted and proper sanitary conditions prevail throughout."[40]

In the Midwest, where temperance advocates and strict Christian beliefs dominated, many parks did not serve alcohol at all and advertised that fact. Idora Park in Youngstown, Ohio, not only celebrated its alcohol ban but when questions arose that the park's ice cream vendor elsewhere marketed a type of beer, the park hosted notorious temperance advocate Carrie Nation as a speaker.[41] When Alamo Park (1906–1910) in Cedar Rapids, Iowa, revoked its ban on alcohol and gambling in 1909, it actually lost business. Alamo's former patrons, farmers and small-town citizens within a fifty-mile radius in eastern Iowa, complained the park had become "nothing but a hootchy-kootchy affair" and stayed away.[42] The park shut down the following season.

Interestingly enough, the traction companies' response—at least philosophically—to controversies over the intermingling of classes and the consumption of alcohol by the working classes was to build more parks. One reason many traction companies in medium to large cities may have owned more than one amusement park was not just to drop an excuse for travel to the end of each of its lines extending out from the city hub but to sort out amusement parks by class and "standards." The editors of the *Street Railway Journal* applauded this separation: "[We support] providing cheaper amusements in one resort while the better class of entertainments . . . that appeal to the higher-grade of patrons may be maintained in an entirely separate place. . . . In general, we do not believe it is wise to attempt to make people of widely different types, socially and intellectually, mix in amusement resorts."[43] For example, higher-class parks frequently engaged orchestras or military bands as a wholesome, artistically uplifting type of park entertainment with which to identify their parks and to attract a better clientele. These ensembles comprised brass, reed, woodwind, and percussion instruments and played standards and military marches in large band shells or amphitheaters. Such concerts could double or even triple park attendance (fig. 2.6) when a celebrity conductor like the long-haired Kryl, Creatore, or Liberati was present, and parks frequently advertised the concerts in local newspapers. John Philip Sousa, the self-styled "march king of America," appeared regularly at Willow Grove (1896–1976) in Philadelphia and made special guest appearances from time to time at other amusement parks. Orchestral entertainment stood in stark contrast to brass band concerts, consisting of cakewalks, ragtime, ballads, and other popular Tin Pan Alley hits that catered to working-class tastes in small gazebos often located in the middle of a park's grove or courtyard. So, while Sousa and his orchestra appeared regularly at Willow Grove, Chestnut Hill Park (1898–1912), seven miles away from Willow Grove, employed a brass band specifically to differentiate itself from Willow Grove and to draw more working-class crowds. (Ironically, the wealthy residents of the Chestnut Hill neighborhood so lamented the park's success as cheap entertainment for the working class that they bought the park in 1912 only to demolish it.)

Higher-class parks also relied on electrical illuminations or fireworks shows combined with illuminated fountains and living statue displays as aesthetically uplifting entertainment. New Jersey's Newark Electric Park (1903–1912), Kansas City's Carnival Park (1907–1909), Gloucester City's Washington Park (1895–1913), and Philadelphia's Willow Grove all hosted magnificent tableaux vivant at their nightly fountain shows (fig. 2.7). They nightly recreated three or four famous historical paintings (e.g., *Washington*

2.6. TYPICAL WILLOW GROVE AUDIENCE, WILLOW GROVE PARK, PHILADELPHIA, C. 1907. AUTHOR'S PRIVATE COLLECTION.

Crossing the Delaware) and statuary, as portrayed by comely actresses. Willow Grove and Washington Park elevators mechanically lifted the stages so that they seemed to appear magically in the center of the fountain amid multicolored illuminated jets of water. Such grandiose spectacle, enabled by mechanical developments in the manipulation of stage machinery and by chemical advances in combustible materials, combined edifying value meant to appeal to middle-class audiences critical of cheap sensations while still being a raw spectacle. Some parks thus transcended categories of vulgar entertainment, whereas others were targeted as cheap, vice-filled places. A significant part of what made amusement parks so successful as a national adaptation to modern life was, therefore, the opposite of what historian David Nasaw claims for Coney Island's "totalizing" effect in erasing social boundaries.[44] Across the country, amusement parks often flourished because they developed strategies for maintaining social divisions of race, and class and, in doing so, they were able to include everyone in learning technological accommodation and urban modernist perceptions.

In a smaller city with only one park the park itself could still be organized so that immigrant and working classes spent their time differently from the middle class once inside the park's grounds. Some entertainments charged greater sums in order to attract a higher-class crowd to theater shows,

NIGHT VIEW OF LAKE AND FOUNTAIN, WILLOW GROVE PARK.   Photo. Copyright 1907 J. M. Canfield.

2.7. NIGHT VIEW OF LAKE AND FOUNTAIN, WILLOW GROVE PARK, PHILADELPHIA, 1907. POSTCARD. AUTHOR'S PRIVATE COLLECTION.

musical concerts, and other performances. Many parks actually relied on their motion picture theaters to differentiate the classes within the amusement park. Parks accomplished this strategy both by locating theaters adjacent to beer gardens and cafes where alcohol was consumed during the show and by the types of movies that were exhibited. For example, a theater showing scenics or travel pictures was expected to attract a higher class of patrons, whereas those exhibiting westerns and melodramas targeted the working class and immigrants. Since many parks offered multiple movie theaters, they could tactically attract different audiences to different parts of the park, thereby rearranging the crowds into more homogeneous social groups.[45] Such a hierarchical notion of parkgoers shored up rather than broke down class, racial, and ethnic divisions—as was already evident in the segregationist practices employed by amusement parks across the country.

Among African American communities such arguments about class distinction regarding parks that served beer, offered up games of chance, and included dance halls were particularly salient. In the Washington, D.C., area, black newspapers like the *Washington Bee* and the *Washington Colored American* held up the African American–owned Washington Park (1901–

1924) as an example for reinforcing white racism toward African Americans as "intemperate in drink, dress, amusement, and speech."[46] When the local black chapter of the Masons held its annual picnic, the group opted for a Jim Crow Day at the segregated River View Park (1898–1929) rather than the all-black Washington Park. Like the white middle-class clergy, reformers, and cultural elitists who worried that white amusement parks fostered immorality and vice among immigrants and the working class, an African American middle class fretted about the unwholesome atmosphere and behavior at African American amusement parks. But, for a black middle class embracing an ideology of racial uplift, they expressed greater concern that negative associations of black amusement parks would drag down public opinion of all African Americans. As historian Andrew W. Kahrl neatly summarizes, "Rather than viewing [black-owned Washington Park] as a rebuke to white exclusion and a visible symbol of black initiative, many community leaders believed that Washington Park and the crowds it attracted would corroborate white stereotypes and serve as a force that would collapse the class differences that groups such as the Masons, through their leisurely pursuits, strove so hard to accentuate."[47]

As amusement parks became important targets for debate about modern urban culture, they provided a focus for defining what counted as social values. While, for some, the amusement park may have symbolized the democratic ideals of a melting pot society,[48] reformers more frequently complained to the opposite effect: the parks' cheap sensations contributed to the relaxation of codes of conduct, and their sale of alcohol encouraged immoral sexual behavior, which could only result in a devalued mongrel culture. As both a commercialized perversion of play and a playground for "spectatoritis," amusement parks were both branded as a vice and likened to a disease whose only cure, according to the reformers who campaigned against them, lay in recreational activities that would be government regulated and uphold the traditions of middle-class culture and values, emphasizing intellect, self-control, and good moral character.[49] Arts critic James Huneker put it succinctly in 1915: "In a word, it is not a question of restriction but of regulation; decency, good taste, and semibarbarism should not be allowed to go unchecked. Coney Island . . . is a disgrace to our civilization. It should be abolished, and something else substituted."[50] What was at stake throughout was America's future and what the amusement park contributed to it.

THE SPECTACLE OF BODIES ON DISPLAY

The parks' dramatic spectacle of technologically induced delirium, of seeing and being seen, and of sexual display and intemperate behavior depended not only on machinery in motion and alcohol consumption. Like the moving pictures that changed regularly and provided continuing novelty, other types of shows, stunts, and performances contributed to the overall environment and crowd behavior. Movies and live acts were fundamental to the parks' success not only for helping to construct homogeneous social groups within the park but for their economic viability as well. Since mechanical rides could not often be changed, park owners believed that a steady stream of changing shows would maintain the freshness and variety that would encourage patrons to make repeat trips to their parks. Acrobats, trapeze artists, animal tricks, bareback riders and other equestrians, and all manner of circus acts were regularly featured entertainment on outdoor stages. Among this live entertainment, daredevil stunts also highlighted the transcendence of physics itself through coupling the human body with new types of mechanical transportation: bicycle riders, biplane aviators, and automobile drivers leapt gaps, made loop the loops, or performed other antics in their machines.[51]

The purpose of many performances was to hypostatize the past or the faraway, the gigantic or the miniature, the grotesque or the exquisite. Performances and performers at the parks conveyed new lessons about race and racism, gender and sexuality, national identity and foreign inferiority, and technology and the limits of the body. Some types of performances accomplished this better than others, of course, and these were often the ones that thrived at amusement parks. In particular, exotic dancers, ethnological villages or displays, and pyrodramas or disaster shows best facilitated an ideological program about contemporary American industrial progress and its new visions of empire.

Among the most popular live attractions, shows of dancing girls—whether named *Paris by Night, Streets of Delhi, Street of Cairo, Turkish Theater*, or *Oriental Theatre*—offered up women in tight, translucent dresses. Music halls, cabarets, burlesque, and vaudeville had all previously put on shows of scantily clad women dancing in sexually suggestive fashion. Amusement parks built on this tradition, as well as on the current fad of exotic foreign dances made popular at the Turkish and Asian theaters of the 1893 Chicago World's Columbian Exposition and the 1904 St. Louis Louisiana Purchase Exposition. The star performers all had names like La Neta, Princess LaTurkia, Princess Olga, Cleopatra, Saslika, or La Belle Iola.[52] They claimed to be demonstrating authentic dances from the Middle East and India, such as belly dances or "danses du ventres" (dances of the veils). They featured sensual, sexy wriggling unseen outside cheap theaters, and what they accomplished (beyond sexual titillation) was the association of an openly expressive, even hyperactive female sexuality with foreign preindustrialized cultures. In their assertive sexual gestures and skimpy outfits (by Western clothing standards), these women represented the Middle East and the Far East as more openly sexual and therefore less civilized, less refined, and more barbaric than Europe and the United States.

It was easy to equate openly sexy women with inferior foreign cultures as an illusion of stereotyping. The dancers, however, were more often than not American girls wearing wigs, makeup, and costumes. For example, when police raided Coney Island Dreamland's Turkish Theatre and arrested "Corita" for her "dance of the seven veils," the newspaper identified Corita not as a Turkish visitor but as Cora Cadwell, a native New Yorker.[53] (Of course, such regular police raids and well-publicized arrests on indecency charges only enhanced a show's reputation and helped its attendance.) The shows claimed legitimacy as depictions of Middle Eastern and Asian cultures that were still regarded as savage, potentially even dangerous, and therefore in need of American influence. But these dances were never authentic rituals or ethnographic displays; instead, they became known as "hootchy-kootchy" or "cooch" dances designed to please and excite male patrons. They were a case of instilling sexual desire as a substitute or front for imperialist desires.

Although it is difficult to know much about the specifics of these shows, there is some extant evidence despite the fact that neither the shows nor the girls who worked in them were understood as culturally legitimate enough for their records to be saved. Early movies depict this genre of dances, if not always actual amusement park shows: *Turkish Dance, Ella Lola* (Edison, 1898) features the famous vaudeville dancer Boston-born Ella Lola performing a belly dance. *Princess Rajah Dance* (American Mutoscope and Biograph, 1904) depicts a dancer who first did this "hootchy-kootchy" act at Coney Island and then featured it on the Pike at the 1904 St. Louisiana Purchase Exposition, where the film was shot. Princess Rajah's "cooch" dance (fig. 2.8) consists of her shaking her bust and butt and then balancing

2.8. SHOTS FROM *PRINCESS RAJAH DANCE* (AMERICAN MUTOSCOPE AND BIOGRAPH, 1904). PAPER PRINT COLLECTION, MOTION PICTURE, BROADCASTING, AND RECORDED SOUND DIVISION, LIBRARY OF CONGRESS, WASHINGTON, DC.

a chair gripped in her teeth! Like other exotic dancers, Princess Rajah represented some vague, ill-defined, mysterious Asian country.

Nan Aspinwall Gable, a white small-town Nebraska girl, regularly transformed herself into Princess Omene. Princess Omene was a parks and vaudeville exotic dancer who (at different times and locations) boasted she was Egyptian, East Indian, Spanish, Italian, Algerian, or Parisian (fig. 2.9).[54] Gable's subsequent celebrity as Two-Gun Nan, a sharpshooter and cowgirl who appeared with Buffalo Bill's Wild West show and on the western vaudeville circuit, eclipsed her earlier career as a dancer. But because she was proud of her latter, nationally celebrated persona (which even overlapped with her performances as Princess Omene), the career clippings that she saved made their way into an archival collection.[55] They preserve important aspects of her first vocation as an amusement park exotic dancer.

2.9. NAN ASPINWALL AND THE ORIENTAL DANCE TROUPE THEATER POSTER, NAN ASPINWALL GABLE SCRAPBOOK, ASPINWALL FAMILY COLLECTION. COURTESY OF NEBRASKA STATE HISTORICAL SOCIETY, LINCOLN, NE.

Sometime after the 1904 St. Louis world's fair, Gable began to perform as Princess Omene. It is unclear whether she performed at the 1904 fair or simply visited it—although her scrapbook contains photographs of the exotic theater "Mysterious Asia" and of Princess Rajah, who performed in the theater. What is clear is that shortly afterward, she became Princess Omene, a self-advertised "Oriental Dancer" who appeared at amusement parks in the summer (fig. 2.10) and in vaudeville houses during the winter. Wearing a long black wig and using heavy eye makeup (fig. 2.11), the natural blonde performed "a number of artistic dances and poses" that were "muscle dances" and "danses du ventre," according to her publicity. One notice describes her act: "Princess Omene, the East Indian dancer is also a general favorite, with her dances and eastern costumes. She appears in a different costume each night. She also has a number of sweet sounding bells which she rings while dancing."

2.10. "ORIENTAL THEATER," NAN ASPINWALL AND THE ORIENTAL DANCE TROUPE, FEATUR-
ING PRINCESS OMENE, UNKNOWN AMUSEMENT PARK. NAN ASPINWALL GABLE SCRAPBOOK,
ASPINWALL FAMILY COLLECTION. COURTESY OF NEBRASKA STATE HISTORICAL SOCIETY,
LINCOLN, NE.

2.11. NAN ASPINWALL AS PRINCESS OMENE, NAN ASPINWALL GABLE SCRAPBOOK, ASPIN-
WALL FAMILY COLLECTION. COURTESY OF NEBRASKA STATE HISTORICAL SOCIETY, LINCOLN,
NE.

Although there is no indication that she had any formal dance training, Aspinwall Gable modeled herself after stage dancer Ruth St. Denis, who made a sensation appearing in *Radha* (1906), a vaudeville hit that claimed to represent authentic Indian poses and religious dances. Although it is unlikely that Gable ever saw *Radha*, she collected popular portraits of St. Denis in this and other roles, and her own studio and advertising photographs openly mimic St. Denis's poses. Princess Omene's publicity often emphasized that her "touch of the oriental . . . will not offend any lady . . . [and] is the original untrammeled dance of the orient." Aspinwall Gable and her Princess Omene act, which continued through at least 1908, offer a unique perspective on this representation of female sexuality conjoined with xenophobic overtones at the amusement park as Gable attempted to inject the context of St. Denis's more "highbrow art" into her act. Mitigating the kind of movements that brought obscenity charges against Corita with a more refined approach and publicity notices, Aspinwall Gable was seemingly able to champion the exoticism popularly associated with the East and Orientalism without vulgar overtones that tipped Eastern cultures into the category of barbarism.

Like the dancing girls who represented exotic, foreign cultures while putting on a display that transgressed all Victorian norms, ethnological villages also frequently featured scantily clad men and women who performed dances and other activities. These villages or exhibits of living peoples purported to be scientific, anthropological presentations of indigenous peoples. They were a legacy of international expositions, where "living village" displays of African, South Seas, and Native American populations dramatized the difference between industrialized, civilized Europe or North America and the colonies of Western empires or Native American tribes. Among popular ethnographic displays were reconstructed Japanese villages, Native American villages, and plantation shows of antebellum African American life. Alison Griffiths and Fatimah Tobing Rony have written convincingly of the tensions that existed in these displays between "anthropological accuracy and prurient appeal" even when they were at international expositions.[56] Interestingly, both Griffiths and Tobing Rony conclude that cinema, rather than circulating reconstructed villages where live villagers perform with some unpredictability and stare back at the audience, would ultimately provide Western audiences with a more satisfying, truly voyeuristic encounter with foreign otherness.

Despite seeing ethnological displays as a potentially threatening spectacle since the performers not only looked back at their audiences but might also mingle with them "offstage," so to speak, Griffiths and Tobing Rony do not account for their continuing popularity in the United States and merely acknowledge that such troupes frequently toured as popular "fairground attractions" after the conclusion of international expositions. Griffiths and Tobing Rony do not consider how the changed context of an amusement park might shift the delicate balance of science and entertainment carefully cultivated at an international exposition. Indeed, the best-known example of an ethnological display—the Igorots, an indigenous Philippine tribe that first achieved notoriety at the St. Louis world's fair—remained as traveling performers in the United States for several years.[57] When the fair was concluded, the Igorots did not return home but crisscrossed the country's amusement parks and state fairs.[58] At many parks they were the top-drawing attraction for the season.[59] (In 1910 Coney Island's Borneo Village mimicked the Igorots' success with a living village display of inhabitants from Singapore.)[60]

By the end of the 1906 summer season the Igorots were both so financially successful and so entrenched in the United States that a legal battle ensued over their lives and U.S. earnings.[61] While the lawsuit centered on competing claims from the current and former managers of the thirty-six-member troupe, the result was that a Chicago judge ruled the Igorots, as people of a recently acquired U.S. territory, had full citizenship rights in the States and could not be forced back "into servitude" to their former manager. Consequently, with their U.S. citizenship secured, the Igorots continued to tour the country's amusement parks, playing savage foreigners despite their legalization as civilized American citizens. The anthropological discourses that contained their initial appearance seemed to matter less and less as they performed the characters of simple, salacious primitives at amusement park shows while they assimilated into American life as increasingly educated, sophisticated Westerners.

One variation of the ethnological display, the plantation show, demonstrates in an even more pronounced way the entirely performative, artificial nature of those entertainments that defined racial identities at amusement parks. The plantation show was largely an offshoot or imitation of *Black America*, a successful living display held in Ambrose Park (Thirty-Seventh Street and Third Avenue) in Brooklyn in 1895. (The prior season, Buffalo Bill's Wild West show played at the same location for the entire summer.) Initially organized as a means to employ African American performers during the summer, when most theaters closed because of the heat, *Black*

America imported bales of cotton, livestock, a working cotton gin, small cabins, and a cast of five hundred to create a believable depiction of slave quarters on an antebellum southern plantation.[62]

Billed as an ethnological display depicting southern rural simplicity, *Black America* claimed authenticity. Contemporary descriptions heralded the way that the "cabin life of negroes [was] faithfully and picturesquely re-produced" so that it created a voyeuristic, touristic impression as though one were simply passing through rural, antebellum Virginia or Carolina.[63] The *New York Times* reinforced such an impact: "A fat, black mammy, with a red handkerchief on her head, sits outside one of the little cabins, knitting; a dusky damsel, all in pale blue, makes a picture of herself standing in the square frame of an open cabin window."[64] The paper called on the two opposing stereotypes of African American womanhood—nonthreatening maternity and hypersexuality—as evidence of the show's authenticity although it simply underscores the show's tautological logic: *Black America*'s authenticity depended on reinforcing existing racist myths and stereotypes.

Furthermore, the plantation show did not rely solely on its actors' "living statue" displays but incorporated music, dance, athletic performances, and songs. "Inhabitants" performed Jew's harp and violin melodies, cakewalks, songs, juggling, and boxing matches, as though entertainment was part of the "natural" fabric of everyday life, even while the reality was that all the performers were seasoned theater professionals playing scripted roles. (In many other ethnological displays actors may not have been "authentic" representatives of the group being represented. For example, critics praised Coney Island's North Pole display and described one of its most captivating inhabitants, "Miss Esther Leventhal is one of the charming Esquimaux who . . . also often speak[s] in her native tongue."[65] Yiddish, perhaps?) After the success of *Black America*, smaller plantation shows became a staple at amusement parks across the country. These live entertainment shows generally played to racist stereotyping that encouraged park patrons, regardless of their own ethnic ties, to identify with whiteness and to see all other ethnic and racial identities as exotically framed, inferior, and other.

PYRODRAMAS AND DISASTER SHOWS: THE AMUSEMENT PARK'S BIGGEST MULTIMEDIA EXTRAVAGANZAS

The apotheosis of theatrical spectacle resided in parks' disaster shows and pyrodramas. Electrical illuminations, fireworks shows, tableaux vivant, band or orchestra concerts, dancers, ethnological inhabitants, and even daredevil stuntmen were all "lesser cousins" to the amusement parks' greatest productions, which often combined all of the former entertainments as elements of one show. Inasmuch as disaster shows and pyrodramas were important contextual and intermedial models for new moving pictures, they also still outscaled the new medium for optical effects, grandiose tableaux, and sheer sensation. As an amalgam of theater, circus, modern panorama, fireworks show, and magic tricks, the disaster show and pyrodrama was the largest-scale, most multisensory spectacle of the period.

Defined by an 1897 magic book as the fusion of theater and fireworks display, pyrodramas were colossal theatrical performances of "unprecedented scale, realism, and intensity" that relied on audience grandstand seating in large outdoor amphitheaters, ornately painted stage sets, moving scrolls or panoramas as backdrops, casts of hundreds who sang and danced in elaborately staged musical numbers, actors, special effects equipment, and fireworks.[66] Among the most popular of these shows were *The Last Days of Pompeii*, *The Destruction of Messina*, and *The Battle of the Monitor and Merrimac*. The pyrodrama's "cousin," the disaster show, also theatrically recreated events that culminated in "some stirring catastrophe . . . [or] awful cataclysm" that could be reenacted with the aid of "colored fire."[67] Popular disaster shows most often recreated disasters of urban tenement life (fire) or of natural catastrophes like earthquakes and floods. Whereas some disaster shows like *Fighting the Flames*, *The Destruction of San Francisco by Earthquake*, and *The Galveston Flood* flirted with contemporary recreations of newsworthy events, pyrodramas more often took up historical reenactments—often battles or adaptations of epic novels and plays—as their subject matter.

But pyrodramas and disaster shows were both melodramas less dependent on the spoken word and foregrounding of actors and their artistry than on special effects that created wind, water, explosions, and fire. In fact, when Chicago's White City discontinued its *Destruction of Messina* after the 1909 season, it tried to sell its large number of effects machines: "ten electric lamps, cloud, flame, wave and sunrise effects . . . drum, wind machine, crashes, guns, organ and chimes."[68] Pyrodramas and disaster shows were costly to produce and required big spaces and big casts, which meant they occurred far more frequently at bigger amusement parks.

But where they did occur, they were in the earliest years of the twentieth century among the top park concessions. *The Battle of the Monitor and*

Merrimac was popular at Denver's Elitch Pleasure Gardens (1904–present), as well as at Chicago's Riverview Park and Boston's Wonderland (1896–1996).[69] In Jackson, Michigan, Hague Park's *Battle of Manila*, which recreated Admiral Dewey's victory in the Spanish-American War, played only on special occasions but drew as many as twenty-five thousand to a single performance.[70] In a single day at Coney Island one could witness both Rome and Moscow burn, "experience" several naval battles and episodes from the Boer War, and watch Galveston flood, San Francisco quake, and Vesuvius erupt.[71] *The Johnstown Flood, The Destruction of San Francisco by Earthquake*, and *The Galveston Flood* played to crowds at Boston, Columbus, Detroit, Chicago, Indianapolis, Minneapolis, Milwaukee, Kansas City, and New York City parks. At Indianapolis's Wonderland (1906–1911), the painted scenes, narration, and illuminated effects that reenacted the 1889 Johnstown, Pennsylvania, flood made for one of the park's most popular attractions.[72]

Battle in the Clouds, a pyrodrama about a futuristic Martian invasion that featured biplanes and balloons, as well as the usual effects of destruction, occurred at both Coney Island and Chicago's Riverview Park.[73] *Fire and Flames* was popular at Carnival Park in Kansas City, Kansas, as well as at Wonderland in Boston. Chicago's White City *Fighting the Flames* was among its most popular attractions.[74] At Coney Island both Luna Park's *Fire and Flames* and Dreamland's *Fighting the Flames* were the most popular attractions during the 1904 and 1905 seasons.[75] Pyrodramas and disaster shows so cleverly fused literary or historically edifying content with effects that were entirely sensational that they were popular across class lines; one historian even called them "a psychological addiction for the metropolitan public."[76]

All amusement park disaster shows and pyrodramas developed from and capitalized on strategies originated by the most famous, ambitious producer of pyrodramas—James Pain. Pain, a British impresario who originally produced pyrodramas on different historical (often war) reenactments in Britain, first brought *The Last Days of Pompeii* to Manhattan Beach near Coney Island in 1879. *The Last Days of Pompeii* provided outdoor grandstand seating and standing room for as many as ten thousand spectators. The grandstand sloped down to a narrow, shallow moat or lake 260 feet long and 70 feet wide that separated the audience from an elaborate stage.[77] Historian David Mayer notes that the lake served a practical function both as a protective barrier from "falling fireworks debris and sparks" (even though there were reports of occasional injuries and burns) and as a reflective surface for the visual sensation.[78] But, more important, Mayer argues for how the lake provided an important spectatorial separation between the audience and the pyrodrama, creating an illusion that was "at once immediate and remote."[79] Photographs of the stage itself reveal a large-scale facade of Pompeiian buildings set in front of a prominent, snowcapped mountain.

The limited plot enacted a story based on a popular 1834 novel about star-crossed lovers caught amid conflict between the Romans and the Christians. Mayer compares Pain's adaptation to the original for the ways that Pain eliminated the novel's supporting characters, nuanced and complex characterizations, and class and political issues of the 1830s. The actors were more important as accessories to the unfolding drama of destruction and grand-scale spectacle. Mayer argues that Pain provided just enough historical fact and characters categorized purely as decadent Romans or virtuous Christians so that the cataclysmic interruption of Vesuvius's eruption and flowing lava provided a satisfying combination of "historical education, Christian morality, and fiery entertainment."[80]

The Last Days of Pompeii was only the first Pain pyrodrama to show in the United States. It played continuously at Manhattan Beach in the summer until 1914, and Dreamland also constructed an elaborate *Last Days of Pompeii* show nearby in 1904. The show also toured in as many as thirty other U.S. cities. Although Pain initiated the packaging and marketing of pyrodramas, he sold his U.S. business in 1897 to Harry Bishop Thearle, who hired local casts and crews at parks across the country. As Mayer notes, in cities like Buffalo, St. Louis, Peoria, Chicago, Cincinnati, Cleveland, and Fort Worth, Pain's Fire Works arrived at local amusement parks and "excavated lakes and built stages and grandstands, trained and costumed casts . . . provided promotional materials . . . [as well as directors and bandmasters]" while arranging for spectacular pyrotechnics to be shipped and stored onsite.[81] For example, Pain's Fire Works produced the Civil War reenactment *Bombardment of Ft. Sumter* at Indianapolis's Wonderland in July 1907 in the park's shoot-the-chutes lagoon with model battleships firing at each other and at a specially built fort's battlements.[82] The local newspaper heralded the production as "the most pretentious exhibition of fireworks yet."[83] Other Pain productions, including *The Storming of Vicksburg*, *The Fall of Sebastopol*, *The Fall of the Bastille*, and *Battle in the Clouds*, were popular across the country for the ways that they relegated actors to the sidelines, interrupted the narrative for a range of variety acts (in the tradition of the touring theatrical combination company), and "reconceived fireworks as a mass spectacle to be produced by experts and consumed at a distance by audiences."[84] In their disregard for lofty speeches and reliance on sensational optical effects, they epitomized the microbial cause of spectatoritis.

Indeed, the local *New York Times* critics regarded the shows as important enough that they annually reviewed the seasonal attractions, and they rarely mentioned anything of the plot or drama in Pain's shows. Instead, they emphasized both the variety show and spectacular aspects of the performances. Since these were shows of pure sensation—fireworks, special effects, and magic tricks—what mattered most was audiovisual spectacle:

> Before the temples stands an army of mail-clad warriors, with glittering weapons and armor, before whom passes a procession of priests, dancing girls, Senators, and slaves, all in brilliant and fanciful costumes, escorting Arbaces, who walks under a gorgeous canopy. After he has been seated games are played. There are foot races, acrobatic performances, dancing by the fantastically attired girls, and then a confused combat, in the midst of which Vesuvius vomits forth a volume of lava; there is a tremendous earthquake, the buildings totter and fall, the populace rushes wildly about and chaos is wrought in very short order.[85]

These shows were all action and hyperbole. As stated by a 1904 Coney Island guidebook describing *The Galveston Flood*, "Thunder, lightning, the fury of the wind until the maddened waters leap from the depths, rush wildly over the city, carrying death before it, leaving a scene of despair after it—all of which forms an exhibition entirely new in the annals of the European or American stage."[86] A contemporary critic more pointedly summarized the story development of *Fighting the Flames*:

> You look out upon a tenement street, which swarms with guttersnipes, factory girls, policemen. . . . But see! A wisp of smoke curls upward from Cohen's pawnshop! Then flames, and more flames. The alarm rings out, shouts rend the air, and in a moment the Department, with two steamers, a hose cart, a chemical, and a hook-and-ladder truck, comes charging through the throng, and attacks the conflagration, which has spread to adjoining buildings, at whose windows some forty women stand screaming. Up go the ladders, out spread the life nets. Girls leap headlong and are caught in safety. Others the firemen carry shrieking down their ladders. And all this, remember, amid clouds of smoke and frequent explosions.[87]

At the heart of these descriptions of sensational dramas is the spectacle of destruction, the central importance of machines as both "stars" and deus ex machinas, a carefully scripted ballet of chaos, fire and noise, and the subordination of individual actors to the totality of the event. Whether a historical reenactment or an illustration of modern urban dangers, the disaster show and pyrodrama depended less on individual heroes than on the sensations of devastation and the awesome sight of apocalyptic fury as produced by mechanical apparatus.

American battle reenactments especially illustrate how pyrodramas provided both a satisfying "narrative" and sensational climax. In the naval battles patriotism always triumphed over calamity. The end result, however, was not the consequence of individual or even team heroic actions in battle but the sight of "Old Glory" rising majestically among smoke, noise, and fireworks illuminations—an outcome of pure sensation that was the equivalent of so many patriotic "flag-raising" films that brought vaudeville audiences to their feet during the Spanish-American War.[88] Lagoon Park (1895–1918), outside Cincinnati, even remade its Civil War naval battle in subsequent seasons into the *Battle of Manila* and then the *Battle of Santiago*, staging more recent U.S. naval battles in the Philippines and Cuba in 1898.[89] Employing the same actors, fireworks, and patriotic script, the park merely refitted the boats for the same large scenery, grand actions, and blasts that always ended in the triumphant raising of the American flag against the backdrop of a pyrotechnic display. Kristen Whissel suggests that such a powerful, emotional conclusion was possible because "one of the hallmarks of turn-of-the-century battle reenactment[s] . . . was the creation of a perilous point of view that helped audiences imaginatively to place themselves in the crossfire on the scene of history, thereby providing the brief sensation of witnessing well-known dramas of nation formation and imperial expansion."[90] Thus, the audience was actively engaged as dramatic eyewitnesses within a highly ideological scenario yet safely separated and detached from the physical destruction itself. Such a point of view encourages the perception of the world as a "picture set up before a subject," an "enframed totality," which Whissel argues indicates a readiness for understanding America's imperial position of justified geographic expansionism at the turn of the century.[91]

Other shows like *The Chicago Fire* at Chicago's White City likewise ended on a triumphant note that rationalized industrial progress despite the show's emphasis on wide-scale destruction: *The Chicago Fire* culminated with a phoenix "amidst flames and illuminations" disappearing so that a miniature Chicago of 1906 could rise in its place.[92] *The Last Days of Pompeii* ended with the Christian hero escaping and the decadent, wealthy Romans perishing. Thus, the spectacle was always a "double pleasure": a vision of Armageddon in which a spectator felt safely immersed and experienced the "moral satisfaction" of witnessing triumph over adversity, a triumph itself that frequently celebrated the politics of industrial and technological expansion.[93]

One of the most interesting subgenres of the disaster show that heroicized the union of man and machine involved the grand displays about modern firefighting. Firemen were already popular turn-of-the-century mythic urban figures. There were parades, live theatrical performances (e.g., *Hale's Fire Fighters*), and a number of early films that extolled the firefighter and his modern steam engine for pumping water.[94] As one historian summarizes the fire disaster show, "The entire spectacle defines the dark side of Metropolis as an astronomical increase in the potential for disaster only just exceeded by an equally astronomical increase in the ability to avert it."[95] Unlike local policemen who were generally viewed as corrupt bullies, firefighters of this era received considerable publicity as true American heroes, and they dramatically employed modern technology to solve problems generally wrought by modern urban living conditions. The fire show illustrates that a pyrodrama or disaster show was always more than the visual stylization of fire and smoke. It spectacularized the union of modern technology (horse-drawn steam engines) with circuslike choreography of performers, in this instance hundreds of firemen rushing the scene while men climbed up ladders to the tops of the buildings and acrobats slid down ropes and jumped into nets. Chicago White City's *Fighting the Flames*, for example, employed 250 actors, 14 horses, 5 cabs, several fire wagons, 2 automobiles, and 2 trolley cars to battle a fictional hotel fire.[96]

Shows about floods, earthquakes, volcanic eruptions, and fires all coordinated casts of hundreds who faced Armageddon and leaped, somersaulted, and vaulted to safety amid mechanical special effects, deafening sound, music, and, of course, fireworks and smoke. Indeed, when the *New York Times* reviewed the opening of Pain's *Battle in the Clouds*, it hailed the airship (the modern machine) as the star of this aerial combat pyrodrama while enthusiastically reporting on the grand ballet and acrobats that were a requisite part of the show.[97] Disaster shows and pyrodramas, in many respects, resembled a twenty-first-century Cirque du Soleil–styled ode to twentieth-century industrial technology more than the tragic site of a fatal disaster.

Indeed, the choreography and action of disaster shows were suitable material for motion pictures. New York City film manufacturers Edison Manufacturing Company and American Mutoscope and Biograph filmed the Coney Island fire shows and widely distributed these acts. As profilmic events for the movies, the shows themselves were therefore doubly cinematic—extravagant multimedia spectacles themselves cinematic in their assaults on the viewer at a distance with grandiose visions, audiovisual effects, and motion-filled dramas while simultaneously the actual content of exciting protonarrative films. As movies, the unfolding of the actual stage shows *Fighting the Flames, Dreamland* (American Mutoscope and Biograph, 1904), and *Fire and Flames at Luna Park* (Edison, 1904) played to audiences across the country both in amusement parks and in vaudeville theaters, thereby spreading the disaster show beyond the confines of Brooklyn and the other larger amusement parks.

By 1910, however, the *Billboard* lamented that all these live shows were unable to compete with the mechanical attractions at the parks themselves.[98] Indeed, disaster shows and pyrodramas were the top park attractions generally only until 1906 although many successfully maintained profits until well into the 1910s. In 1906 *Hale's Tours and Scenes of the World* replaced some disaster shows as the top or near-top attraction at the parks while nickel movie theaters or nickelodeons became widely prevalent along commercial strips and in amusement parks as well.

The grand spectacle of the disaster shows and pyrodramas along with their mix of live action, bombardment of the senses, and emphasis on movement still helped to contextualize and set expectations for the cinematic virtual reality of *Hale's Tours*, as well as for an increasingly narrative cinema in general. As Mayer observes, "Pyrodramas . . . conditioned audiences to observe and understand extended narrative intelligible only through action, minimal facial expression, and gesture performed with the emotion-informing assistance of accompanying orchestral music. With both media, the eye and the ear collaborated, between them inferring all meaning apart from what might be gathered from either a few shouted words or brief inter-titles."[99] Contemporaneous with cinema itself entering the amusement parks, pyrodramas and disaster shows established that a notion of the "cinematic" at the amusement park was not merely an ontology affixed to a new medium but always a new mode of perception linking spectacular vision and motion across modes of entertainment.

DISASTER AND DEMISE OF AMUSEMENT PARKS

The disaster show's true irony is that it focused on fiery cataclysms while the amusement parks and movie theaters in which the audiences sat posed much greater risk for out-of-control fires. In 1903 the Iroquois Theater fire in Chicago claimed more than six hundred lives when an arc light started a blaze, and it remained a symbol for some time of how building safety violations and lack of safety preventions could lead to tragedy. Beginning in 1906, movie nickelodeons similarly violated lighting, exit, and maximum capacity safety regulations even while projection booths and highly flammable film stock posed an even greater safety threat than a legitimate theater.

Fires plagued amusement parks throughout this period. The *Billboard* annually reported blazes at parks, and the causes ran the gamut from careless smoking to combustibles like coal tar and oily rags to electrical malfunctions to arson to "causes unknown." (Fire presents a significant amusement park hazard up to the present day.) While preparing for a Memorial Day opening on May 27, 1911, workers at Coney Island's Dreamland accidentally ignited the Hell Gate attraction when they tipped over a bucket of tar and lightbulbs burst. The park rather famously burnt to the ground and was never rebuilt. Two days later, at the opposite end of the country, fire broke out at The Chutes (1910–1911) in San Francisco. This fire killed four people and many animals, and it destroyed the park, which had only been in operation for one season.[100]

As if that were not enough, the *Billboard* also reported a third May amusement park fire. At Oletangy Park (1896–1937) in Columbus, Duke (the dog appearing in the *Johnstown Flood* disaster show) alerted park workers to a fire in the Old Mill ride and managed to avert the park's destruction. Unfortunately, two months later, in July, another fire that started in the Old Mill wiped out five buildings, including Duke's place of employment—*The Johnstown Flood*.[101] In the same season Chester Park (dates unknown) in Cincinnati also experienced a major fire (August 14), and smaller fires occurred at eight other amusement parks.[102] Even after the close of the season, Boston's Paragon Park (1904–1985) and both Paradise and Luna Parks in New York suffered small fires.[103]

These were not isolated instances where fire threatened an entire amusement park. Half of Des Moines's Ingersoll Park burnt in 1906.[104] Coney Island's Steeplechase Park burnt to the ground in 1907. White City (1906–1908) in Indianapolis burnt in 1908. Both Buffalo's (1904–1909) and Pittsburgh's Luna Parks (1905–1909) burnt in 1909.[105] Open for only one year, Baltimore's Luna Park burnt in 1910.[106] Los Angeles's Ocean Park pier (1905–1969) burnt in 1912 and again in 1915, 1920, and 1924. Washington Park in Gloucester City, New Jersey, was destroyed by fire in 1913. Forest Park in Chicago burnt in 1922. Much of Hague Park in Jackson, Michigan, burnt in 1923. Al Fresco Park (1905–1925) in Peoria and Electric Park (1907–1925) in Kansas City each burnt in 1925. Perhaps the saddest fiery end to a park was Omaha's Loop Park, open for only three weeks in 1906, when it completely burnt to the ground.[107]

Amusement parks also were not immune to the kinds of natural disasters that were the subject of their other disaster shows. Flooding, tornados, and earthquakes frequently damaged parks and sometimes destroyed them. Amusement parks may have been more vulnerable to flooding in this period because many were located on river islands or adjacent to rivers in flood zones that ultimately convinced both their owners and civic authorities not to rebuild and to use the land for greater flood control of the cities. For example, Island Park (dates unknown) in Easton, Pennsylvania, was located on an island in the LeHigh River that was accessible by a trolley bridge. Regular flooding eventually forced the park's closure and removal of its attractions to nearby Bushkill Park (1902–present), which, although still technically in operation, has not been open since 2006.[108] Perhaps the best example of a flood-prone amusement park is Coney Island (1896–1972), Cincinnati. Situated along the Ohio River, Coney Island experienced major floods in 1913, 1937, and 1964, and it rebuilt each time. The most dramatic example of amusement park flooding occurred in Union Park (1890s–1934) in Dubuque, Iowa, in July 1919, when a sudden change in the weather resulted in heavy thunderstorms and a flash flood from the nearby creek. Parts of the park became submerged under more than twenty feet of water, and five park patrons died from being hit by building debris or from drowning. Although the park rebuilt, it never recovered from the stigma of this tragedy.

Equally dramatic but without the fatalities are the parks that suffered tornados. Cleveland's White City (1897–1907) was destroyed by a storm. Baltimore's River View Park suffered a cyclone in June of 1911.[109] Lagoon Park on the Kentucky and Ohio border was largely destroyed in a 1915 tornado. In Charlotte, North Carolina, Lakewood (1910–1936) was destroyed by a tornado.[110] While calamities by fire or natural means did not occur regularly at parks and their theaters across the country, they happened often enough and posed enough of a threat that the disaster shows' portents of wholesale historical destructions addressed reasonable social anxieties but transposed them onto objects that were rendered exotic or fanciful (e.g., the Roman-era eruption of Mt. Vesuvius during a sybaritic Roman feast, a Martian invasion set in the future), distant in memory (e.g., the 1889 Johnstown Flood, the 1871 Chicago fire), or "disposable" insofar as slums represented the worst of urban living conditions and their inhabitants the least sympathetic Americans.

Of course, many parks closed for reasons other than burning to the ground, becoming submerged, or being blown down. By 1935 only about three hundred parks remained nationwide. As early as World War I, traction company owners had begun to realize that selling park sites for suburban real estate was more profitable than maintaining unprofitable parks merely to sell train tickets. In addition these very same street railway companies became increasingly reorganized as public utility transportation companies and their land assets sold off. By the end of the 1920s even more of these companies declined and could not compete with the automobile and its domination of city streets. The Depression further forced many remaining parks out of business.

CONCLUSIONS: AFTER THE FALL

The story of the rise and fall of amusement parks between 1893 and the Great Depression is not the only story there is to tell about amusement parks. Amusement parks were a key component in the proliferation of American popular culture exported around the world at the beginning of a new era of Americanization abroad. While the trend may have famously begun with Buffalo Bill's Wild West tours of Europe in the late 1880s and 1890s and was completed in the global domination of American-made movies by the end of World War I, amusement parks played a role in powering the ascendancy of American popular culture as a dominant international force.[111] As historians Robert W. Rydell and Rob Kroes explain, this story is complex: "There is hardly ever a one-to-one relation between the ideological program of American culture as Americans willfully project it abroad and the ideological reading given to it at the receiving end."[112] So, although the story of the influence of American amusement parks in Europe and other continents lies beyond the scope of this volume, it is worth noting that among the first legacies of the turn-of-the-century amusement park was its exportation of an American nationalist modern identity.

Within a few years of the successes of the first American amusement parks, there were foreign imitators. Britain's most famous amusement park, Blackpool Pleasure Beach, was founded in 1896 by an English businessman who had recently been in New York and wanted to create an American-style amusement park. Elsewhere in Britain there were White City parks in London (1908–1914) and Manchester (1907–1928). There were a string of amusement parks across Canada; the best known of these were Dominion Park (1906–1929) in Montreal; Crystal Beach (1908–1989), Hanlan's Point (1905–1937), and Scarboro Beach or White City (1907–1925) in Toronto; and Happyland (1906–1922) in Winnipeg. In Europe, Luna Parks became generically synonymous with the Americanness of amusement parks, and Lunas were built in Paris (1909–1931), Cologne (1909–1927), Geneva (1912–1918), Leipzig (1911–1918), Hamburg (1913, 1917–1923), and St. Petersburg (1916–1924).

It is not simply that foreign countries mimicked the American amusement park. In many cases American businessmen designed and built the parks and furnished many of the mechanical attractions. Frederick Ingersoll, known as "the man most responsible for spreading amusement parks around the world," expanded his string of parks in Pennsylvania, Ohio, and other American states; he built Luna Parks abroad in Athens, Berlin, Bombay, Buenos Aires, Honolulu, Lisbon, Madrid, Melbourne, Mexico City, and Rome.[113] These were not trolley parks organized around the local and regional synergistic political economy of transportation companies and commercial leisure inasmuch as they represented the spread of American investments abroad at a time when American companies generally became more international in scope. Once they had achieved a kind of American saturation, American ride manufacturers like the Philadelphia Toboggan Company, the Traver Engineering Company, the T. M. Harton Company, and the Allen Herschell Company expressly sought more customers for their scenic railways, circle swings, fun houses, and carousels, and they made international markets a prime target for expanding their businesses. The American amusement park industry cultivated sites around the world.

Perhaps, the phenomenon of how a specifically American modernist perception and ideology could be internationalized can best be explored in the microcosm of *Hale's Tours and Scenes of the World*. As the single ride at the turn-of-the-century amusement park that offered a fusion of motion pictures and mechanized movement, *Hale's Tours* epitomizes the function of the intersection between movies and amusement parks. More interesting, it grafted contemporary travelogue genres and a vernacular of armchair travel onto its perceptual apparatus so that it literally accomplished new views of the world for its patrons and new subject sensibilities of the rider as a tourist consumer. Its representational, perceptual, and ideological strategies condense the work of the amusement park into one crystallizing moment for understanding the amusement park as a nationalist, modernist project, and the story of the turn-of-the-century amusement park yet remains incomplete until we turn next to the dynamics of *Hale's Tours and Scenes of the World*.

But we can draw some preliminary conclusions about the American amusement park. The turn-of-the-century amusement park's modernity lay in its visual overstimulation, sensory involvement, and kinesthesia that made new industrial technologies pleasurable to ambivalent audiences. In this regard the amusement park outfitted citizens for a new world through the reassurances of fantasy. By dazzling its participants and viewers as itself a technological spectacle, the amusement park helped to win popular consent to the new mass society.

Regardless of their locations across the United States, amusement parks helped to absorb ruralite and urbanite alike into a more urban-industrial society. Despite twenty-first-century historians' claims that amusement parks were democratic playgrounds, amusement parks both appealed to and resisted "melting pot" culture in important ways: (1) They served as a symbol of revolt from traditional, genteel cultural standards. (2) They offered new forms of spectacle for individuals and families whose lives were increasingly organized by the time clock, technologies, and pressures of an industrial society. (3) They tamed and turned people's fears of new technologies and *of each other* into more tightly integrated routines and rhythms of work and leisure. (4) They helped to teach men and women how to cope with women's increasing autonomy and independence and how to contain it through visual surveillance. (5) They promoted identification and unity with American nationalist values while spatially and structurally maintaining social divisions of race and class: they more often upheld social segregation over social integration. The phenomenon of the amusement park was always a local ideological drama and more than something distinctly local: it was a nationwide event of embracing urban modernism no matter how heterogeneous the population. Amusement parks accustomed Americans across class, ethnic and racial divisions to urban shocks while defining and making pleasurable modern sexuality in relation to public space, the act of looking, and consumerism.

Thrill Ride Cinema

HALE'S TOURS AND SCENES OF THE WORLD

My poor body, madam, requires it. I am driven on by the flesh; and he must needs go that the devil drives.

—WILLIAM SHAKESPEARE, *ALL'S WELL THAT ENDS WELL*

A COMBINATION MOVIE AND AMUSEMENT PARK THRILL RIDE, *Hale's Tours and Scenes of the World* coordinated sounds, motion pictures, and mechanical movement to present a new sense of being in the world. Heir to a popular type of early film depicting the moving point-of-view from the front of a train (the phantom train ride), as well as to the virtual voyages of panoramas, scenic railways and pyrodramas, *Hale's Tours* recreated the range of perceptions, social relations, expectations, and fears connected with the experience of travel. *Hale's Tours* contributed to democratizing and modernizing attitudes about tourism, as people in the twentieth century increasingly had access and means to travel as a form of leisure.

A word whose usage can be traced back to 1811, *tourism* denigrated those who toured but maintained a kind of distinctive subject-object, superior relationship to the environs and denizens of their travels. By depicting experiences of travel, including the sensations of crossing landscapes and viewing distant countries and the social interactions among travelers themselves, *Hale's Tours* amplified this detached subject-object experience, purposefully disseminating the pleasurable sensation of tourism to the wide, varied audiences that populated amusement parks. Beginning in 1905 and disappearing sometime before 1915, *Hale's Tours* was a thrill ride or travel ride that simulated railroad or auto travel in order to foreground the body itself as a site for sensory experience. It articulated a seemingly contradictory process for the spectator: it attempted to dematerialize the subject's body through its extension into the cinematic field while it repeatedly emphasized the corporeality of the body in all its fixity and in the physical delirium of the senses.

If culture critics of the early twentieth century linked issues of "spectatoritis," voyeurism, and tourism to visiting amusement parks and moviegoing, then *Hale's Tours* represents not just the intersection of the amusement park and motion pictures in a single movie thrill ride but the condensation of these issues in the experience of one attraction. Its goal was to fabricate the cheap sensations, absorption of the self in spectacle, and superficiality of tourist travel more generally associated with the environments and atmospheres of amusement parks and movies. It unified the related perceptual conditions offered by these two cultural phenomena in one highly theatricalized instance.

PANORAMAS AND OTHER PRECURSORS *TO HALE'S TOURS AND SCENES OF THE WORLD*

The conceptual origins of *Hale's Tours* have remained shrouded in conflicting accounts and mystery. In the first scholarly treatment of *Hale's Tours*, in the mid-1950s, film historian Raymond Fielding asserted that the show premiered at the 1904 Louisiana Purchase Exposition in St. Louis despite the fact that no guidebook or official account of the fair includes *Hale's Tours*.[1] It is more likely that Fielding's informants were either confusing *Hale's Tours* with its popular progenitor at the exposition, the Trans-Siberian Railway that incorporated moving panoramas and the creation of different rates of speed, or conflating it with the scenic railway and George C. Hale's firefighting disaster show, which was a hit at the fair.[2] The first record of a *Hale's Tours and Scenes of the World* operation was in May 1905 (fig. 3.1), when Hale and his partner opened the virtual motion picture voyage ride at Kansas City's new Electric Park. The ride's roots, however, do lie directly in exposition spectacles at the turn of the century—in the virtual voyage attractions at the 1904 St. Louis Exposition, the 1901 Buffalo Pan-American Exposition, and the earlier 1900 Paris Exposition—as well as in the ideological,

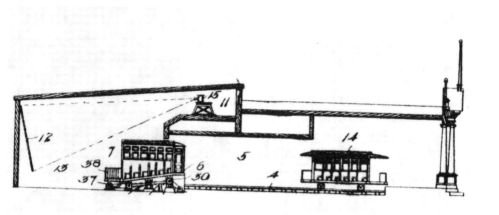

aesthetic, and perceptual economies of late nineteenth-century panoramic viewing that grounded these spectacles.

World's fairs were an important staging ground at the end of the nineteenth century and the beginning of the twentieth for teaching people about and familiarizing them with not only new mechanical technologies but ways they could adapt their perceptual experience through the use of those technologies. World's fairs, therefore, represent an important antecedent to amusement parks not just for their examples of commercial, technologized entertainment zones that purported to represent the world but also in teaching people *how to see* that world. In this aspect they provided periodic models for both amusement park attractions and motion pictures, and nowhere is this better expressed than in the panoramas (already a popular commercial entertainment) that dotted the exposition landscape and even added actors, tricks, and other effects to improve upon the medium. As cultural historian Stephan Oettermann notes, "Panoramas became a medium of instruction on how to see, an optical stimulator in which the extreme sensory impression, the sensational new experience, could be practiced over and over."[3]

By 1900, panoramas and moving panoramas were familiar illusionistic commercial entertainment. Panoramas were large-scale, often 360-degree paintings whose subject matter could be a historical military battle, a natural disaster, or even a faraway landscape (travelogue). Panoramas were originally popularized in England and France in the early 1800s, when they were housed in multistory, circular (drumlike) buildings (often called cycloramas) where spectators could walk up and down ramps to contemplate the expansive scenes. Moving panoramas were also large-scale paintings, generally canvases wound on a spool and unraveled before a seated audience. While most of these played to audiences seated in front of a proscenium stage, novelty attractions like the Trans-Siberian Railway adapted the moving panorama to unravel behind a window frame in order to create the illusion of passing landscape for a traveler seated in a railroad coach car. In the latter half of the nineteenth century, panoramas became immensely popular in the United States—both as fixed installations and as traveling shows.

Panoramas spread a painting beyond the spectator's peripheral vision and, as an oversized spatial illusion, overwhelmed the spectator's whole body, thus encompassing him or her in the field of the representation. Oettermann reinforces this analysis in his characterization of the perceptual experience of a panorama: "While seeming to offer an unconfined view of a genuine landscape, it [a panorama] in fact surrounds observers completely and hems them in. . . . It is a complete prison for the eye. The eye cannot range beyond the frame, because there is no frame."[4] Film scholar Alison Griffiths also cites this unique mode of spectatorship—engaging both the eye and the body—produced by the panorama's scale and multiperspectival rendering as a definitive feature that separated panoramic experience from any perceptual or ideological claims of nineteenth-century easel painting. She argues that it is not only their "immersive" quality that made panoramic viewings unique but also the panoramas' exhibition contexts and ontological status as "technologies of virtual transport and invocation of presence." Like amusement park rides, they offered up a kind of traveler's "learning with the body" but without the real mobility of actual transportation.[5]

Panoramas subjected spectators to multimedia environments in architectonic spaces that powerfully emphasized the body itself as the physical center for absorbing sensory shocks—shifting the audience's attention from fascination with the fantasy to "virtual" participation. Despite the limitations posed by being a static, frozen image that could at best oscillate between being "lifelike and drained of life" even with all the special effects gimmicks and addition of live performers, panoramas promised their viewers something that would be more powerful than and would replace their own memories of the subject matter.[6] In the late nineteenth-century United States this promise extended most frequently to reenactments of Civil War battles (e.g., *Panorama of the Battle of Gettysburg*, 1884) and scenic landscape travelogues (e.g., the numerous moving panoramas of the Mississippi River).[7] Reinstalling new, better cultural memories during the period when the country was trying to rebuild a sense of national unity was a significant project.[8]

George Hale capitalized on panoramas and their promise by expanding the virtual voyage both to a simulation of a transportation conveyance and to actual moving pictures. In attendance at both the 1900 and 1904 expositions (he staged his popular live-action show *Hale's Fire Fighters* at both fairs), Hale would have been familiar with the popular Trans-Siberian Railway carriage and its simulated journey of moving panoramas outside the windows since it, too, played at both fairs. In addition he might well have attended or heard about other panorama and movie attractions at the 1900 Paris Exposition: the Lumière brothers' *Maréorama* (fig. 3.2) was a phantom ship panorama installation, *Le ballon Cinéorama* was a 360-degree motion picture virtual aerial voyage from the point of view of an airborne hot-air balloon, and *Tour du monde* was a moving panorama attraction depicting exotic travel locations. According to Ralph Hyde the *Maréorama* offered an audience seated on a ship's deck the experience of two rolling moving panoramas on either side in order to recreate a Mediterranean cruise from Villefranche-sur-Mer to Constantinople that included a storm "en route."[9]

Cinéorama consisted of ten projectors playing ten synchronized hand-tinted films in a circle. The films depicted travel in five European cities and in the Sahara Desert and opened and closed with footage shot from the gondola of a hot-air balloon. Film viewers sat in an imitation gondola above the circle of movies being projected. An English-language guidebook to the Paris Exposition describes the effect of *Cinéorama*: "By the magic of a . . . passage which annihilates distance, one could glean a series of lively impressions such as are only obtained by an ordinary traveler crossing the old continents for several months, regardless of time or money."[10] While *Cinéorama* represents a model for what *Hale's Tours* hoped to achieve, it played for only two days before fire marshals shut the operation down because of the extreme heat generated by ten early motion picture projectors. Unfortunately, while the legend of the *Cinéorama* may have come to Hale's attention and even intrigued him, it is unlikely that he actually experienced it.[11]

Hale may have not only attended but may have borrowed the name of the Paris Exposition's *Tour du monde* (across the Champ de Mars from the *Cinéorama*). *Tour du monde* was a successful moving panorama in which one was seated on a platform and watched painted views of Japan, China, the Indian Ocean, the Suez Canal, and the Mediterranean (those same parts of the world represented by exotic dancers elsewhere at the expositions

3.2. MARÉORAMA, *SCIENTIFIC AMERICAN*, 29 SEPTEMBER 1900.

and at the amusement parks) as they were unspooled from a long canvas attached to a pole. The *New York Times* reporter to the fair said, "At the *Tour du Monde* you have bits of China and Japan and Russia and all sorts of out of the way places, each with its local color and vegetation, and in front of the canvas are groups of living natives from the various countries represented—Cingalese, Red Indians, Japanese, and what not, wearing their native costumes and whiling away the weary hours with cards and expectoration."[12] Combining ethnological display and virtual travel vis-à-vis a moving panorama, *Tour du monde* belonged to that category of entertainments the reporter labeled "sideshow ramas" that offered fake journeys in abundance at the exposition.

All of these exposition virtual voyages tried to heighten the verisimilitude of leisure travel through various gimmicks. What they accomplished at a world's fair touting new technologies and new ways of seeing the world was the adoption of novel vantage points for depicting travel to new destinations. Condensing time and fragmenting an actual journey into short, intense, theatricalized spectacles, they offered up parts of the world previously considered distant, less civilized than the West (as evidenced by the *Times* reviewer's comments on inhabitants), and culturally unfamiliar.

An even more fantastic version of such virtual travel was *A Trip to the Moon*, the most successful illusion ride show on the Buffalo 1901 Exposition's midway. (Hale's knowledge of popular panorama "rides" also likely extended to *A Trip to the Moon*.) Later rebuilt by its creators at Coney Island's Stee-plechase, *A Trip to the Moon* was a simulation of a trip to the moon using panoramas, magic lantern slides, and other lighting effects. Patrons boarded an aircraft with propellers and wings. The ship rocked and swayed in a simulation of air travel while moving panoramas and electrical lighting effects played. The ship "landed" on the moon, where a cast of "moon people" sang and danced.[13] Well-known American author Albert Bigelow Paine described his visit to the attraction:

> The great wings lifted and fell, the aerodrome heaved, the earth dropped down from sight, and we felt that we were soaring far above on our lunar journey. Suddenly there was a darkening, followed by complete blackness. Lightning flashed across the sky. Thunder rolled and crashed, and there was fierce rain on the awning overhead. . . . The rain slackened, the thunder died away, the stars came out; then there was a pink glow in the sky. It was a rare illusion that rushed up to meet us—morning on the moon. The moon inhabitants, however, did not prove altogether satisfying; and the fact that they were given to vocal music did not add to their interest.[14]

A Trip to the Moon thus represents but one of a number of conceptually similar, technologically varied virtual voyages that conflated the edifying and pedagogical values of geographical knowledge and distant civilizations with the "cheap sensations" of the exotic and fantastic.

All these panorama examples—with or without additional effects and regardless of their site installation—represent imitations of travel. They overwhelmed the spectator's senses while offering up novel points of view that allowed for experiencing a landscape from a distant, high vantage point or even an aerial one. They were "both a surrogate for nature and a simulator, an apparatus for teaching people how to see [nature]."[15] In short, they replaced human limits of vision and subjective sensory experience of a scene with a touristic, spectacular substitute. Rather than emphasize the sensation of the world bounded by the horizon and the edges of one's peripheral vision, panoramas exploited the sensation of being engulfed or immersed in a simulation of the world replete with sound, motion, lighting, and other effects in order to provide a surfeit of sensory information. As Ralph Hyde points out, "The panorama supplied a substitute for travel and a supplement to the newspaper."[16] At a time when America's role in the world was dramatically changing as it became an imperial power, *Hale's Tours* assumed an ideological function of surpassing the panorama at the amusement park and in downtown entertainment zones as a teacher about tourism in this world and about how to understand tourism through one's bodily involvement.

THE RISE OF *HALE'S TOURS AND SCENES OF THE WORLD*

George Hale's foray into the illusion ride business began sometime in 1904 when he crossed paths with a St. Louis inventor. William Keefe had designed "an entertainment pavilion, circular in shape, around the periphery of which an open-sided railroad car was made to run on tracks within a dark tunnel. The wall of the tunnel which faced inward toward the center of the pavilion was to be a continuous screen . . . onto which could be projected motion pictures or still images from projectors located either at the center of the pavilion or mounted on the railway car itself."[17] Keefe wanted to patent this entertainment apparatus (fig. 3.3) in March 1904, presumably in time for it to be used at the St. Louis Exposition. But, as Fielding reports, Keefe needed financial backing to make his invention and approached Kansas City magistrate Fred W. Gifford. Gifford, a close personal friend of Hale's, brought Hale into the partnership.[18] Hale and Gifford ultimately bought out Keefe's share and pursued a business practice of licensing and granting territorial rights of the installation to others.

In 1906 Hale and Gifford sold the rights east of Pittsburgh to famed showman William A. Brady of New York and Edward B. Grossmann of Chicago for $50,000 (fig. 3.4).[19] (Brady brought in young penny arcade owner Adolph Zukor to run several of his installations. *Hale's Tours* served as Zukor's bridge from marketing cheap mass entertainment to a more ambitious career in motion pictures, realized ultimately in his subsequent years as founder of Famous Players–Lasky Productions and president of Paramount Pictures.)[20] Hale and Gifford sold the southern states rights to Wells, Dunne,

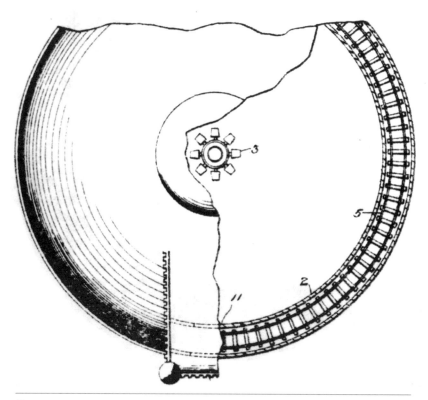

3.3. PATENT ILLUSTRATION, WILLIAM J. KEEFE, "AMUSEMENT DEVICE," PATENT 767,281. U.S. PATENT OFFICE, 22 MARCH 1904.

and Harlan of New York. They sold additional licenses to C. W. Parker Co. of Abilene, Kansas, for traveling carnival companies. They sold the Pacific and northwestern states' rights to a group of men who incorporated as "The Northwest Hale's Tourist Amusement Company" in Portland, Oregon.[21]

Hale and Gifford retired comfortably with their profits, leaving the regional entrepreneurs to run *Hale's Tours* installations at storefront theaters and amusement parks with at first dramatic success and then, in succeeding years, with financial reverses. Initially, *Hale's Tours* spread rapidly across the United States. Within a short period there were more than five hundred *Hale's Tours* at amusement parks and storefront theaters. Storefront *Hale's Tours* installations sat adjacent to nickelodeons, dance halls, cheap vaudeville houses, and saloons in downtown and ethnic working-class commercial strips. Amusement park installations rapidly appeared at approximately one-third of the estimated number of existing amusement parks (fig. 3.5), where they became instantly popular. Hale and Gifford's East Coast licensee, the Brady-Grossmann Company, installed at least three *Hale's Tours* at New

3.4. *HALE'S TOURS AND SCENES OF THE WORLD* ADVERTISEMENT, *BILLBOARD*, 10 FEBRUARY 1906.

York's Coney Island (at Dreamland, Luna Park, and on Surf Avenue), one nearby at Brighton Beach, one at Rockaway Beach in Queens, and others in downtown Manhattan storefront theaters.[22] In Chicago *Hale's Tours* appeared in the entertainment district on lower State Street and at both the White City and Riverview amusement parks.[23] Parks in Washington, D.C., Georgia, North Carolina, Ohio, Pennsylvania, Illinois, Wisconsin, Minnesota, Iowa, and Kansas also all immediately reported *Hale's Tours* among their top-grossing concessions.[24] Even though the novelty lingered for several years, the popularity of the attraction peaked in 1906 and 1907 in the United States only to flag soon thereafter in some places and more slowly in others until it is likely that the increased systematization and consolidation of the movie industry made it first difficult and then altogether impossible to obtain new phantom train ride movie products (what we today would call the "software" for the enterprise). Its importance therefore lies not in its longevity but in its immediate impact.

Hale's Tours itself consisted of one or more theater cars, each seating sixty to seventy-two "passengers." The company advertised that an installation could "handle as many as 1250 persons per hour with ease."[25] Admission for a ten-to-twenty-minute show was ten cents. The movies that showed out the front end of the car offered a filmed point of view from the front or rear of a moving train. The goal was to create the sensory illusion of movement into or away from a scene, accentuated by mechanical apparatuses and levers that simultaneously vibrated, rocked, oscillated, and tilted the car. There were also ambient sounds associated with the visual movement forward into the landscape—wheels clattering, paddle-wheels churning—punctuated by the announcements of whistles for braking and stopping, and bells or horns that served as fictional "warnings" timed to coordinate with the visual appearances of pedestrians or animals on the street or tracks. Fans blew blasts of air at the travelers from the rear of the car.[26] Some installations included lecturers who commented on the scenery and tourist points of interest along the journey. Adolph Zukor, one of the earliest operators of *Hale's Tours* shows, wrote to Fielding in 1957 that his theaters in New York, Pittsburgh, Newark, and Boston included lecturers.[27] In addition a photograph of the interior of an unidentified British *Hale's Tours* car shows a lecturer gesticulating to the audience.[28]

Hale's Tours offered subjective point-of-view journeys to scenic spots in the United States (including Niagara Falls, the Catskill Mountains, the Rocky Mountains, Northern California, the Black Hills, and the Yukon); to Canada, South America, and Europe; to foreign lands that were especially remote or preindustrial (China, Ceylon, Japan, Samoa, the Fiji Islands, Borneo); and even to urban centers via trolley or subway.[29] Representative titles of American films made for *Hale's Tours* include *A Trip on the Catskill Mt. Railway* (American Mutoscope and Biograph, 1906), *Into the Heart of the Catskills* (American Mutoscope and Biograph, 1906), *A Trip Down Mt. Tamalpais* (Miles Brothers, 1906), *The Hold-Up of the Rocky Mountain Express* (American Mutoscope and Biograph, 1906), *Ute Pass from a Freight Train* (Selig Polyscope, 1906), and *Trip Through the Black Hills* (Selig Polyscope, 1907).

Hale's Tours' cars also relied on existing phantom train ride films—short movies made from the point of view of the front of a train (e.g., *Haverstraw Tunnel*, American Mutoscope and Biograph, 1897). Despite the fact that some of the earliest phantom train ride films were almost ten years old, they resurfaced in *Hale's Tours'* cars.[30] American Mutoscope and Biograph advertised older phantom train films as "attractive railroad pictures which have been found highly successful with tour car schemes," thereby recycling a product that had otherwise lost its novelty value.[31] Numerous catalogues recommended such titles as the popular *Haverstraw Tunnel*, views of New York City from the elevated train (e.g., *New York to Brooklyn via Brooklyn Bridge, No. 1* [Edison, 1899]; *104th Street Curve, New York, Elevated Railway*

[Edison, 1899]); views of Niagara Falls (e.g., *Arrival at Falls View Station* [American Mutoscope and Biograph, 1901]; *Lower Rapids, Niagara* [American Mutoscope and Biograph, 1896]); and train rides through mountains and tunnels (*The Gap, Entrance to the Rocky Mountains* [American Mutoscope and Biograph, 1899]; *Frazer Canyon* [American Mutoscope and Biograph, 1899]). *Hale's Tours* finally fulfilled the potential of virtual railway tourism across the United States initially expressed in the desires of the movie reviewers of *Haverstraw Tunnel* in 1897.

By the end of the 1906 summer season, *Hale's Tours* had also spread to leading world capitals—there are records of installations in Mexico City, Havana, Melbourne, Paris, London, Berlin, Bremen, Hamburg, Hong Kong, and Johannesburg.[32] Hale and Gifford reportedly sold the British territorial rights for $100,000, and *Hale's Tours* enjoyed great popularity in Great Britain, a success perhaps due in no small part to the cresting popularity of phantom train ride films there.[33] In London a *Hale's Tours* storefront installation opened at 165 Oxford Street. By 1908 there were three other installations in downtown London, as well as in Bristol and Leeds.[34] *Hale's Tours* were also constructed at several English amusement parks, including Manchester's White City, Blackpool Pleasure Beach, Brighton's Palace Pier, and Nottingham's White City. *Hale's Tours* in England and Ireland appears to have outlived its American counterparts and to have enjoyed continuing popularity until at least 1910 and perhaps until 1912. For citizens in all these countries *Hale's Tours* represented the first permanent, widespread venue to show motion pictures exclusively, and it was *Hale's Tours* that most often introduced the first generation of moviegoers to the phenomenon of motion pictures.

Its longer life in Britain may be accounted for by several speculative explanations. As an extension of phantom train rides, *Hale's Tours* capitalized on a type of cinema that one could argue was simply always more popular and in greater demand in Britain than in the United States. One could hypothesize that virtual tourism to remote locales in preindustrial, colonial lands served a different cultural purpose for a country like Great Britain, in the wake of the Boer War, struggling with maintaining its sense of empire as opposed to the United States, which had not yet come to terms with its emerging identity as a world empire. But, most important, U.S. film manufacturers increasingly exported story films in the period from 1906 to 1912, and by 1911 these made up 60 percent of the market in Britain.[35] Many British manufacturers did not try to compete and instead differentiated themselves by offering up growing numbers of scenics, travelogues, and the kinds of appropriate *Hale's Tours* fare that was getting harder to acquire in the domestic U.S. market.

The British motion picture industry newspapers *Bioscope* and *Optical Lantern and Cinematograph Journal* report no shortage of train travel films; British urban trolley, subway, or omnibus rides; and sea travel films throughout this period. They list dozens of such films offered by Warwick, Gaumont, Pathé Frères, Charles Urban, Nordisk, Éclair, and Hepworth at the same time that American trade newspapers identify no similarly available fare. Representative titles from this period include: *A Ride Through the Ardennes* (Hepworth, 1906), *Ascent and Descent of the Dolomite Towers* (Charles Urban, 1907), *A Trip on the Metropolitan Railway from Baker St. to Uxbridge and Aylesbury* (manufacturer unknown, 1910), *A Trip Through British Borneo* (Charles Urban, 1907), *Phantom Ride from Chamonix to Vallorcine* (Éclair, 1910), and *Ride on the Gothard Railway* (Warwick, 1910).[36] A *Hale's Tours of the World* advertisement for the London installation even details the value of simulated travel to the Italian lakes as "the new style of honeymoon" while also recognizing the distinctive quality of British travel in the empire vis-à-vis *Hale's Tours*: "We can visit the Colonies or any part of the world (without luggage!) and return within fifteen minutes."[37]

Within months of *Hale's Tours'* initial success, imitators and variants quickly followed. In New York and Chicago there were *Palace Touring Cars, Hurst's Touring New York,* and *Cessna's Sightseeing Auto Tours. Citron's Overland Flyer* was a spring-supported railway car that could bounce or rock passengers; it had revolving rollers underneath the car to create "a rumbling sound like the travel of wheels over a track."[38] Although this ride relied on a technically different mechanical system for its motion effects (Hale and Gifford eventually bought out Citron's patent for this mechanism),[39] the ride experience was essentially the same as *Hale's Tours* except that it opened and closed curtains at the side windows in synchronization with the beginning and end of the motion and sound effects.[40] *Trolley Car Tours,* which also opened during the 1906 season at storefront theaters and amusement parks, relied less on slight mechanical differences than on democratic rhetorical appeals to differentiate itself from the *Hale's Tours* experience of a luxury train. *Trolley Car Tours* advertisements trumpeted, "Our car is the latest and best in a car device for travels and tours—the most natural way to the masses. Few ride in Pullmans; everybody hits the trolley."[41]

Other competitors also varied the mode of transportation or enhanced the *Hale's Tours* phenomenon of showing point-of-view moving pictures out a front window. *Auto Tours of the World and Sightseeing in the Principal Cities* changed the vehicle to a large touring automobile and added painted moving panoramas to the sides of the open car (fig. 3.6). *Auto Tours* described in detail its combination of moving panorama and motion picture display: "The illusion of seeing the various countries and cities from an automobile is produced by a panorama of moving scenes attached to the wall beside the Sightseeing Auto upon which are seated the 'Sightseers,' and the throwing upon a screen in front of the Sightseeing Auto the moving pictures which were taken from a moving automobile, by this company, and which are the property of the Sightseeing Auto Co."[42]

In addition *Auto Tours* "stopped the car" midway through the show in order to deliver passengers to an adjacent electric theater showing a variety of moving pictures rather than only point-of-view travelogues. An advertisement explained the purpose of this sideshow: "'Sightseers' are given a side trip which enables them to view a variety of moving pictures, thus taking away from the patrons of the Sightseeing Autos that 'tired feeling' which is produced by a repetition of the same kind and character of moving pictures they would be forced to witness should they always remain on the auto."[43] In adapting the moving panorama experience of the nineteenth century for new twentieth-century forms of luxury travel, *Auto Tours* eased its customers into a new simulated mode of travel by carrying forward a familiar immersive experience. At the same time, *Auto Tours* combined the past with the future by giving customers both a simulated motion travel experience and a nickelodeon program.

Pullman trains and automobiles, both generally luxury means of travel in 1906, were not the only vehicles adapted for motion-simulated movie rides. Some simulated hot-air balloon travel, including one patented in 1906 by Philadelphia film manufacturer Sigmund Lubin.[44] *White & Langever's Steamboat Tours of the World* applied the *Hale's Tours* concept to water travel, beginning in the 1907 season. It employed an actual ferry to transport patrons to a "marine-illusion boat," where moving pictures were projected in the front of a stationary boat that seated up to two hundred people. Mechanical apparatus rocked and oscillated the mock boat, rotating paddle wheels beneath the deck "simulat[ed] the sound of paddle-wheels employed for propulsion," and fans blew breezes in the faces of the audience to "give the impression that they are traveling."[45] The illusion boat included a steam calliope as well.

Hruby & Plummer's Tours and Scenes of the World (fig. 3.7) appropriated *all* these concepts but made them more generic for traveling carnivals. That

SIGHTSEEING AUTOS!

Auto Tours of the World and Sightseeing in the Principal Cities

WE MAKE OUR OWN FILMS.   OTHER PEOPLE RENT THE ONES THEY SHOW.

ONE OF OUR FRONTS.

Our Moving Picture Shows Are Original, Instructive, Novel and Amusing.

ABOVE ALL, THE BIGGEST MONEY-MAKER OF ANY PICTURE SHOW IN THE UNITED STATES

Our pictures, which are taken from automobiles in the principal cities of the world, and along famous auto routes of both the old and the new worlds, are shown to the "Sightseers" from a Sightseeing Auto. The illusion of seeing the various countries and cities from an automobile is produced by a panorama of moving scenes attached to the wall beside the Sightseeing Auto upon which are seated the "Sightseers," and the throwing upon a screen in front of the Sightseeing Auto the moving pictures which were taken from a moving automobile, by this company, and which are the property of the Sightseeing Auto Co. By an original and clever idea the "Sightseers" are given a side trip which enables them to view a variety of moving pictures, thus taking away from the patrons of the Sightseeing Autos that "tired feeling" which is produced by a repetition of the same kind and character of moving pictures they would be forced to witness should they always remain on the auto. Our ideas concerning the manner in which the pictures are shown were thought of sufficient value by a leading firm of patent lawyers in Chicago that by their advice plans and specifications of same have been forwarded to Washington, and patents are now pending.

PARK MANAGERS WHO DESIRE THE "BIG THING" WRITE US.

Any person who can secure a concession for showing the Auto Tours of the World and Sightseeing in the Principal Cities, write for terms. You can do business with us, and we don't want it all, either. We will install and grant the license to operate for a percentage of the gross receipts; or we will install in parks and give a percentage of the gross for the privilege; or we will sell plans, giving right to operate, furnish fronts, and make you a proposition that will bring you a monthly rental of $150. This you will have every month in your pocket before you start business. We furnish the films at a weekly rental of $15. For full particulars address

CHAS. W. CESSNA,
Gen. Manager Sight Seeing Auto Co.,
DECATUR, ILLINOIS

or W. H. LABB CONSTRUCTION CO.,
Gen. Agents for U. S.,
State Life Bldg., INDIANAPOLIS, IND.

© 3.6. *AUTO TOURS OF THE WORLD AND SIGHTSEEING IN THE PRINCIPAL CITIES* ADVERTISEMENT, *BILLBOARD*, 27 JANUARY 1906. ©

3.7. *HRUBY & PLUMMER TOURS AND SCENES OF THE WORLD* ADVERTISEMENT, *BILLBOARD*, 3 MARCH 1906.

way, itinerant showmen were not dependent on a permanent installation and could easily set up and tear down a train, boat, or automobile. *Hruby* advertisements defined the installation: "A moving picture show in a knock-down portable canvas car, boat, vehicle or ordinary tent that can be easily set up, quickly pulled down, readily transported, yet mechanically arranged [so] that the bell, the whistle, and the swing of a moving train, boat or vehicle is produced. Trips or views can be constantly changed to suit your fancy, scenes of any railroad vehicle or boat ride, on land or water, produced with full sensation of the ride, together with 'Sightseers' sightseeing side trips covering Principal Cities of the world."[46] *Hruby*'s also rocked and oscillated both the seat bases and the upper portions of the chairs. It was outfitted with Edison films and projector, a motion simulation apparatus, a portable structure for housing the entirety, an advertising front, and portable generator for powering the exhibition.[47]

A Trip to California over Land and Sea, however, may have been even more ingenious than *Hruby*'s. It combined railway and marine illusion travel, offering first the fantasy of a cross-country rail journey from the East Coast to California and then the sensation of the car dropped into the water to turn the vehicle into a boat for travel down the California coast. Its advertisement proclaimed that the effect was "the car being instantaneously transformed into a beautiful vessel which gives you a boat ride along the coast, the performance ending with a sensational climax (a Naval Battle and Storm at Sea)"—despite the fact that no known naval battles had ever taken place off the coast of California![48]

Early accounts of these movie rides are reminiscent of the inventive reports regarding the reception of the earliest Lumière films: "The illusion was so good that . . . members of the audience frequently yelled at pedestrians to get out of the way or be run down."[49] It is noteworthy that in this report spectators do not jump out of the way (as they did in the hyperbolic reports about Lumière film showings) since they do not understand things coming at them inasmuch as they understand themselves moving forward; they instead yell at onscreen pedestrians to get out of the way. (Actually, audience catcalls further imply an acoustic space that defines their participation in the movie.) Film historian Noël Burch summarized: "These spectators . . . were already in another world than those who, ten years earlier, had jumped up in terror at the filmed arrival of a train in a station: [they] . . . are masters of the situation, they are ready to *go through the peephole*."[50] But Burch makes the mistake of thinking that *Hale's Tours* depended entirely on its capacity to effect this visual, out-of-body projection into the diegesis. He fails to see that these illusion rides were always *more than* movies; they were about a physiological and psychological experience associated with travel.

Hale's Tours riders themselves may have recognized this element. A reporter describes one rider: "One demented fellow even kept coming back to the same show, day after day. Sooner or later, he figured, the engineer would make a mistake and he would get to see a train wreck."[51] The "demented fellow" may have actually recognized the delicious terror of *Hale's Tours* better than Burch or even the reporter since it is precisely the anticipation of disaster that provides the thrill at the heart of *Hale's Tours.* The reporter only understood the irony since the ride controlled the fact that disaster would not happen and that the "demented fellow" would always experience anticipation safely. Obviously a fan of *Hale's Tours*, the "demented fellow" may have been exhibiting less of a dementia than the delirious effect produced by this and other rides at the amusement park, and he may indeed be kin to the modern thrill ride or roller coaster aficionado, who professes a fondness for repeat rides, for "collecting" ride experiences at different locations, and for the thrill.

It is also important to point out, in deference to the "demented fellow," that the new mode of railway travel that *Hale's Tours* and others worked so hard to simulate was not necessarily always safe. Indeed, Lynne Kirby persuasively argues that *Hale's Tours* best unified "the perceptual overlap between the railroad and the cinema."[52] But more than overlap railroad and cinema, *Hale's Tours'* "imagination of disaster" fused the experience of the parkgoer as both a railway traveler and moviegoer, bringing into focus the larger fantasy of the amusement park of seeing technology go out of control and the pleasure in the resulting terror.

Illusion ride manufacturers understood this fact. Their advertisements promoted the motion effects and the physical sensation of travel over the movies themselves. (Their patent applications, after all, asked to cover the motion effects and the installation rather than the projectors and screens that were already patented to other companies and, indeed, the installations relied on a variety of different motion picture projectors.) Several noted the importance of fans blowing air on the audience for making realistic the physical sensation of travel. There is little detail about the kinds of bells, whistles, and calliopes being sold with these outfits, and there is even less information about how these sound makers operated during a *Hale's Tours* or *Trip to California* show. Yet the sound makers were included among the advertised paraphernalia of the show, always there as if to serve some unspecified but integral function, and the patent applications always included a sound device for simulating the sound of forward movement.

Like the loop-de-loops and scenic railways, illusion rides emphasized the traveler's body as the center of an environment of action and excitement but added the illusion of travel in an actual worldly location outside the park. They extended a multiplicity of effects *on* the body—the novelty of moving images, loud sounds, and physical sensations of motion shocks and wind effects. The installation manufacturers who belonged to the industry of thrill ride manufacturers and carnival or fair concession producers rather than to developing networks of motion picture and apparatus manufacturers repeatedly emphasized the synchronization of visual, kinesthetic, and sound effects as the unique property of their apparatus. They were less interested in the business of "what was viewed out the window." Rather, they organized a theatrical experience for the cognitive convergence of sensory information as the basis for the illusion that "you are really there."

THE ESSENTIAL EXPEDITION OF *HALE'S TOURS*:
A NARRATION OF TOURISM

Hale's Tours therefore was not just "a movie" but was always a movie ride. *Hale's Tours'* latent content assumed a newly commercialized tourism—the traveler made over into a spectator by taking a virtual journey specifically to consume the unfamiliar, whether that was the new industrial city, the foreign preindustrial, or picturesque Nature. The subjects of *Hale's Tours'* travel films assumed a series of binary values already in place about Nature and Civilization and the function of tourism for flirting with those oppositions.

Hale's Tours capitalized on and extended the popular phantom train ride films made from the late 1890s on (e.g., *Haverstraw Tunnel*). Yet its most significant filmic precursor is another "attraction" linked to a world's fair. *A Trip Around the Pan American Exposition* (Edison, 1901) is a three-reel phantom ride shot from onboard an electric boat launch at the 1901 Buffalo fair. Offering a traveler's point of view from a gondola that stops and starts as it makes its way through the exposition canals and past the fair's attractions, *A Trip* allowed theatergoers at vaudeville houses around the country to participate in a distant tourist destination as they experienced a virtual boat ride along the circuitous route of the fair's canals. Kristen Whissel argues for the film as a visual trope of how electricity and traffic "flow" converge in American modernity, providing a key lesson on the perception of technological modernity.[53] Thus, audiences were ready for *Hale's Tours'* "enhancement" of the virtual voyage and were already accustomed to spectatorial viewing that engaged touristic sensation and spectacle as key to modernist perception.

The films shown in *Hale's Tours* and other motion travel cars typically featured the landscape as the vehicle picked up speed, so that details accelerating into the foreground were the featured information. The films employed both editing and camera movements but usually only after presenting an extended shot (often one to two minutes or longer in a seven- to eight-minute film) organized by the locomotion of the camera. The initial effect was a continuous flow of objects rushing toward the camera, the same cinematographic practice as the earliest phantom train ride films.

The camera, usually mounted at a slightly tipped angle, showed the railroad tracks in the foreground as parallel lines that converge at the horizon, an important indicator of perspectival depth. Telephone poles, bridges, tunnels, and other environmental markers in the frame also marked continuous flow according to the lines of perspective. Passing through tunnels effected a particularly dramatic difference of darkness and light, moving image or no image, and interruption and flow. As Fielding aptly describes it, "The moving image of the tracks slipped away under the forward edge of the coach."[54] The repetition of all these elements contributed to an overall impression that the perceptual experience of camera motion is a recreation of the flow of the environment.

The ambient sounds associated with the visual movement forward into the landscape provided a sound envelope that also made the realism of the ride possible because it contributed to a cognitive convergence and blending of the discrete and somewhat disparate sensory information provided by motion and vision. If, as Barbara Maria Stafford has argued in her discussion of aesthetic illusion and multimedia, it is cognitively impossible for the brain to process simultaneous discrete sensory information so that coherent thinking depends on a synthetic convergence performed mentally, one may hypothesize it is the sound cues that hypostatized that union.[55]

The films, however, did not always maintain a strict cowcatcher point of view and synchronized sound information to get across their sensations. Changes of locale occurred abruptly through editing, the camera position was moved, or the perspective from the front or rear of the train was altogether abandoned. For example, *Ute Pass from a Freight Train* depicts in turn an engineer and fireman at work on a train up ahead on the tracks, Pike's Peak, and the view out the back of the train from the caboose. In another example, one of the earliest *Hale's Tours* train travel shows reported at Coney Island was rather incongruously *A Trip in a Balloon* (manufacturer and date unknown), an "imaginary sky voyage" that featured *aerial* cinematographic views of New York made during aeronaut Leo Stevens's recent balloon trip.[56]

Moreover, *Hale's Tours* often expanded the travel format with views of tourist attractions or panoramas. Increasingly, films made for *Hale's Tours* after 1906 stretched the travelogue with comic or dramatic scenes that typically featured mingling between men and women, one class and another, farmers and urbanites, train employees and civilians, ordinary citizens and outlaws. (And, of course, programs like *Automobile Tours of the World* simply moved the audience from its *Hale's Tours*-esque fare to the variety format of an electric theater.) As early as 1906, a *Hale's Tours* advertisement in the *New York Clipper* listed five "humorous railway scenes" that could be included in *Hale's Tours* programs.[57] *Trip Through the Black Hills* (Selig Polyscope, 1907) covered "the difficulties of trying to dress in a Pullman berth."[58] Films like *Trip Through the Black Hills* often ended with shots of arriving at the train station.

In addition, simple story films associated with railroad travel—for example, *The Great Train Robbery* (Edison, 1903), *What Happened in the Tunnel* (Edison, 1903), *The Deadwood Sleeper* (a comic film about the nighttime antics of trying to sleep in a Pullman sleeping car that ends with a robbery [American Mutoscope and Biograph, 1905])—also played in *Hale's Tours* cars. Zukor reported that when revenues began to wane, he showed *The Great Train Robbery* at his Manhattan *Hale's Tours*, and he discovered that attendance was so good for this adaptation of the popular theatrical melodrama that he did not need the gimmick of a simulated railroad car to show motion pictures.[59] (He subsequently converted his installation into a nickelodeon.)

Therefore, it was not unusual for the films to cut regularly to the interior of a railroad car, producing a "mirror image" of the social space in which the *Hale's Tours* patron was seated. These films were not purely travelogues, then, but were also about the social relations and expectations connected with the experience of travel. They suggest that what was fundamental to the event was not merely the sight of the "destination," and the sensation and sound of immersion in it, but the *experience*—both physical and social—of being in that place.

For example, *The Hold-Up of the Rocky Mountain Express* begins with a long shot of the train station platform, and then the camera slowly and smoothly moves forward.[60] The point of view is the front of a departing train. As the train/camera picks up speed and leaves the station, people on the tracks jump out of the way. The train/camera passes through a town and then into the scenic rural landscape. The voyage through the picturesque snow-covered fields and trees continues for a few minutes.

Then there is an abrupt cut to the inside of a coach, obviously a studio set of a passenger car. This is the first shift of address that the film effects: it changes the point of view from the cowcatcher to the backseat of a railway coach. Inside the coach two men sit across from two women. Behind the women, another woman tries to flirt with the men. Oblivious to her efforts, one of the men trades places with the woman opposite him so that the four become paired off in two heterosexual couples. The frustrated flirt hits the porter (an actor in blackface) over the head and knocks him down. The conductor arrives and intervenes. Both railroad employees exit.

Next, a tramp crawls out from under the seat behind the couple on the left. Unobserved by the passengers, he sits down next to the lone woman (in effect, producing a third heterosexual coupling and realizing her goal although the humor here resides in the impropriety of this pairing). She reacts in horror and attacks him until the conductor reappears and throws him out of the car.

At this point the film returns to the cowcatcher point of view. But the camera/train soon stops moving because a log is laid across the tracks. Two railroad men enter from the foreground to move the log but instead are held up by outlaws. The film then returns to the interior of the passenger car. Travelers looking out of the window to see the cause of the delay are disturbed by one of the thieves entering the car. He lines up the passengers, robs them, and one of the women faints. The film returns to the point of view of the tracks and depicts the criminals getting away on a handcar; the train starts up and pursues them. Here the point of view of forward locomotion serves narrative rather than picturesque purposes.[61] As the vehicles approach a station, the bandits are apprehended, and the film ends. The station is the scenic destination, the dramatic story is concluded, and the spectator made over into a traveler has reached the end of the "journey." When one considers as well the typical environment for a *Hale's Tours* installation at an amusement park, the "virtual voyage" and visceral experience may now be easily understood as a novel motion picture variant consistent with the rhythms and subjects of the park's other thrill rides.

Grand Hotel to Big Indian (American Mutoscope and Biograph, 1906) is a variant of *The Hold-Up of the Rocky Mountain Express*. Its title depends on familiarity with well-known summer resort landmarks in the Catskill Mountains of New York. Like *Rocky Mountain Express*, the film begins with an extended shot of a cowcatcher-traveling point of view along the famous Horseshoe Loop on the New York state Ulster and Delaware Railway.

The film then cuts to the train interior where men and women are seated on opposite sides of the aisle (fig. 3.8). The conductor walks through the car while, outside the windows on each side, mattes of traveling landscape "flow" past. A porter enters and seats a well-dressed man in a place just vacated by another passenger. The newcomer (the *New York World's* comic strip character Mr. Butt-In come-to-life) tips his hat to a young girl across the aisle; she gives him the cold shoulder and tells her papa, who crosses the aisle to give the masher a hard time. No sooner has that action been completed than the man who initially vacated his seat returns and wants his seat back. A fight in the aisle ensues; it is broken up by the conductor and the porter, and each man is sent back to his seat. The film then cuts back to the cowcatcher point of view.

Other such narrative "interruptions" of the continuous flow of locomotion in this film include a man who cannot get his horse to move off the tracks. Similar to the shot of the train men entering the foreground in *The Hold-Up of the Rocky Mountain Express*, the engineer and fireman alight in front of the train and try to help the man pull his horse off the tracks. The engineer squirts oil from a can onto the wheels of the wagon and onto the horse's legs! Mr. Butt-In, the gentleman who caused a comic struggle in the interior, arrives, and another fight ensues. The railroad employees carry off Mr. Butt-In, and the man in the wagon urges his horse off the tracks. After a pause the train starts up again and continues on its journey.

Grand Hotel to Big Indian improves on the formula of *The Hold-Up of the Rocky Mountain Express* to the extent that it mixes vicarious scenic tourism with dramatic social intercourse *and* the fantasy of the newspaper comic strip come to life (demonstrated the same year in Edison's *The Dream of a Rarebit Fiend*). The space of the *Hale's Tours* car provided the spectator-travelers the pleasure of a fantasy born out of modern life. It allowed the movie spectator to become immersed in a spectacle that combined worlds of fiction and the real and, in the process, to blur the distinction between the two.

© 3.8. SHOTS FROM *GRAND HOTEL TO BIG INDIAN* (AMERICAN MUTOSCOPE AND BIOGRAPH, 1906). PAPER PRINT COLLECTION, MOTION PICTURE, BROADCASTING, AND RECORDED SOUND DIVISION, LIBRARY OF CONGRESS, WASHINGTON, DC. ©

The *Hale's Tours* film that takes such blurring to its logical conclusion is *When the Devil Drives* (Charles Urban, 1907), a British movie unlikely to have been imported into the States but one of many European-made films for showing in British and continental *Hale's Tours* cars. Although there is no evidence to support that the film played in the Unites States, *When the Devil Drives* demonstrates the degree to which the *Hale's Tours* phenomenon incorporated increasingly sophisticated multishot films whose object was not the "realism" of the setting but the realistic sensation of tourist travel fantasies that were also fantasies increasingly made out of the materials of mass media.

When the Devil Drives borrows self-consciously from and blurs the nascent genres of trick film, *Hale's Tours*-esque travelogue, comedy, and animation. It begins with a story prelude of two couples packing their trunks into a horse-drawn cab for hire. Based on their personal appearances, the two couples are apparently husband and wife and daughter and son-in-law. The fact that this will be a comedy is made explicit not only in the gestures they employ and in the antics of packing the carriage but in the character of the domineering wife, played by a man "in drag." The carriage driver, barely visible in a dark top hat and large cloak, sits quietly throughout the preparations but is "transformed" (through stop-motion) into the devil just as soon he drives away. (Such a transformation hints at the Méliès trick-film influence that will become more pronounced later in the film.) He careens wildly through the streets while his passengers stick their heads out the windows and protest vigorously. He stops the cab, and the two couples alight while making physical protests. The devil driver laughs, and he and the carriage vanish, leaving the couples stranded with their trunks on the street.

The next shot is a view from the passenger platform of a train entering a railroad station—a clichéd and much repeated view some twelve years after the Lumière brothers' first rendering of the same material. The film then cuts to a studio interior view of a train compartment, where the two couples chat with other passengers. Again, the film cuts to an exterior shot of a train entering the railroad yard, and again, the film cuts to an interior studio shot—this time depicting the engineer and fireman at work shoveling coal. An explosion and a cloud of black smoke knock down the crew, and the devil emerges from the cloud. He throws the men off the train and folds his arms in satisfaction.

Only at this point does the film finally introduce the cowcatcher point of view as the train begins its journey out of the railroad station. Unlike other *Hale's Tours* films, *When the Devil Drives* reverses the order and hierarchy of mode and presentation: other *Hale's Tours* films that incorporate story elements *begin* with an extended phantom train ride showcasing the scenery and effect of locomotion before introducing character or plot. *When the Devil Drives* establishes its comic personae and story about a family journey *before* it becomes a phantom train ride. By overturning the conventions, it incorporates the spectacle effect into the contours of narrative.

Once the phantom train ride is established, the film cuts to what is obviously a toy train moving along tracks on a flat matte landscape. As the toy train makes its way *off* the rails, it continues its journey across flat, painted mountains thanks to stop-motion cinematography. The view is reminiscent of similar ones in Georges Méliès's earlier films *Voyage à travers l'impossible* [*The Impossible Voyage*] (Star Films, 1904) and *Le Raid Paris–Monte Carlo en deux heures* [*From Paris to Monte Carlo*] (Star Films, 1905).[62] The toy train runs out of rails and plunges into a body of water. Shots of the toy train now moving underwater in an aquarium are intercut with reaction shots of the four passengers watching fish swim by their window.

Sound effects would also have contributed to narrative realism. The chief purpose of the ambient sound effects of wheels clattering or water swirling, whistles shrieking, and bells ringing may have been to cover or smooth over the disparity between the *physical* sensation of motion and the *visual* perception of hurtling into space. But other sound effects could also have enhanced and reinforced narrative elements.[63] In other words the realism of the *Hale's Tours* films was never purely a cinematographic reproduction of nature but a combined program that produced a theatrical effect of perceptual and emotional immersion and involvement.

From this point in *When the Devil Drives* things only go from bad to worse: the train compartment appears to tilt and get turned upside down. After much business the train rights itself and gets back on the tracks only to leave the terra firma for the sky, where it floats upside down. As a finale, the train makes a circle and spins. The film ends with the spinning circle first superimposed and then dissolved into an emblematic shot of the devil laughing. Like *Grand Hotel*'s depiction of travel challenged by comic book characters come to life and *The Hold-Up of the Rocky Mountain Express*'s drama straight out of a dime novel, *When the Devil Drives* simulates trick-film fantasies of Méliès-like magic. Ultimately, the rhetoric of verisimilitude associated with these films is conflated with both worldly travel and fantasy.

CONCLUSION

If *Hale's Tours* movie installations put a novel "thrill" into motion pictures by making movies a multimedia visceral experience, they in many ways simply extended the work of movies in general. At amusement parks, *Hale's Tours* were a mechanical ride that transformed parkgoers who could not afford affluent luxury travel into travelers enjoying recreational escapes. *Hale's Tours* thus offered up nature and fantasy as an antidote for the overstimulation of modern life. It allowed the spectator passengers to pretend that, as railway tourists, they could master and take pleasure in *all* those environments (both real and fictional) to which society was claiming new access. *Hale's Tours* reinforced that the world is an object lesson in pleasure—a lesson in which the preindustrial, the distant, the colonial, as well as the fictional, are all exotic, accessible spaces that could be consumed. By emphasizing the commercial nature of railroad travel into these reaches, *Hale's Tours* defined a new kind of traveler for whom manifest destiny meant inevitably possessing a geographically expanded playground.

Hale's Tours "trips," moreover, may be said to have initiated men and women into their new standing within the system of commodity production, converting them from private individuals into a mass culture consuming machine, travel, and Nature alike. In this regard *Hale's Tours* supported this process, transforming the status of a mechanical conveyance into a seemingly limitless commodity of pleasure and excitement. But by establishing a link between movies and the amusement park ride, the excesses, and the sensations of tourism, *Hale's Tours* provided sensory verification of the turmoil increasingly associated with modernity, the new century, and urban life.

The Miniature and the Giant

POSTCARDS AND EARLY CINEMA

Both [the miniature and the giant] involve the selection of elements that will be transformed and displayed in an exaggerated relation to the social construction of reality. . . . While fantasy in the miniature moves toward an individualized interiority, fantasy in the gigantic exteriorizes and communalizes.

—Susan Stewart, On Longing

FROM THEIR OUTSETS BOTH POSTCARDS (THE MINIATURE) and movies (the gigantic) took on the amusement park—as subject matter and as a location for their dissemination. Movies depicted the parks, the mechanical rides, and the patrons' unrestrained behavior while the films of these attractions played at the parks themselves. Picture postcards likewise illustrated the parks, their contents, and their participants and were a staple at amusement parks, where they were sold as souvenirs. Postcards and movies promoted amusement parks well beyond the confines of the parks and widely circulated views of them as new icons. They commodified the parks and made them transportable. They offered idealized pictures of them that framed expectations and perspectives while relying on physical involvement as a way to make a popular argument about the parks. Because of their sweeping dissemination and ubiquity, cinema and postcards helped to further decenter urban modernity from the largest cities so that rural, small-town, medium-sized-city, and working-class people from multiple regions and social or ethnic locations were included in the emergence of a national modernity. Rather than be excluded or seen as belated foils to a process often historicized as city-centered and top-down, diverse Americans across far-flung sites participated vicariously in a new urban modernity vis-à-vis postcards and movies.

From the 1890s through the first decades of the twentieth century, both cinema and picture postcards flourished. The story of early cinema—its relationship to such antecedent pictorial forms as photography, painting, and panoramas and its correlation to contemporary representational and social practices in theaters, fairs, museums, and even morgues—is well known.[1] But little has been said about cinema's bonds to the other chief new popular mode simultaneously turning vision itself into a trade item for a new mass consumption—picture postcards. A comparison between early cinema and postcards, however dissimilar the material objects initially seem, reveals an important ideological coalescence in accommodating an embodied perceptual experience to new lessons about tourism and nation-building. The miniaturization of views that is key to the picture postcard complements the enlargement of views central to motion pictures (including and especially *Hale's Tours*) so that together they represent the twin poles of metaphorically adapting one's body to the emergence of modernity.

A THEORY OF POSTCARD AND CINEMA SPECTACLE

Perhaps any comparison between movies and postcards seems counterintuitive and has heretofore escaped historians' attention because so long as postcards and movies are understood merely as material objects—the things seen—they seem to have little in common. The picture postcard, a static photograph small in size and scale, renders its subject matter diminutive in relationship to the spectator. Indeed, above all else, a picture postcard is itself a material object, a *three*-dimensional thing that has volume, shape, and tactility, as Elizabeth Edwards and Janice Hart note in their study of the photograph as a material object.[2] Movies seemingly accomplish the opposite: the spectator cannot touch or possess the actual image, pictorial material so large that perception of so much detail always yields to movement, to the trace of presence through time. One offers views easily enclosed and controlled by the body of the person looking at it; the other yields oversized sights that literally overshadow the spectator. One affords only a single static, frozen, motionless scene, whereas the other celebrates movement and mobile, wandering, often panoramic vision. One is predominantly a personally interactive experience: a postcard is purchased, owned, traded and/or made into a gift, written upon, and then most often encountered secondhand in the intimacy of the home; movies are a more ephemeral experience, best understood as part of a social collective, semipublic viewing space.

When we reconsider the nature of their spectacles, however, not as materialized in the object itself but as a particular relationship produced between observer and observed, the postcard and the cinema (which emerged at the same historical moment) are both novelty mechanical accommodations to the shocks of the new. They both construct visual perception as a more complex phenomenon than an ahistorical identification with the "eye" of the picturing apparatus and an inscribed position produced by the object. Movies and postcards were not the first such "toys" of the industrial age to accomplish this consideration and not the first to bifurcate the process itself into the twin poles of miniaturization and enlargement. They do represent an important flourishing of a phenomenological relationship to objects viewed that began earlier in the nineteenth century. The stereopticon, a handheld magic lantern for viewing photographs that gave off three-dimensional effects, was a popular late nineteenth-century parlor toy that may be seen as one material predecessor to the postcard. Its counterpoint was both the magic lantern show, where similar images would be projected onto a screen in front of an audience, and the panorama. As Jonathan Crary has argued, such entertainments of a new industrial age ask us to reconsider representation as less about "the world out there" than about the physiological grafting of vision to attention, fascination, and even distraction as embodied cognitive processes.[3] Within this new historicized model of spectatorship such novelties as motion pictures and postcards both effected and promised embodiment as a prophylactic against a world that heralded an increasing sense of disembodiment. Indeed, a new generation of postcard scholars agrees that the postcard likewise emerged "as a mediator of modernity, a means to identify and possess the totality of the city at a time when it was in fact fragmenting physically and socially."[4] Both cinema and postcards reconciled bodily experience and cognitive understanding to the ascendancy of vision as the privileged self-sufficient source of perceptual knowledge when modernity's novelty and radical social heterogeneity threatened physical anxiety and alienation.

Now, the very features of postcards and cinema that seem to suffuse them differently may be recast as the comparable ways the body is compensated for linking vision to other physiological perceptions in an attempt to ameliorate modernity's conditions. Postcards offer miniaturized scenes that are easily enveloped and contained by the body of the spectator. Their static, frozen, visual field presented in a frontal display of direct address may be perceptually unified through a single glance; thus, they center the body as an attentive subject. They rely on perspective, positioning the camera above ground level so that the camera's eye dominates the viewed space while the person holding the card also dominates the little card with her or his physical being, inscribing a prosthetic alliance between the viewing subject and object. Postcards are seemingly omnipresent perpetrators of an all-seeing masterful gaze. Susan Stewart explains the function of the postcard: "The souvenir [postcard] reduces the public, the monumental, and the three-dimensional into the miniature, that which can be enveloped by the body, or into the two-dimensional representation, that which can be appropriated within the privatized view of the individual subject."[5] All danger of a world beyond the comprehending subject is momentarily overcome by aesthetically subsuming it to the superior epistemological position of the postcard observer and the observer's agency in a world of commodity relations. She characterizes the experience as a metaphor for celebrating the individual's sense of interiority.

The postcard reduced the new urban industrialized world in dimension and made it into a packaged *personal* event, one that promised a satisfactory relationship to a shadow of the thing itself. In this regard both the purchase of the postcard and its receipt as a gift authenticate a remote (urban) viewing experience. Thus, as Edwards and Hart claim, the presentational form of a postcard matters even more than the nature of the image material itself for its social significance.[6] An individual undertakes a private experience in the card's purchase in which the subject recovers a sense of agency through consumerism, inscribing a handwritten message on the card, and becoming a point of ersatz production in making this card over into a gift. The individual who receives the card and its handwritten greeting is asked to experience a desire for the virtual vision eminently knowable in its miniaturized, silently visual, aestheticized form. The fact that so many people collected these views at the turn of the century legitimates the postcard's role for surprising and capturing viewers into a reverie of places, people, and events that existed nowhere but represented traces of the real displaced onto the sublime.

In a similar relay of surprise and capture, cinema expanded the visual field of the postcard and produced an opposite perceptual effect: cinema yields gigantic sights that may well threaten to overwhelm the body of the spectator (and there is sufficient discussion of this phenomenon, the train-rushing-the-onlookers effect). Early cinema's exhibitionist aesthetic of frontal display and direct address, as Tom Gunning has argued, however, produces delight rather than fear. Gunning describes this effect in terms of the image as the magic of the illusion itself: "In its double nature, its transformation of still image into moving illusion, [early cinema] expresses an attitude in which astonishment and knowledge perform a vertiginous dance, and pleasure derives from the energy released by the play between the shock caused by this illusion of danger and delight in its pure illusion. The jolt experienced becomes a shock of recognition."[7]

What needs to be more forcefully asserted from Gunning's logic is the embodied spectatorship that this argument assumes; Gunning even uses a vocabulary that recognizes physiological affect although there is a slippage between vertigo, shock, and jolt of the image and of the same sensations in the audience. What follows of importance is that the audience responds not merely to the panic of being overwhelmed, absorbed, and in some cases overrun by the image (the shock of danger) but to the thrill of subjugating *all* senses to a hyperbolic field of visual information. Like the postcard, early cinema is not a simple reality effect. It metaphorically ingratiates the subject to one's own exteriority by integrating the virtual space of visual observation and the physical space of bodily cognition to produce wonder.

HISTORY OF THE PICTURE POSTCARD

If the history of early cinema is well documented, it is not so well known that picture postcards, in both the United States and western Europe, easily rivaled early movies in popularity. They became fashionable initially because of the affordable, reproduced pictures themselves rather than because of the cards' function as "cheap" letters. Prior to the turn of the century, people primarily communicated across distances through sealed messages. The idea of unsealed communication that anyone—especially servants who were present in most middle-class households—could read was not generally a welcome or even proper notion.

Postcards instead became a market function of new reproductive technologies that made printing cheap enough for small handheld pictures to be mass-produced and distributed. Inexpensive chromolithographic prints and trade cards were already popular and widely distributed. (Austria printed the first picture postcard in 1869.) In the United States the 1893 Chicago World's Columbian Exposition provided a singular event that made miniaturized pictures desirable as affordable keepsakes on a mass scale as well as mementoes to share with others.[8] The world's fair strictly regulated and licensed all photography (including that of amateurs) on its grounds and instead encouraged its tourists to memorialize their experience through buying photograph albums, printed illustrations, and miniature cards. One may see this as connected to a wider cultural shift and purpose for the fair in which fairgoers were addressed as tourists whose burgeoning importance lay in their role as consumers. With color chromolithography already an important international business dominated by German firms, the Chicago Columbian Exposition printed a series of small pictorial cards (fig. 4.1) commemorating the exposition that could be purchased and mailed directly from its grounds.

In 1898 the U.S. government authorized new postal privileges to these types of cards, allowing picture cards to be mailed for a penny apiece (half the cost of sending a letter). Initially, these postcards relayed only the view, and the backside contained space only for the addresses of the sender and recipient. The postcards themselves were either brightly colored chromolithographs or what were known as "real photos" printed from actual photographic negatives and then frequently hand-tinted in factories. While postcards were initially a means to share *images*, senders informally began to scribble brief messages alongside the margins, tops, and even the backsides of the pictures. At a time when no more than one household out of a dozen had a telephone, people turned to these cheap cards not only as means to register their tourist experiences but as a way to communicate rapidly with friends and relatives. Many cards inscribe brief messages that simply make explicit a connection between the space depicted and the sender: "We visited here yesterday. Love to all from all, Bessie," was handwritten across an image of Electric Park, in Montgomery, Alabama. A card from Denver's Elitch Gardens has written on it: "This is where we go on a real warm day. All well. From Della." A parkgoer at Chicago's White City remembered to write his mother: "Dear Mother, We were out here this afternoon and liked it fine."[9]

4.1. OFFICIAL SOUVENIR POSTAL, WORLD'S COLUMBIAN EXPOSITION, 1893. POSTCARD.
AUTHOR'S PRIVATE COLLECTION.

But many handwritten expressions, no mater how brief, suggest more wistful thoughts about separation from family members and friends. Across a chromolithograph of crowds along the pier at Long Beach, California, a Miss Margaret Caldwell of Los Angeles wrote to Miss Esta Shrader in Milo, Iowa, on July 12, 1907: "Do you remember all the walks we had once here?" (fig. 4.2). One J. O. Fenwick signed an image of Forest Park Highlands, "Greetings from St. Louis, Mo. August is here. Frances is not—is Frances coming? Say yes—'aint it.' Lovingly, J. O. Fenwick." One writer from New York in September of 1906 wrote across a postcard of Luna Park at Coney Island: "I received your welcome letter last evening. You can write again. Am well. Give love to Gracie." The card was addressed to Mrs. Frank Gunther in Leetonia, Ohio. A card from Riverside Park in Indianapolis reads: "Dear Pearl, How is everything going on? Tell Edna to write a letter, if only a few lines. Love to all from Aunt Lena." On an image of the *Fire and Flames Show, White City, Chicago,* another sender wrote: "Dear Frank, How is the world treating you? Are you still lonesome? Ida." The authors of these cards are not only individuals who, as was common practice, may have moved to nearby larger metropolises to live and work away from family and friends. There are quite simply countless expressions of remembrances, greetings, and requests for letters and visits to others quite far away and across regional lines.

End of Pleasure Pier,
Long Beach, Cal.

4.2. END OF PLEASURE PIER, LONG BEACH, CAL., WITH HANDWRITTEN MESSAGE, 1907. POSTCARD. AUTHOR'S PRIVATE COLLECTION.

In 1907 the government allowed the backs of postcards to be imprinted with a border dividing the card in half so that personal messages could be penned on the left-hand side and the right-hand side reserved for the address.[10] At a time when mail delivery occurred multiple times daily in many locales, the messages now authorized on the postcards not only became somewhat more extensive descriptions of longing and separation, but they also served another purpose. In many instances the card itself became a handy object for sending notice or requests for appointments, dates, or simply to inquire about someone. Of course, the messages continued to memorialize the experience of being at the parks depicted on the reverse sides. But not all postcard messages sent from amusement parks or even of views of amusement parks were about going to amusement parks.

What is most important is that postcard sending and collecting these views in albums soon became a national past time. Historians estimate that by 1906, 770 million postcards were mailed, and by 1909, 968 million postcards were mailed annually.[11] Postcards depicted an array of views and topics, including "children, cats, historic figures, famous personalities, and poetry," as characterized by one historian.[12] But the new medium was dominated by local views, especially "main streets," communal landmarks and monuments, commercial buildings and businesses—the trappings associated with newly modern urban America.

The triumph of the postcard is best understood, however, not merely in the views produced but in the public mania for buying, sending, and collecting postcards. A trade magazine reported that 175,000 cards had been mailed from Coney Island the first four days of September 1906 and 200,000 more on September 7 alone.[13] The selling and posting of cards was big business at all amusement parks, and the proliferation of these cards thus circulated views and images of the parks everywhere.

The postcard craze was not without opposition. Critics pathologized the phenomenon: in the United States one writer referred to "postal carditis" as a 1906 epidemic of the "ravages of the microbe postale universelle."[14] Another called them "pernicious postals" and an "insidious temptation."[15] In Great Britain a journalist wrote: "The illustrated postcard craze, like the influenza, has spread to these islands from the Continent, where it has been raging with considerable severity."[16] It is especially revealing that culture critics of the time linked the public fascination to a disease, to an invisible invasion of the body, since postcards functioned to reinscribe the body in new modes of seeing.

The only time that postcards escaped criticism from culture critics was in columns and magazines addressing female audiences. In women's magazines like Ladies' Home Journal, women received advice about how to arrange postcard collections and about the virtues of postcard writing and collecting for encouraging good manners, expressive restraint, and the broadening of education.[17] In sum, postcards may well have accrued some association with the feminine, doubling the importance of distancing their broader subjective function through metaphors of disease, infection, and germ invasion.

Collecting was a significant Victorian leisure activity advocated and practiced by many. Historian Ellen Garvey points to how Victorian authors praised collecting for teaching children valuable skills of observation and discernment. But, more important, she observes how the types of collections themselves served to bifurcate gender roles and thus acquired different negative and positive connotations. Boys and men collected stamps, for example, which she says immersed males in "the discourse of commerce and nationalism" as they learned the satisfaction of the language of national commodities, trading, and economic value.[18] While this type of collecting was praised, scrapbooks that arranged advertising trade cards, social calling cards, bits of memorabilia, newspaper or magazine clippings, greeting cards, and eventually postcards acquired more negative and feminine associations. Garvey argues for how scrapbooking as a collecting activity taught women and young girls their new roles as consumers in a late nineteenth-century marketplace where more and more production activities had departed from the home. In her study of late nineteenth-century scrapbooks of trade cards she concludes that such collections are not about material acquisitions per se but about desire for a particular relationship to the world as expressed through the cards that are collected: "Girls learned to fantasize within the images of consumption provided."[19] Although Garvey is focused on how advertising trade card scrapbooks supported women's new roles as department store shoppers by providing pleasure through domestic fantasies of consumption, her conclusions may easily be extended to postcard collecting as well. Female postcard collectors learned how to imagine themselves in the new role of tourist, a new type of consumer consuming both amusements and physical spaces in the world at large.

The millions of picture postcards that were sold, mailed, and circulated as souvenirs in the first decades of the twentieth century produced miniaturizations of the parks, secondhand experiences that allowed anyone who bought a card and everyone who received one a sense of inclusion, mastery, and pleasure over this new spatial-temporal configuration. As the novelist Walker Percy commented in his essay "The Loss of the Creature," the tourist and postcard recipient alike in the new modern technical society surrendered a sovereignty of the self; they had been refashioned into subjects for desiring and consuming experiences and objects.[20] The postcard and collecting postcards are both products of and servant to this transformation.

In the way they represented these subjects, postcards idealized places, people, and events so that their visions of the park existed nowhere except in the reverie of the card. Yet they represent actual places, the real dislocated into fantasy. Regardless of which of the hundreds of parks is being depicted, the postcard views tend to follow the same conventions and formulaic points of view. They generally adhere to codes of commercial photography whose primary purpose is to advertise and to display pride in industrialized modernity. Such cheap miniature photographs afforded travelers and local visitors alike the opportunity to become and to commodify their status as tourists, to savor or to transmit to family and friends a fetish of their leisure. These edited views and ready-made objects provided a more perfect vision of destinations frozen in time, a souvenir that emphasized monumentality, novel vantage points, spaciousness, and visual charm and interest. In short, they promised an antidote to the chaos, sensory overstimulation, and psychological alienation threatened by the city because they preserved and circulated the idea that modern cities and industrial life also contained their own sublime order—oases of space and time for exoticizing all that was considered modern.

REPRESENTATION OF AMUSEMENT PARKS
IN POSTCARDS AND CINEMA

Both cinema and postcards counted amusement parks among their first subjects.[21] Most early films depict Coney Island and Atlantic City because of the parks' proximity to a number of early film producers. Coney Island also offered Thomas Edison's film company a chance for some additional advertising of electricity itself (e.g., Edison's 1905 *Coney Island at Night*). Postcards encompassed a broader geographic range: probably every amusement park, no matter how small, had at least one postcard view, and most made available multiple views from various vantage points. But both modes approached the amusement park through a range of representational strategies that borrowed from existing media while reconfiguring the new and novel.

A large number of postcards simply reproduced a *monumental view* that celebrated the amusement park as a civic shrine, an architectural spectacle in a tiny format. These cards are stylistically derivative of the pictorial presentations of the 1893 Chicago Exposition and other contemporary world's fairs. Numerous official photographs of the 1893 fair, as well as watercolors and drawings featured in souvenir albums, framed the exposition's Court of Honor as a splendid Beaux Arts architectural backdrop for interconnected, shimmering lagoons. Such views are distanced, frontal, highly symmetrical scenes in Renaissance perspective. Like these spatial views popularized by the 1893 fair, amusement park postcards feature an axial organization around a water basin and the shoot-the-chutes ride centrally located at the parks. Chicago's White City, named after the 1893 exposition, literally reproduced the same high angle, so familiar in that fair's photographs and drawings (fig. 4.3). These views not only allow the viewer to take in the entire park grounds with one glance, but they emphasize detailed, Beaux Arts architecture against the Chicago horizon. Other parks, like Milwaukee's Wonderland, reproduced the same visual and stylistic organization in their postcards, going so far as to imprint on them "panoramic view" (fig. 4.4).

4.3. WHITE CITY, CHICAGO, 1910. POSTCARD. AUTHOR'S PRIVATE COLLECTION.

4.4. PANORAMIC VIEW, "WONDERLAND," MILWAUKEE, 1905. POSTCARD. AUTHOR'S PRIVATE COLLECTION.

They unify park geography by stretching and extending the park across the line of the horizon, transforming park space into miniaturized handheld phantasmagorias.

Some cards depict architectural views where the park entrance—featuring an arch, ticket window, park name, and outlines of lights—is centered. For example, Wheeling Park in Wheeling, West Virginia, offers a grand white architectural arch that fills the frame of the postcard. The arch is decorated with red and white striped bunting, striped awnings, and American flags. The park's name in electric bulbs and a sculptural eagle sit centrally atop the structure's pediment. Scranton's Luna Park entrance postcard centers a white arch outlined in light bulbs against a background of foliage (fig. 4.5). A crescent moon adorns the top of the arch, and the letters spelling out Luna Park's name stretch out across the pediment. Four male uniformed ticket-takers pose in front of two stands at the entrance, and the windows in each base of the arch are framed by the words "tickets, 10 cents." In each window a female cashier looks out directly at the viewer. A more vernacular squared-off arch at Ohio's Indianola Park in Columbus is obviously made of wood and painted green so that it looks like a barn door entrance, and a postcard view of it reproduces the same grand visual style, despite this park's humbler architectural pretentions. In this view the pediment still includes a circular portrait relief, and the ticket windows in each side of the arch have hand-colored red awnings. American flags on poles extend up and beyond the entrance. The entrance itself is framed against red-flowering bushes and trees in the foreground and park architecture in the background. All these views define the parks as patriotic, aesthetically uplifting, palatial courtyards reminiscent of the Court of Honor, a symbol of the achievement of American industrial civilization to that generation.

In opposition, other postcards simultaneously also offer *romantic* views of parks as a pastoral oasis of trees, promenades, flowers, and water. By likening the park to a nature preserve, views like "Board Walk and Beach, Cedar Point, Sandusky, Ohio" (fig. 4.6) adapt conventions of landscape painting to commercial photography and rely on dynamic compositions, rich colors, and organic subjects to literalize the amusement park's bucolic, soothing nature away from the stresses and shocks of the city. Just as the 1893 Chicago World's Columbian Exposition incorporated its own antidote to the overstimulation of mechanized industrialization in its peaceful Wooded Island, so did amusement park postcard representations likewise promise spaces that heralded industrial modernity as well as a remedy to it. "The Grove, Big

N.y Aug Entrance to Luna Park, Scranton, Pa. 1006

This is the new park in

4.5. ENTRANCE TO LUNA PARK, SCRANTON, PA, 1907. POSTCARD. AUTHOR'S PRIVATE COLLECTION.

Island Park, Lake Minnetonka, Minneapolis, Minn." (fig. 4.7) frames crowds of men, women, and children strolling among tall trees, and the title suggestively summarizes the amusement park's continuing function as a romantic nature retreat. Some views, like one of Electric Park, Kansas City, Mo. (fig. 4.8), center a colorful flower bed framed by park benches and the white pillars, tower, and arcade of the architecture. The scenic railway—the intrusion of the mechanically modern—is only visible in the background as a continuation of the encircling white frame of the park's architecture. Some views go even further and reproduce an angle that leaves one wondering whether the park contains any mechanical modern rides at all: a postcard view of Melville Park's entrance allows for a penny arcade façade on the left but sets its grand entrance arch as a backdrop to the sculpture, flower bed, and lawn framed in the foreground (fig. 4.9). While all these parks made available other postcards that depict mechanical attractions, they also offered up the pastoral oasis and garden as an antidote to the excitement and monumentality of the modern they otherwise celebrated.

The dialectical tension between the pastoral ideal and the mechanically modern finds its synthesis, however, in the many images of park entrances

2286. Board Walk and Beach, Cedar Point, O.

4.6. BOARD WALK AND BEACH, CEDAR POINT, O., C. 1907. POSTCARD AUTHOR'S PRIVATE COLLECTION.

THE GROVE, BIG ISLAND PARK,
LAKE MINNETONKA,
MINNEAPOLIS, MINN.

4.7. THE GROVE, BIG ISLAND PARK, LAKE MINNETONKA, MINNEAPOLIS, MINN., 1907. POST-CARD. AUTHOR'S PRIVATE COLLECTION.

Electric Park, Kansas City, Mo.

4.8. ELECTRIC PARK, KANSAS CITY, MO., 1910. POSTCARD. AUTHOR'S PRIVATE COLLECTION.

MELVILLE PARK, ENTRANCE AND PENNY ARCADE.

BAYONNE, N.J.

PENNY ARCADE

4.9. MELVILLE PARK, ENTRANCE AND PENNY ARCADE, BAYONNE, N.J., 1907. POSTCARD.
AUTHOR'S PRIVATE COLLECTION.

that literalize what cultural historian Leo Marx called "the machine in the garden"—the railroad car or trolley and its tracks that abut the park's natural landscape setting.[22] Although Marx's trope has been generously applied to nineteenth-century American literature, painting, and popular culture as the chief representational means for conveying the conflict between burgeoning industrial American power and a nostalgic premodern agrarianism, the figure of the machine generally represents an intrusion, a disturbance in the American Eden. Nowhere better than in these park entrance postcards, however, does the amusement park itself signify the successful marriage of the pastoral and the mechanical and the victory of the "machine in the garden" as a celebration of the future. Since most parks were owned by railroad and trolley companies, these picture postcards doubly advertised the parks and the transportation to them. More important, however, they naturalized a relationship between nature and the mechanically modern and blurred the boundaries and distinctions between the two.

A typical view can be found in a postcard of Ontario Beach in Rochester, New York (fig. 4.10). An open, panoramic view of the park from a high angle above the sandy beach shows the boardwalk as a sharp diagonal across the beach in the foreground. Rhythmically punctuated by vertical street lamps, the boardwalk hosts fashionable crowds who walk along its expanse or sit at benches. The postcard's center is entirely filled by the semicircle of cars of a stopped passenger train. Even thicker crowds fill in the space between the train and the pavilions in the background. Tree lines and scaffolding are barely visible at the horizon line beyond the buildings. The colorful peaked rooftops of the buildings—with a prominent American flag atop one—are reminiscent of the outline of a circus tent. The implied motion of the people and the dynamic composition reinforce the setting's carnival atmosphere and qualities, all emanating from the center ring, where the stationary train is the star of this circus.

Numerous picture postcards offer variations on this theme. "Crowds Arriving at Saltair Beach, Utah" (fig. 4.11), is a brightly hued view of the Salt Lake & Los Angeles Railway cars disgorging crowds of people fancifully dressed in reds, pinks, whites, and black onto a pier. The pier occupies much of the picture frame and extends from the foreground into the background. To its left are the turquoise waters of Salt Lake. To its right are the brown railroad cars. Centered in the background where all sightlines converge are the green-topped domes of the Saltair Pavilion, its rounded tops a contrast

4.10. ONTARIO BEACH PARK, ROCHESTER, N.Y., 1906. POSTCARD. AUTHOR'S PRIVATE COLLECTION.

5329. Crowds arriving at Saltair Beach, Utah.

4.11. CROWDS ARRIVING AT SALTAIR BEACH, UTAH, 1915. POSTCARD. AUTHOR'S PRIVATE COLLECTION.

to the straight lines of the pier and train and its color a striking comple-
ment to the fashionable attire of the crowds. In this instance nature has
been absorbed into the overall gaiety produced by the vision of the train, its
disembarking passengers, and their destination.

Even in postcards that are not such visually rich commentaries on the
interrelationships among parkgoers, nature, the amusement park, and
the train, the presence of the train at the "door" to the park is an often-
repeated view. Sometimes these postcards depict views taken from high
angles above the park so that the railroad car and its tracks, park architecture, and expanse of natural landscape perfectly balance each other. Other
times, the railroad car is nestled in and among the scaffolding of the park's
architecture so that it is a seamless extension of the modern amusements.
In the case of "Entrance to Delmar Park, Oklahoma City, Okla.," the car
is visible primarily because it and the expansive lawn in the foreground
are tinted green, whereas the park's architecture consists of white buildings with red rooftops. In "Entrance to Ocean View, Va." (fig. 4.12), two
open trolley cars in the middle ground of the picture are dominated by
the horizontal emphasis of the low-lying, sweeping architectural facade
and train tracks in the foreground. Strong vertical lines of the electrical
poles and the circle swing scaffolding in the background balance out the
frame. Here it is rather the metonymic markers of electricity that are given
more importance than the trolleys themselves, lost among the other items
of visual interest.

Although cinema early on expressed a fascination for trains traveling
through picturesque landscapes, a fascination that reached its culmination
in *Hale's Tours and Scenes of the World*, movies depicting actual amusement
parks took a different route. They generally bypassed architectural and
nature views of the parks and emphasized instead the novelty of motion
that was integral both to individual mechanical rides at the parks and to
the medium of movies itself. Shoot-the-chutes at Coney Island was among
the earliest popular Edison subjects in 1896 (*Shooting the Chutes*), and both
Edison and American Mutoscope and Biograph reshot it several times over
the next ten years.[23] Films that depicted mechanical rides (fig. 4.13) were
above all else portraits of the motion, dips, spins, and turns produced by the
thrill rides.[24] In contrast, postcard views like "Finish on Steeple Chase, Forest
Park, Chicago, Illinois" (fig. 4.14) emphasize through their very stillness the
exposed wood and metal skeletal structures of the rides, even when a car
of the ride is frozen in motion. Any implied motion of the arrested vehicle

Entrance to Ocean View, Va.

4.12. ENTRANCE TO OCEAN VIEW, VA., 1913. POSTCARD. AUTHOR'S PRIVATE COLLECTION.

4.13. SHOTS FROM *STEEPLECHASE, CONEY ISLAND* (AMERICAN MUTOSCOPE AND BIO-GRAPH, 1897). PAPER PRINT COLLECTION, MOTION PICTURE, BROADCASTING, AND RECORDED SOUND DIVISION, LIBRARY OF CONGRESS.

FINISH ON STEEPLE CHASE
FOREST PARK

4.14. FINISH ON STEEPLE CHASE, FOREST PARK, CHICAGO, 1911. POSTCARD. AUTHOR'S PRIVATE COLLECTION.

is always less commanding, smaller in scale than the ride's scaffolding that fills the postcard frame.

The shoot-the-chutes ride, however, offers both postcards and cinema an opportunity for simultaneously producing for their spectators a magisterial, possessive gaze over the park. Postcards like "Luna Park, Pittsburgh" regularly show a "top of the chutes" view (fig. 4.15) or "bird's-eye view" as an elevated vantage point for a panoramic, almost aerial view of the park's skyline. Movies like *Shoot the Chutes Series* (Edison, 1899) reproduce the same effect, offering the spectator a visual sweep of the park. This film also begins one section with its vantage point from the top of the chutes and then moves with the point of view of the boat as it goes down the chutes, a traveling point of view akin to the phantom train ride and *Hale's Tours'* subsequent views.

Interestingly enough, there is no evidence that either postcards or movies ever photographically depicted true aerial views of amusement parks. The Edison Manufacturing Company did film aerial views on occasion (e.g., *Bird's Eye View of San Francisco, Cal., from a Balloon* [1902]; *Panoramic View of Electric Tower from a Balloon* [1901]) but did not seek out an opportunity to film Coney Island or other nearby amusement parks from this vantage

LUNA PARK, PITTSBURGH, PA.   8069

ⓒ 4.15. LUNA PARK, PITTSBURGH, PA, 1907. POSTCARD. AUTHOR'S PRIVATE COLLECTION. ⓢ

point. Postcards, however, did offer up true bird's-eye view images but not as actually experienced aerially, photographically, or even from a unified point of view. Postcard aerial views like "Council Crest, Portland, Oregon" (fig. 4.16) are fanciful, almost maplike, drawings. They offer a whimsically styl-ized depiction of detail and contemporaneous events, in this case, balloonist stunts and circus performances. The primitive, anti-illusionistic rendering of flat surfaces imitates folk painterly style, leading to an association with the vernacular and with representational traditions that are prephotographic.

Council Crest, the Dreamland of Portland, Oregon.

Rather than one all-embracing view, aerial views like this one offer multiple vantage points that condense fictional mobility. In this regard the spectator may literally be static, but this more painterly, nostalgic view also argues for a mobile body incorporated into perspective. Above all, both postcards and movies represented the amusement park as a panoramic spectacle that afforded a magisterial gaze over the park as a phantasmagorical urban oasis.

PLEASURE SEEKERS: THE MOBILE HUMAN FIGURE
AT AMUSEMENT PARKS

In addition to representations of park spaces and structures that invited an immersive—even mobile—view, depictions of the human figure in life and in action were equally important for defining the amusement park as characterized by the energy and looking relationships of the crowd.[25] Postcards featuring the human figure in action usually depicted crowd scenes or riders on the mechanical displays. In these images figures are recognizable as middle-class types via fashion and posture. But these images lack the personal distinguishing details that are the hallmark of the picture portrait. Often captured in pairs and small groups, people may be seen strolling a park boulevard, playing on the beach, or seated in pairs in the car of a ride. In all cases the images similarly draw on photographic and painting traditions for depicting the bourgeoisie at leisure. For example, "Promenade, Willow Grove Park, Philadelphia, Pennsylvania" (fig. 4.17) is a typical depiction of fashionably dressed people who are caught candidly and frozen in the middle of their actions rather than posed frontally, acknowledging the presence of the camera and presenting themselves to the viewer. Such commercial views stand in stark contrast to the amateur photographs that John Kasson examined for his 1978 book *Amusing the Million*, where he argues parkgoers faced the camera and exhibited a *joie de vivre* that was specifically linked to their new identities as happy consumers of leisure rather than as productive laborers.[26] In these images, the same for both white and African American parks, it is the experience of the crowd that matters most as a feature of the amusement parks.[27]

Whereas international expositions fostered countless stereographs and photographs of foreign, nonwhite racial and national typologies from their ethnological displays or living villages, amusement parks seem not to have commemorated their Old Plantations, Igorot shows, Japanese bazaars, Indian villages, or Asian theaters in commercial portrait postcards for sale. There are exceptions to this rule, or course, especially in several postcard views of Coney Island's Midget City. In addition individual performers like Princess Omene commissioned her own portraits as advertising cards or as souvenirs. But, in general, the full-length portrait of a "foreign national" as representative of a "primitive native type" was not made available at the parks. Perhaps this is because—as I have already argued—any claims for authenticity regarding ethnological displays or foreign theaters were simply dismissed at the parks as willing suspensions of disbelief. Without the scientific educational discourses of anthropology and racial hierarchy that undergirded international expositions' displays, amusement parks traded chiefly on the sensationalism, exoticism, and even salaciousness of these attractions.

If park postcards apparently forwent any claims for regularly depicting racial typologies, movies do display both "foreign" performers and parkgoers enjoying rides, especially training the moviegoer to the pleasure of looking at others as among the pleasures of both the amusement park and the cinema. But films about foreign performers are less about their status as outsiders than about their movement-filled performances. *Arab Act, Luna Park* (American Mutoscope and Biograph, 1903) positions its stationary camera

too far away from the actors to reveal any details of physiognomy and is instead about the constant tumbling, somersaulting, and motion of a troupe of performing acrobats. The only traces of Arab identity are the stereotyped costumes and fezzes, which do not serve to underscore racial difference so much as to associate the low artistic form of the carnivalesque circus show with foreign, exotic elements.

In most instances it is more important that the relay of looks central to cinema spectatorship forms the basis for the movies about the human figure in action. *Double Ring Act, Luna Park* (American Mutoscope and Biograph, 1903) is another view caught by a stationary camera of a circus act at Luna Park: a costumed man and woman perform tricks while riding bareback on a horse in a ring. The horse's circular cantering around the ring continues nonstop in the short film. But central to this film, as so many others, male bystanders, whose heads are visible in the foreground, alternate between watching the circus act and turning their heads to gaze directly at the camera.

In other films, watching a performance transfers from the performers in legitimate stage acts at the amusement park to the park participants themselves. In *Bamboo Slide* (American Mutoscope and Biograph, 1903), an all-male crowd intently watches the men and women as they come down the slide and tumble into each other at the bottom; the onlookers alternate their glances between the riders and the camera (fig. 4.18). It is through a triangulated series of visual exchanges—onscreen male spectators watch male and female riders, onscreen male spectators turn and stare at the movie theater audience, the movie's audience stares at both men and women onscreen— that a hierarchy of looking power relations is established with the audience spectator at the top of the hierarchy.

Such a tacit structure is not unique to this one film (or even to early films about amusement parks). It is, however, unique to cinema. As early as 1897, *Aerial Slide at Coney Island* (American Mutoscope and Biograph) featured pretty models costumed as bathing beauties flying down the slide. Looking directly at the camera, in this film as well as in such other more obvious performances (e.g., *Princess Rajah Dance*), is less about naive "actors" who have not yet learned to ignore the camera than about the onscreen establishment of an implied contractual agreement that the performer agrees to be the object of the audience's gaze. As has been well documented in film history, the further establishment of an onscreen "looker" removes the tacit contract between the onscreen performer who gazes directly outward and the audience and instead places the onscreen actor who is doubly looked at in a position of being the object of a voyeurism mediated by the onscreen lookers.[28] Both practices occurred simultaneously in early films, setting cinema as a medium more fully capable than postcards of emphasizing amusement parks as about acts of pleasurable looking—both in emphasis on parkgoers looking and acting and in movie spectators' increasingly voyeuristic relationship to the subjects.

RUBE AND MANDY AT CONEY ISLAND (1903)

As cinema incorporated elements of narrative and seemingly staked out a spectatorial voyeurism as its dominant strategy, nascent story films between 1903 and 1908 repeatedly organized this hierarchy of looking relations while roaming amusement park landscapes as themselves the site of spectacle. Coney Island thus provided early cinema's efforts at narrative with multiple valences: its mise-en-scène is a modern electrified, highly cinematic display of extravagant architectural shapes, lights, and movements; it temporally unfolds a series of machines in motion that engage bodies in comic contortions; its patrons openly and alternately gawk at both other parkgoers and at

4.18. SHOTS FROM *BAMBOO SLIDE* (AMERICAN MUTOSCOPE AND BIOGRAPH, 1904). PAPER PRINT COLLECTION, MOTION PICTURE, BROADCASTING, AND RECORDED SOUND DIVISION, LIBRARY OF CONGRESS, WASHINGTON, DC.

the motion picture camera. Increasingly addressing the movie spectator as a voyeur, these motion pictures combine the human body interacting with the mechanical and the panoramas of amusement parks as an argument for detached, magisterial observation coupled with unabashed titillation, sexual and humorous—calling for a despatialized gaze that masks corporeal affect.

Rube and Mandy at Coney Island (Edison, 1903) is one such example. *Rube and Mandy* follows two country bumpkins through their arrival and participation at the amusement park. The use of two stock vaudevillian objects of ridicule puts on display here bodies that were well-known caricatures of rural folks unfamiliar with new technologies and technological procedures. The "bumpkin" or "rube" (short for Reuben) was a figure that unreasonably clung to anachronistic ways in a modern industrial, more technologized world. "Rube" was a close relative to Uncle Josh, a caricature popularized by Cal Stewart on the vaudeville circuit and through phonograph recordings made for Edison beginning in 1898. Edison even made a series of Uncle Josh films between 1900 and 1902 featuring their own actor playing Uncle Josh (Charles Manley), who similarly had run-ins with "new-fangled" machines and institutions. Uncle Josh's well-known comic monologues made jokes about his befuddlement with new technologies like the automobile or the Victrola or with modern spaces and institutions like New York City, Coney Island, the department store, or the famous restaurant Delmonico's. Inasmuch as Rube and Uncle Josh comically represented the rural as backward to both city dwellers and ruralites, they yet granted a position of intellectual and social superiority to their entire audience while their binarism asked the audience to identify with the urban modern.

Edison's 1903 film illustrates this position. As immediate recognition of Rube's and Mandy's status as country bumpkins, the film begins with the couple's arrival at Coney Island astride their dairy cow. This symbol of nineteenth-century rural farm life separates them from the urbanites—in actuality, both city dwellers and farmers—who will arrive by train.[29] Their exaggerated dress, makeup, and facial gestures further type them as comic outsiders. The film then follows them through the park as they try out the attractions (fig. 4.19). The film as an attraction offers up Rube and Mandy surrendering to a series of strange phenomena that physically disorient them. As backward and unsophisticated, they are more bewildered than pleased at the conclusion of each ride. On at least one occasion they are also punished: when Rube gets too close to Professor Wormwood's show of acrobatic dogs, the professor beats Rube over the head.

Of course, the film also advertises the park itself. Early on, several wide panoramic shots establish the park space as the profilmic event, documenting and inscribing Coney Island as the film's subject on a par with Rube's and Mandy's antics. As Charles Musser summarizes the film's purpose: "In one scene the couple are barely noticeable as they tour the amusement park . . . allowing the panning camera to caress the spectacular locale. In a later scene the couple themselves become spectacle, not only for the camera but for the amusement seekers in the background."[30] Jonathan Auerbach further contends that the mobile camera's "promiscuous and indiscriminate" roaming between these "rival spectacles" results in the dissolution of the borders between fiction and actuality.[31]

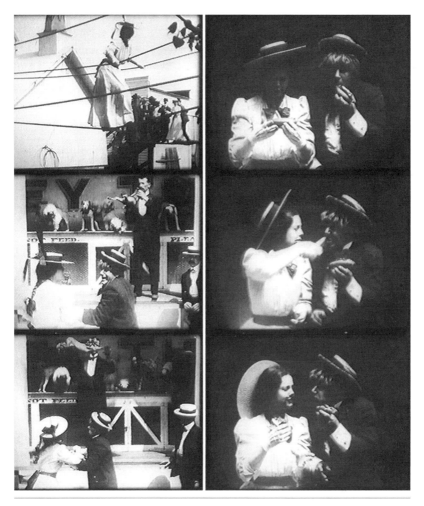

4.19. SHOTS FROM *RUBE AND MANDY AT CONEY ISLAND* (EDISON, 1903). PAPER PRINT COL-
LECTION, MOTION PICTURE, BROADCASTING, AND RECORDED SOUND DIVISION, LIBRARY OF
CONGRESS, WASHINGTON, DC.

The film's "fiction" is less a story than a comic performance by Rube and
Mandy, who have not yet learned how to submit their bodies to the park's
machines. Their reactions at the novelty of doing so throughout the film
produce a series of moving poses, grimaces, and awkward motions that suggest it is already the normalization of the other parkgoers physically intertwined with machines that makes Rube and Mandy so comic and out of
place. Here the humor lies in their bodies making repetitive, involuntary,
uncontrolled movements. Mechanical motion has already won out, and this
is basically an opportunity to mediate new technologies, urban leisure, and

alienation through a visual structure focused on the awkward, out-of-control body. As Auerbach notes:

> The film in effect portrays three kinds of performance, which become increasingly difficult to keep separate: the reaction shots of park patrons in crowds and small clusters, who laugh at the antics of the silly couple, the broad slapstick physical humor of Rube and Mandy themselves, and the various stage acts that the two watch and sometimes aggressively disrupt. . . . In this serial watching, with strolling patrons, comic couple, and park performers all looking at each other as well as directly at the camera on occasion, the borders between actuality and fiction dissolve amid a sea of milling bodies.[32]

The display of these bodies also becomes, more than the mere sight of Rube and Mandy as comic protagonists, part of a relay of authorized looking that integrates the moviegoer with the performers onscreen.

The film ends with an emblematic shot, a "waist-up" shot of Rube and Mandy in front of a studio interior flat (such a shot could be attached by the exhibitor at either the beginning or end of the film). The two stuff their faces with Coney Island hot dogs, a new and popular mass-produced food. It appears to be the only moment of real pleasure for the couple, whose grotesquery while eating now becomes the exhibition itself as they enact gluttony, stuffing their open mouths, shoving food in each other's faces, and smearing ketchup and mustard all over themselves. (It also borrows from contemporary facial gesture films that are close-ups of grimacing or laughing faces.)

This shot is distinctive and contrasts with the rest of the film. In addition to being the sole studio interior shot, the depiction of corporeal overindulgence in consumption stands apart from the clean, rhythmic, mechanical pleasures of the amusement park. In this conclusion Rube and Mandy appear as rural peasants of a preindustrial era. Their bodies bridge the carnivalesque folk cultures of the past and the mechanical production of physical affect in industrialized modern leisure. The "ending" returns the spectator to that singular position of direct, confrontational looking in which the performers know they are performing for the camera and stare directly at the audience. It releases the spectator from any voyeuristic position to one of that tacit performance contract between looking subject and looked-at object and, as such, it finalizes Rube and Mandy as premodern buffoons in contrast to their audience as modern and urbane.

Boarding School Girls (1905)

By 1905 Edison's *Boarding School Girls* (fig. 4.20) took the surveillance of park space and park performers to a logical extension of spectator viewing—the sexual pleasure of the female body displayed in motion. There are two extant full versions of this film (at the Library of Congress [LOC]) and at the Museum of Modern Art [MOMA]), each slightly different from the other. Indeed, a detailed comparison of the two versions accentuates the way this film expands on the spectatorial purpose established by *Rube and Mandy*.

Both versions begin in the same way, with the girls descending the stairs of their finishing school and boarding a charabanc (an early open-topped sightseeing bus). The shot establishes the decorum, genteel deportment, and orderliness of the girls. (Only the LOC version includes a lengthy shot of the bus's trip down the street while the girls daintily wave handkerchiefs at passersby.)[33] Both versions depict the carriage's arrival at Coney Island, the girls' disembarkation, and their entrance into the park. However, the two versions handle the physical displays of live action and the space of Coney Island in subtly dissimilar ways.

Only the LOC version shows the girls breaking from their pack and running wildly out of the frame. After they run offscreen to the left, spatial continuity is preserved in the next shot, which shows them continuing from right to left as they clamber onto the miniature railroad. Their teacher and chaperone, Miss Knapp, appears and runs after the departing train. Across two continuous shots a chase is motivated and established. The pattern continues then for a sequence of ten shots in which the girls appear in the frame, try out a ride, and Miss Knapp arrives to try to catch them.

In the MOMA version, however, the same ten shots appear in a different order and have often been trimmed so that the girls do not rush in from offscreen: they are already inside the frame, either getting on or already aboard a ride. The MOMA version preserves haptic space contained within each discrete shot rather than imagining a Coney Island landscape as a topography united by continuous action, something that will be fundamental to the slapstick comedies of the 1910s that feature Coney Island comedies. The result is the heightening of the bodies on display in each shot or block as they engage with the mechanical attractions. The chase itself becomes more gratuitous than causal. It was thus not only possible at the time to treat the shots as discrete units but also not even to recognize what the chase film

4.20. SHOTS FROM *BOARDING SCHOOL GIRLS* (EDISON, 1905). PAPER PRINT COLLECTION, MOTION PICTURE, BROADCASTING, AND RECORDED SOUND DIVISION, LIBRARY OF CONGRESS, WASHINGTON, DC.

has been understood as establishing in film aesthetics—a sense of narrative necessity from one shot to the next. Available to exhibitors who arranged and ordered the shots, the film of Coney Island bodies on display experiencing the mechanical rides triumphs over the development of a uniquely modernist cinematic syntax.

What is central to both versions is that the bodies are acted upon, out of control, given over to shaking and jerking movements that produce a kind of unrestrained, sensual motion of the body rather than of individual will or subject control. It is the girls' bodily presence through the entire surface of their bodies that is the subject matter of the film. While the girls may be costars with the park, it is the concert of bodies and mechanically induced motions that offers up a physical antidote to the formality of Victorian deportment and manners, in this case one that also signifies the unleashing of repressed female sexuality.

Miss Knapp, however, is portrayed by a male actor in drag. Her stiff upright carriage and ungainly running (as opposed to the fluid, relaxed movement of the girls in motion) are a caricature of the spinster and invert the expression of heightened sexuality. In the end of both versions (although with shots trimmed in the MOMA version), the girls dig a hole in the sand at the beach and cover it with a towel. Miss Knapp walks over it and clumsily falls down. It is the penultimate comic instance of watching her dignity deflated. Then the girls propel her toward the ocean and pull her into the waves.[34]

Boarding School Girls establishes three types of bodily motion as more important than any development of narrative technique: the girls running; the girls on the rides; and Miss Knapp, whose motions, like Rube's and Mandy's, are the most mechanical, jerky, lumbering, clumsy, and therefore laughable for their differentiation from "normal" human grace in motion. The incorporation of Miss Knapp's comic motions and her "difference" mediates open sexuality with the comic. There is not necessarily anything awkward about the girls on the rides. But the chief interest lies in the surveillance of both the rides and the fit and reaction of their otherwise relaxed, pleasure-seeking bodies to the mechanical attractions. Their bodies represent a kind of inversion of Rube's and Mandy's—they are in harmony with the machines in which they engage. The surveillance of teenage girls whose encounters with the mechanical rides produce a relaxation of Victorian codes of conduct, unrestrained self-pleasure, and celebration of their physical movement offers up for the spectator a sexualized voyeurism in addition to a comic pleasure.

VIEWS OF ELECTRIFICATION AT THE AMUSEMENT PARK:
ACHIEVING THE SUBLIME IN POSTCARDS AND MOVIES

A progressive history of early cinema might characterize amusement park films as serving the transformation from the spectacle of an attraction to a container for spectacularizing bodily motion to a setting for the admission of character and narrative causality. Such a stance might well follow the main line of developing cinema ontology but would be misleading for how postcard and cinema views of the amusement park taught their audiences to love the urban modern. Monumental and romantic views of mechanical and bodily motion all did prevail but were often contingent on pervasive views that contextualized the amusement park as the electrified sublime.

Both postcards and cinema *nighttime views* of amusement parks defined new electrically illuminated settings associated with urban spaces as aesthetically awe-inspiring. Postcard views like "Night Scene on the Lake, Forest Park, Chicago, Illinois" (fig. 4.21) focus on the displays of artificially colored lights, rejoicing in the park as a vivid, electrified visual spectacle. Movies like *Coney Island at Night* (Edison, 1905) (fig. 4.22) may not have been able to assault one's senses with dazzling colors but still charged sensory activity through high contrast and the actual panning motion of the brilliant white lights silhouetted against the black night sky.

Following the successes of international expositions at Chicago (1893), Omaha (1898), Paris (1900), Buffalo (1901), and St. Louis (1904), amusement parks made electrification a daily ritual where lights were made visible at dusk, and colored illuminations, spotlights, and subtle patterns of movement imposed a fully coordinated aesthetic design. Modern world's fairs all emphasized dramatic lighting in order to showcase electricity itself as a spectacular effect of progress. Kristen Whissel even notes how these massive electric light displays that outlined buildings, statuary, and fountains with thousands of incandescent lights also allowed for a convergence between the spectacle of artificial illumination and the new medium of cinema, since nighttime illuminations provided so much light that it was possible to shoot movies of them and disseminate these spectacles well beyond the fairgrounds: "Through their cinematic rendering of the [1901 Buffalo] Pan-American's electric light displays, these panoramic films simultaneously enacted and aestheticized technological modernity's transcendence of the natural order through electricity's dissociation of light from time. . . . [They taught] observers and spectators how to imagine the pleasurable power

4.21. NIGHT SCENE ON THE LAKE, FOREST PARK, CHICAGO, 1910. POSTCARD. AUTHOR'S PRIVATE COLLECTION.

4.22. SHOTS FROM *CONEY ISLAND AT NIGHT* (EDISON, 1905). PAPER PRINT COLLECTION, MOTION PICTURE, BROADCASTING, AND RECORDED SOUND DIVISION, LIBRARY OF CONGRESS, WASHINGTON, DC.

of American industry and how to delight in one's incorporation into an expanding electrical network."[35]

The films of the 1901 Buffalo Pan-American Exposition served as a model for later amusement park films that extolled electricity's ability to transform a landscape into a magical city of disembodied lights. *Pan-American Exposition by Night* and *Panorama of Esplanade by Night* (both Edison, 1901) represent a larger number of films that Edwin S. Porter shot for the Edison company at the exposition.[36] Whissel describes their purpose: "The gradual panning action of the camera slowly traces the tendrils of electric light that connect and unite discrete elements of the landscape, creating a visual abstraction of the power lines that were incorporating urban space street by street and block by block in cities and towns across the United States."[37] For Whissel the importance of this technological sublime effect is as a convergent representation of electrical current and camera circular motion that demonstrates an energized traffic flow or circulation as the central figure of modernity.

Whissel's argument for how these views represent an optical experience of electrified traffic overlooks the salient point that they also inscribe a vantage point of considerable distance and altitude from the subject. The promotional literature for actual viewing of the lighting effects, for example, often emphasized the importance of spatial detachment from the illumination for the full effect of bedazzlement, encouraging a distance of one mile or more. David Nye quotes one source: "The distance not only lends enchantment to the view, but mellows the scene to a soft glow, soothing to the eyes. One beholds glowing through the darkness, long lines of little lights, broken here and there into fantastic designs."[38] What is offered as the ideal vantage point would have been difficult to achieve as lived experience dependent on a high, distant elevation uncluttered by obstacles, an optical depth of field not natural to human vision, and an all-seeing gaze for dematerializing the built environment into a vast visual display of radiant electrical energy against a flattened backdrop of blackness. Such guides recommended that the lessons of the technological sublime could not be fully realized from within the crowd encompassed by the light displays but only when the viewer could step outside the lighted arena and could regard it as spectacle—detached, distant, and unified. Movies and postcards effectively transformed these electric illuminations into the luminous panoramic spectacle defined in the promotions, and they became the *only* appropriate way to achieve cognitive integration of the event as a whole. More significant than their onscreen figuration of electrified traffic is the fact that movies and postcards—modern representations—were themselves the secondhand object lessons for achieving modern perception.

Coney Island at Night, for example, used the same approach as the Pan-American films and features a panning shot of an illuminated horizon recorded from a considerable distance. The vantage point and mobile scan of the electrical illumination yields a traveler's gaze, an idealized, detached physical fascination that delivers its utopian promise: illuminations outline neoclassical buildings and the horizontal city preferred by Beaux Arts architects. As Nye says, "Electrical displays gave the visitor an explanatory blueprint for the future, promising to ease work and ban ugliness."[39] But to do so, they required the effects of both idealization and *distance* so that desire could assume a superior illusory position over actual physical participation and proximity.

Numerous film scholars have relied on Nye's assertion of the importance of electrification as a sensory synecdoche for the confluence of technology, excitement, and modernity. Lucy Fischer, Tom Gunning, and Kristen Whissel all argue for a linkage between the illumination displays at the world's fairs of 1893, 1900, 1901, and 1904 and emergent cinema practices.[40] Fischer goes so far as to remind her readers that the sight of electrification itself was a reason that rural audiences attended the movies (as well as amusement parks) when the provinces lagged behind cities for introducing electricity well into the 1930s.[41] She reintroduces the timely argument that amusement parks and movie theaters helped to diffuse one of the chief differences between rural and urban by turning out electrification as a technology of pleasure and acculturating both rural and urban Americans to it.

But beyond these twin sites of electrification, nighttime postcard and movie views of amusement parks capitalized on opportunities to aestheticize electrical illumination and disseminated them as idealized packages of spectacularized desire not only at the sites that provided them but also (in the case of postcards) in one's domestic parlor as mementoes of urban modernity. The numerous postcard nighttime views of amusement parks across the country offered the technological sublime in perfect miniature; the movies constructed it as a gigantic panorama. Both postcards and movies staged in these views *dreams* of modernization that uniquely depended on and existed only in the media that carried them. In these amusement park views, then, tropes of tourist travel, electrification, and bodies overlap and converge. These tropes figure prominently in an era when nature, human power, and technology intersected in the radical social transformations wrought by urban growth, technological development, and colonial expansion—when anxiety about new lived experiences required new reassurances in the forms that perceptual knowledge would assume.

Coney Island Comedies

SLAPSTICK AT THE AMUSEMENT PARK AND THE MOVIES

> Silent American comedy developed a form which drew its inspiration
> from gags, rather than plotting. These gags have their origins in acts of
> anarchy, infantile revolts against authority and propriety. But their explo-
> sive counterlogic also found embodiment in devices of balance and tra-
> jectory, antimachines which harness the laws of physics to overturn the
> rules of behavior. Simultaneously revolt and engineering, these devices
> mine the fascination that spectators of the industrial age had with the
> way things work, the operational aesthetics.
>
> —Tom Gunning, "Crazy Machines in the Garden
> of Forking Paths"

FULL OF POWER-DRIVEN PRATFALLS, REPETITIVE GYRATIONS,
rhythmic punches, and elaborately staged brawls of intersecting parts, slapstick comedy remains one of the best-known genres of motion pictures'
silent era. Even after movies adopted distinct storytelling features of psycho-
logically motivated characters, cause-and-effect plots, and dramatic crises,
slapstick comedy preserved a particular inscription of the cinematic body
both as the spectacular figure-in-motion and as the laughing spectator in
all her or his presence in the theater. Slapstick sustained a more carnal spirit

and upheld an enlarged sense of corporeal delight even during the era when the experience of watching movies became increasingly proscribed by Aristotelian categories associated with "the higher senses." Beginning around 1909, slapstick comedies intertwined bodies (both onscreen and off) with those effects of cinema that produce celebration in the physicality of one's own body. Such visceral sensation often found its best illustration in those slapstick movies featuring amusement parks—that spectacle most closely associated with the body intermingling with the mechanically modern. This special group of films best illustrates not only how cinema overlaps with the amusement park but also how cinema extended the invitation to physical pleasure and bodily thrills available in both institutions.

Even as Hollywood grew in stature and importance as the location for movie production, various film companies shot fictional films at Coney Island. During what is increasingly regarded as "the transitional era" (1909–1917) between early cinema protonarratives and the development of the Hollywood feature film, film companies still operating in New York used the Brooklyn park in both shorts and features: *Cohen at Coney Island* (Vitagraph, 1909), *Cohen's Dream of Coney Island* (Vitagraph, 1909), *Jack Fat and Jim Slim at Coney Island* (Vitagraph, 1910), *Gone to Coney Island* (Thanhauser, 1910), *At Coney Island* (Keystone, dir. Mack Sennett, 1912), *Coney Island* (Comique, dir. Fatty Arbuckle, 1917), and *Tillie Wakes Up* (Peerless, dir. Harry Davenport, 1917). In addition, new film companies on the West Coast likewise shot films using California amusement park locales (*The Cook* [Comique, dir. Fatty Arbuckle, 1918]; *Number, Please?* [Rolin Films, dir. Hal Roach and Fred Newmeyer, 1920]). Fatty Arbuckle's *A Reckless Romeo* (Comique, dir. Fatty Arbuckle, 1917) was actually shot at Palisades Park in New Jersey. Regardless of which actual park was utilized, these films perpetuate the tradition established in earlier films like *Rube and Mandy at Coney Island* and *Boarding School Girls*. But they refine their comic drive of integrating action and the spectacle of bodies united with machinery. These comedies foreground an exaggerated corporeal body while maintaining amusement park spectacle in order to depict relaxation of Victorian codes of conduct, changing gender roles, and comic critique of the institution of marriage.

SLAPSTICK AND PLEASURE SEEKERS

Slapstick comedy got its name from an old theatrical prop consisting of two slats of wood joined together so that they make a loud slapping sound when

one actor hits another with the stick. Donald Crafton, in an important discussion on slapstick, likens the notion of "the slap" to the centrality of physical gags in slapstick movies that have a disruptive impact on the audience.[1]
For Crafton the gags resist integration into the film's narrative and insist that
the form remains a type of popular spectacle that makes slapstick comedies stand apart from increasingly narrative-driven features of the 1910s and
1920s, those films associated with the rise of classical Hollywood cinema. As
an organized show, they may have more in common with the Blowhole Theater and other spectacles of the amusement park crowd as spontaneous performers than they do with evolving film narrative of the 1910s.

In response to Crafton, Tom Gunning demonstrates that slapstick may
indeed be understood as a continuation of early cinema's "cinema of attractions," as the descendant of comic mischief films: slapstick gags provide a
structure of "explosive interruptions" that often require mechanical devices
so that "everything, both devices and human actants, seem to perform like
interlocking gears in a grand machine."[2] Slapstick thus accentuates the
body's relationship to modern industry through its combination with gag
devices. Nowhere is this better illustrated than in the parkgoer's relationship
to the machinery of the amusement park.

Both Crafton and Gunning are preoccupied with the cinematic terms of
slapstick as a dual-focus narrative rather than with its sociohistorical context and function. They attempt to unlock the tensions between the "cen-
trifugal energy" of the comic gag, best represented by the "pie in the face,"
and the "centripetal energy" of narrative, best represented by "the chase."
Whereas Crafton seeks to differentiate slapstick from the classical cinema
that succeeded it, Gunning blurs slapstick with the cinema that preceded it.
Neither addresses specifically the distinctiveness of slapstick as a historical
mode that not only synthesized early comic strategies and influenced later
ones but that also maintained a unique integrity and cultural function.

In addition, their analyses require the presence of not only a laughing,
physically involved spectator but one whose pleasure derives from a mul-
tifaceted fascination rather than the production of knowledge through the
linearity of cause-effect relations. While they suggest that widespread familiarity with popular culture, especially the joke logic of contemporary comic
strips, provided the contextual cultural knowledge necessary for understanding slapstick's antinarrative force, they stop short of explaining that the very
forms that made slapstick legible, so to speak, were also forms that depend
on spectator positions quite antithetical to those of the classical cinema.

Rob King, however, overcomes Crafton's and Gunning's shortcomings in his argument that slapstick was a singular response to modern industrialization, and he convincingly demonstrates (through his case study of the Keystone Film Company) that slapstick comedies of the period helped to displace traditional conceptions of the machine as an instrument of productive labor with a modern conception of the machine as a site of bodily pleasure: "They [the Keystone Film Company] thus participated in the emergence of a distinctly modern comic form that mediated the meanings of mechanization for a public whose own encounters with technology often betrayed startling uncertainties and ambiguities."[3] In this regard slapstick provided a unique filmic format analogous to the experience of the amusement park as described by John Kasson for inverting the usual relations between the body and machine in service of industrial production: here surrender to the machine liberates the body and produces pleasure.[4]

King also recognizes that the pleasures of slapstick comedy—the revelation of the loss of dignity, antinarrative corporeal involvement through violent explosive actions, interaction between devices and human motion that seems to resist laws of physics, and a vision of the world as "a crazy machine"—overlap with the pleasures of the contemporary amusement park. In describing *A Submarine Pirate* (Triangle Films, 1915), he portrays the submarine and the way it is exploited as "more a microcosmic amusement park than a machine of war."[5] The amusement park's mechanical rides, pyrotechnics, and recreations were perhaps a more important example of contemporary popular culture than comic strips for training moviegoers to become fascinated slapstick spectators, to become pleasure seekers at the cinema.

Slapstick comedies in general relied on this model of the amusement park. After acknowledging the amusement park's general significance for acclimatizing the public to modernity, King specifies the amusement park as "the context against which the meanings of Keystone's 'mechanical contrivances' emerges clearly."[6] Jennifer Bean implicitly recognizes what is at stake in overtaking the movie spectator as an amusement parkgoer: "Yet the travesty of order on screen is little more than a prelude for the staggering loss of bodily integrity available to the viewer; one who succumbs first to a 'titter,' devolves toward a 'yowl,' cranks up for a stimulating 'bellylaugh,' and races on to laughter's apotheosis: the 'boffo,' or, 'the laugh that kills.'"[7] Bean's definition of the loss of bodily integrity accurately describes the loss of self-mastery over the corporeal once laughter takes over. But what matters most is that this kind of physiologically engaged spectator who mimics the parkgoer's equally engaged experience—even without actual traveling motion—participates in a new delighted corporeal relationship to technological modernity. King summarizes the situation best: "At Keystone, as at Coney, the image of the world as a crazy machine was a fetish for the modern era, in which cogwheels, levers, and gears meshed to such exhilarating ends that there remained not the slightest gap for confronting the troubling costs of a mechanized environment."[8]

More specifically, the Coney Island comedies *promised* the kind of bodily pleasure that they depicted of amusement park thrill rides onscreen: "We'll just simply rock 'em off their seats," assure Paramount Pictures' Fatty Arbuckle advertisements for 1917, instantiating that the lure of the comic is not only the "boffo" laugh that Bean describes but literally a pleasure of mechanical motion. "Everybody rubbers, and everybody laughs themselves sick," said one summary of *Jack Fat and Jim Slim at Coney Island*. Another called *The Cook* a "mirth factory . . . [that produces] unconfined joy," applying industrial metaphors to the production of a fully embodied, fully engaged spectator. Even the *Moving Picture World* described *Cohen at Coney Island* as "brimful of laughter from start to finish."[9] It is clearly the "gag" structure of these films and their incentive to laugh that provides the substance for all kinds of slapstick comedy advertisements. But the Coney Island comedies assure a melding with machines of pleasure that overturns rules of behavior through the movie itself as a machine absorbed by the body of the raucously laughing spectator.

In addition the Coney Island films also perpetuate the nighttime postcard view and an earlier cinema panoramic spectacle. Integral to their sensation of human motion and physical presence onscreen is the contingent optical experience of an electrified skyline spectacle or a magical city. The *Moving Picture World* recognizes this component in its description of *Jack Fat and Jim Slim at Coney Island*: "Those who have seen Coney Island can rest assured they are looking upon an unusually faithful reproduction."[10] In short, there is a retrograde quality to the Coney Island comedies throughout this period: they not only provide continuity of the earliest spectacle displays, *actualités*, and mischievous gags, but they nostalgically make the connection between the machine apparatus and its mechanical control over the individual in motion both the object (onscreen) and subject (the audience's experience) of the film. In this way they reproduce the original basic drive of cinema wherein the apparatus itself is organized, to quote Francesco Casetti, as a "snare ready to capture whoever enters its radius of activity."[11]

In fact, these films develop outwardly from the most primitive element of narrative: the chase. For Crafton, Gunning, and Charlie Keil the chase represents an important cinematic development between 1903 and 1908 as a means to connect action across disparate spaces and to link discrete shots through spatial and temporal continuity.[12] It is widely understood as an important building block for establishing a narrative sustained across individual shots, as exemplified by *Boarding School Girls*. But the chase as the causal agent in *Jack Fat and Jim Slim at Coney Island* functions remarkably like the chase in *Boarding School Girls*, made five years earlier. By 1910 the chase element had supposedly been absorbed into more sophisticated storytelling techniques. Furthermore, *Jack Fat and Jim Slim*'s chase reemerges with few changes as late as 1917, in *Coney Island*. In other words the narrative charge of these films—no matter how much it expands throughout this period—steadfastly remains "primitive" in relationship to the visual spectacle, physical pleasures of the gag, the body on display and in motion as connected by the novelty of the machine apparatus being represented on the screen either literally or metaphorically.

All the Coney Island comedies preserve the chase subservient to the bodies being acted upon by machines that dominated *Boarding School Girls*. In its protean form *Jack Fat and Jim Slim* introduces the theme of the amusement park as a carnivalesque space in which to escape the repressive bounds of matrimony, elaborating on *Boarding School Girls'* depiction of the topography as a cultural space for open expression of sexuality. Both *Coney Island* and *Tillie Wakes Up* make this theme central for character motivation and behavior but provide this character justification more pointedly as motivation for the display aesthetics of bodies in concert with the mechanical rides.

Jack Fat and Jim Slim at Coney Island (1910)

Jack Fat and Jim Slim has been easily overlooked because while, in its entirety, it does develop character motivation, the logic of the chase and even the narrative regulation of closure, the only extant copy of the film at the Museum of Modern Art is a partial print, with German intertitles, that has edited out all developing principles of narrative. In this version even the motivation for Jack and Jim to go to Coney Island, meet two girls, and then get chased by the girls' beau and their own wives is lost. The extant copy reduces the film to a display of Rube and Mandy–like series of experiences at Coney Island—a different shot for each individual ride that "uses up the space" before each shot ends. If Rube and Mandy represented "different" bodies in their enactment of rural backwardness, Jack and Jim similarly represent extreme and opposing body types of short corpulence and lanky boniness. Even the chase itself is not legible. In this copy a chase film has been reedited into a length of discrete shots of body and machine encounters, suggesting the possibility of a retrograde reception and the success of display attractions of the amusement park (like *Rube and Mandy*) well after films had developed narrative principles of storytelling.

In its full "story," according to the *Moving Picture World*, intertitles appear after the first extant shot of Jack and Jim sitting coatless on their fire escapes: "Whew! Is it hot enough for you, Jim?" "Yes—plenty and a bit more!"[13] Jim looks at his newspaper and shows it to Jack. It is likely that an insert shot appears showing an advertisement of Coney Island. They tiptoe down the fire escape ladders, a precaution not made clear in the full version until their wives later appear on the fire escape and discover their absence. The extant version elides any cause and effect and simply establishes the two characters looking at a newspaper and departing for Coney Island, its location introduced by an intertitle.

In the next shot Jack and Jim depart arm in arm (itself a humorous attraction display of contrasting body extremes) from a train and walk into the foreground. The next shot shows a number of people frolicking in the surf and, among them, Jack and Jim, who are playing with two girls. Ostensibly missing are any shots that the film summary describes: "The gay benedicts meet a couple of sporty ladies who visit the Island with a diminutive beau, whom they lose sight of in the company of Jack and Jim. . . . Their wives discover their absence, find the newspaper, and, seeing the flaming announcement of Coney's allurements, guess the cause of their husbands' sudden disappearance and determine to follow them."[14] The implication of temporal discontinuity and crosscutting, as well as character and chase motivation, is lost, and, instead, the physical presence of Jack and Jim together and in motion presents a model for the film's presentational style of them as a humorous type of amusement park exhibit.

In the following fourteen shots Jack, Jim, and the two girls try out various park mechanical attractions. In many of these a tiny man in white cap and full-length duster (the diminutive beau) follows on the ride, and he himself is followed by two women in exaggerated Victorian spinster-esque costumes who resist the machines and leave the shots raising their fists and waving their arms (the two wives). But, no one in the half-dozen audiences with whom I have seen this film recognized these "chasers" as continuing characters from frame to frame or even understood that they were following the two couples. With Jack, Jim, and the two girls foregrounded quite literally, the shots that dominate the film are about these bodies falling down, exhibiting fluid motion, and tumbling. While most shots do not end with the departure of the two pleasure seeker couples but with the next two or three "riders"—that is, the diminutive beau and the wives—the "chasers" serve as a punctuation mark and hyperbolic physical comedy in relationship to the central bodies on display.

The extant version simply fades to black after the last shot of the husbands slipping on a rolling sidewalk. The film summary describes a more narratively satisfying conclusion, where the wives catch up to their errant husbands at a refreshment stand and then "march them to their homes, where we see them the next day seated on the fire escapes recounting their experiences and laughing."[15]

In addition, although the film's advertisements make numerous claims for the hilarity of Jack's and Jim's appearances on these rides, their bodies in motion are in fact rather graceful. When they and the two girls try to walk through Steeplechase's rolling barrel, they fall down quite gently and easily pick themselves up only to repeat in smooth, fluid movements. While Jim may lurch forward as the camel he is astride stands up and Jack laughs at him, he gracefully carries his sweetheart from the surf to the sand, deftly helps her up the pitching Golden Stairs ride, and otherwise maintains a relatively liquid ease while slipping and sliding and keeping his limbs gracefully moving in connection to his whole torso.

It is rather the diminutive beau and the wives who slam into the sand and fall over at the end of the Helter Skelter slide because they try to maintain rigid spines. The wives' hats fall over their eyes while they grimace in concern over the loss of their dignity. In short, they are not pleasure seekers, and they do not blend harmoniously with the rides—allowing themselves to lose control over decorum, proper carriage, and pride. If one observes it closely, the extant film establishes an important difference between bodies meshing fluidly with machinery so that the attraction of grace in motion contrasts the clumsy recoveries, ungainliness, and quite mechanical movements of those who resist the rides. In this regard Jonathan Auerbach's description of the function of chase film bodily movement is inaccurate. In the chase film, claims Auerbach, the pursued "is less a man than a perpetual running machine, an automaton, at once rendered so by the cinematic chase itself, as well as the thing that makes unmotivated movement possible."[16] *Jack Fat and Jim Slim*, like *Boarding School Girls* before it, argues for more than one kind of motion in relationship to masterful machinery. Its comedy is rooted in the contrast between those who enter each shot *ready for action* and those who do not. Only the latter are rendered as automatons and likened to mechanical objects in their appearance and the depiction of their movements.

CONEY ISLAND (1917)

Coney Island replays the premise of *Jack Fat and Jim Slim* in a more sophisticated synthesis of mischievous gags and display, as well as narrative progression. It is a sublime example of physical motion as interlocking parts of a cosmic machine. Like *Jack Fat and Jim Slim*'s spectacle of the extraordinary body interconnected with the pleasure machines of Coney Island, *Coney Island* contrasts unleashing the sexual repression of the body with the confinements of marriage. Like the experience of the park itself, the pleasures of Coney Island are cinematically rendered both as an accommodation to new technologies that alleviates the alienating effects of modern industrial labor, as well as an allowance for sexual expression in a society whose institutions are otherwise repressive.

The film introduces slapstick comedy star Fatty Arbuckle as a henpecked husband seated next to his wife on the beach, although he soon buries himself in the sand. Fatty's Coney Island is a far cry from the *actualité* beach of *Boarding School Girls* or even of *Jack Fat and Jim Slim*. Although the film is shot on location, the space is open and unpopulated, with no bystanders to look at the camera or get in the way of our view of the performance. Action occurs centrally framed and closer to the camera than in the previous examples. The landscape of the beach functions, just as the park will, as an endlessly open topography for displaying Fatty's obese body against a blank canvas. The mise-en-scène emphasizes openness so that his body is the largest scaled object within the frame—his large girth becomes important—and competes with no randomly placed objects for attention or for showing off the nuances of his actions.

When Fatty's wife discovers that he is missing and runs off to find him, he heads for Coney Island's Luna Park. Skinny Buster Keaton, in his porkpie hat, and his girlfriend, who are introduced watching Coney Island's Mardi Gras parade, also go to Luna. Again, the film intercuts documentary footage of an actual parade, but Buster and his girl only react to it from a contiguous space that frames them and the lamppost that Buster shinnies up for a view. While incorporating actual locations and documentary style, the photographic realism never functions as a subject in and of itself (as *actualité*) and instead cinematically serves character development and narrative legibility.

Since Buster does not have any money, he cannot get into the park. Al St. John, as the perennial rube, pays for Buster's girlfriend and makes off with her inside the park. The guy and the girl get on the Witching Waves ride (fig. 5.1), and Buster (who has sneaked into the park) follows in classic chase form. But the display of the three on the ride represents the chase integrated into a new style. It occurs across multiple shots that allow for a variety of angles and for a close-up of the girl's face as she exhibits symptoms of motion sickness. Eventually, their cars collide, and the two men fight.

Al and the girl leave and seat themselves on a park bench. He leaves her alone in order to buy an ice cream for her. Elsewhere, Buster tries his hand at "hitting the bell," a park game at proving one's strength. While Buster and Al are thus occupied, Fatty meets the girl sitting on the bench and attempts to flirt with her, although she is now trying desperately not to get sick. Again, the edited arrangement of shots figures contiguous spaces while foregrounding character action (fig. 5.2). In returning to the girl, St. John walks through the space where Buster is just getting ready to drop the sledgehammer, and St. John kicks him in the pants. When St. John returns to "his" girl, Fatty takes the two ice cream cones. St. John punches Fatty, and Fatty sprays him with ice cream and pushes him offscreen. St. John lands in the next shot, on top of Buster, who is still at the stand with the sledgehammer. Buster then knocks St. John out of the shot and into the next one of the ice cream stand, where St. John retaliates by throwing scoops of ice cream that, in the next shot, hit Fatty in the face (fig. 5.3). St. John returns to Fatty and the girl, only to have Fatty cause his arrest by a passing policeman. This ballet of action that occurs across contiguous spaces depends not only on editing, angles, and framing but on timing of performances and the shot, as well as on establishing unity across the spaces through eye-line matches. The beauty of this gag structure relies exclusively on a combination of expert acting, timing, and mastery of cinematic syntax that make the sequence a cinematic machine of perfectly interlocking parts. Indeed, this cosmic machine drives contrasting character types of bodies (who duplicate both the comic oppositions of rural/urban and fat/skinny separately depicted in *Rube and Mandy* and *Jack Fat and Jim Slim*)

© 5.1. SHOTS FROM *CONEY ISLAND* (COMIQUE, DIR. FATTY ARBUCKLE, 1917). ©

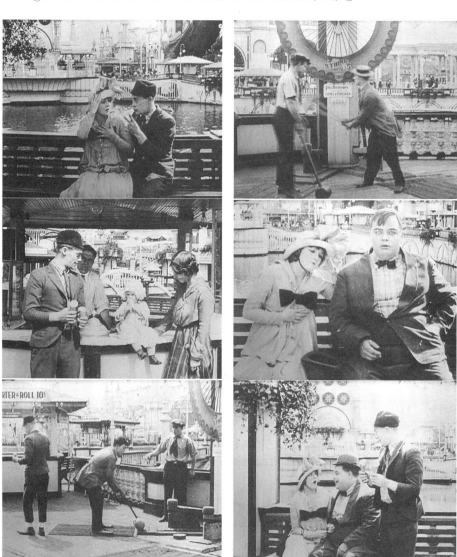

© 5.2. SHOTS FROM *CONEY ISLAND* (COMIQUE, DIR. FATTY ARBUCKLE, 1917). ©

5.3. SHOTS FROM *CONEY ISLAND* (COMIQUE, DIR. FATTY ARBUCKLE, 1917).

as automatons whose very identities hinge on their involvement with both the machines of Coney Island and the "machine" of slapstick energy.

What follows is this: Fatty makes off with Buster's girl, and they ride the shoot-the-chutes, represented as a spatially and temporally fragmented series of shots that occur in relationship to their close-up reactions of fear and delight. In a separate shot Buster looks offscreen at them and notices that the two have fallen out of their boat and into the lagoon. He rushes off to save the girl while Fatty is preoccupied with his own battle with a fish. Buster extends a hand to help Fatty out of the water but is rewarded by being pulled into the pond. Again, a sequence functions less to establish character psychology or motivation and forward narrative movement than to contain a series of interconnected gags that consider physical play between opposite body types that is organized by both the machinery and rhythms associated with modern technology.

In a stunning intermezzo unrelated to the views of park rides, character bodies overtaken by the machines, and a loosely driven chase, Fatty and the girl head for the bathhouse, where Fatty steals the attire of a nearby fat woman. (Interestingly, the two encounter a lifeguard who is a dead ringer for Jim Slim.) In this "middle" of the film Fatty dresses in "drag" and wanders through first the men's and then the women's dressing rooms. It is important here that the camera maintains a close or medium-close relationship to Fatty. The sequence is about his performance, a star turning out "gender bender" antics as he performs to the camera. Abetted by the onscreen presence of the girl, who (like the audience) knows his true identity, Fatty executes a self-conscious drag show (fig. 5.4),

The film sets up its conclusion by finally adhering to a narrative logic of causality and motivation. While Fatty performs, the film alternates the spectacle of his corporeal display with narratively motivated parallel actions: (1) Buster gets a job as a lifeguard; and (2) at the police station Al St. John meets up with Fatty's wife, who is an old friend, and she pays his fine while enlisting his help to find Fatty. Back at the beach Fatty, in drag, and the girl are ready for fun. Buster begins his job as a lifeguard, St. John and Fatty's wife arrive at the beach, and Fatty sees his wife. In a series of close-ups and medium shots organized purely by sightlines several actions occur: Fatty recognizes his wife, St. John abandons the woman in order to flirt with Fatty, and the wife spies the two of them together. Buster reveals Fatty's true identity to all, St. John fights with Fatty, and Buster runs off with his girl. Fatty's wife calls the police, who stumble, trip, and suffer a series of accidents before they finally arrive to arrest the brawling Fatty and St. John, who then join forces and lock up the cops and Fatty's wife. In the last two shots, bridged by action and visual reaction, they reemerge from the station house vowing not to chase women when St. John instantly spies a pretty girl and runs after her.

In *Coney Island* Fatty—centrally framed and emphasized throughout—revels in the pleasures of his own physical performance. He is never so much a character for identification as a model for corporeal self-delight, an instigator of Rube Goldberg–like chain reactions. Through both the time and space of the film his performance mimics and doubles the performance that Tony Bennett attributes to the rider of an amusement park mechanical attraction, wherein the interrelationship between machine and body "suspend[s] the physical laws that normally restrict its [the body's] movement, breaking the social codes that normally regulate its conduct, inverting the usual relations between the body and machinery and generally inscribing the body in relations different from those in which it is caught and held in everyday life."[17] In character and in gag structures *Coney Island* makes human behavior

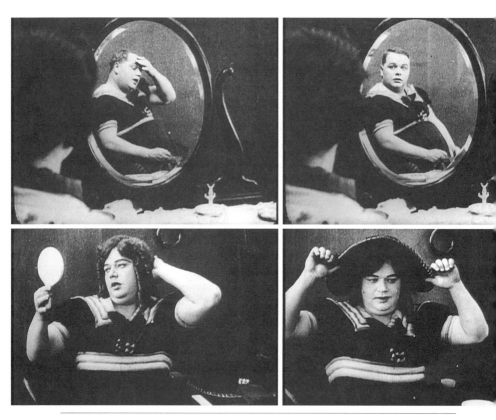

5.4. "FATTY'S 'DRAG SHOW,'" SHOTS FROM *CONEY ISLAND* (COMIQUE, DIR. FATTY ARBUCK-LE, 1917).

and involvement with the pleasure machines at Coney Island attendant on hyperbolizing cinematically the amusement park's "harnessing the laws of physics in order to overturn the rules of behavior."[18]

TILLIE WAKES UP (1917)

Although it was produced the same year as *Coney Island*, *Tillie Wakes Up* extends slapstick comedy at an amusement park from a two-reel comedy to a feature-length film format. Even so, it is less a cohesive dramatic narrative than a story fractured into two parts—a rather conventional comic drama in the first half that satirizes the repressive nature of three marriages all within one apartment building and, in the second, a trip to Coney Island that stalls the narrative and becomes a display of actress Marie Dressler's comic behavior and body in motion. *Tillie Wakes Up* is one of the series of feature-length "Tillie" films that Marie Dressler made in the mid-1910s, all featuring the famous Broadway star in the character role that allowed her to show off, as Jennifer Bean says, her "extraordinary mobility [and] unflinching momentum."[19] Bean argues that the character of Tillie allows for the spectacular display of Dressler's "ability to mimic technology's sublime tics" in the way she brings repetitive motion, running, facial contortions, slips and slides, and a large girth to movements that are comic because they so depart from norms of femininity.[20] Throughout, the film's comedy depends less on anything that Tillie does than on the exhibition of her body being overtaken by the park's various mechanical devices. She synthesizes the oppositions established by Miss Knapp and the girls and by the men and their wives in the earlier comedies. Although she is neither the direct descendant of Rube and Mandy nor a figure for revolt like Arbuckle, she is the crucible for mechanical motion, for automatism rendered because of her contact with modern machinery. Like the thrill rides that act on Tillie, *Tillie Wakes Up* argues that it is through the body and especially the physical comedy of the body on display where modern machinery melds with the will of the person and instigates physical relaxation, spontaneity, the destruction of dignified bearing, and a new kind of grace.

Tillie Wakes Up begins with a lengthy exposition introducing Tillie and her husband, Henry; the nosy neighbors; and the young married couple, J. Mortimer and Luella Pipkin. Both Henry and Luella are philanderers and go off together for a good time, leaving behind their sad spouses. The film crosscuts between Tillie and J. Mortimer, both of whom are in the marital doldrums and want to resuscitate their marriages. After reading an advice column in the newspaper, Tillie decides to enlist J. Mortimer as her "Romeo" to make her husband jealous. They leave, noticed by the neighbors, for a day on the town.

The second half of the film is their day on the town. Like *Tillie's Punctured Romance* (Keystone, 1914), the first feature-length slapstick comedy in the Tillie series, the forward direction of the film depends on alternating narrative detail with comic spectacle.[21] It begins with J. Mortimer's and Tillie's taxicab colliding with another automobile, and Tillie and her beau flee the scene to avoid an afternoon in police court. They catch a ride on the back of an ice wagon and begin to slide back and forth on the ice, foreshadowing their encounter with the mechanical attractions at Coney Island. Once they get off the wagon, so to speak, they are at Coney Island and stop at a beer garden to warm themselves up with a drink. Here, they figuratively fall off the wagon as they proceed to get drunk. As they get increasingly tipsy, the film intercuts between them and their spouses having a good time.

Leaving the table, Tillie begins to waver and grimace. We next see her riding on "the Witching Waves" and then climbing into a vat of peanuts for a nap. J. Mortimer finds her, and they enter Steeplechase Park. The drunken Tillie and Mortimer try out several lurching and rolling rides, where the display of Tillie's weaving, laughing, relaxed body now becomes the main subject, and the movie gives itself over completely to slapstick spectacle.

In much the same way that earlier comedies simply advertise people on one attraction after another, Tillie does not *do* anything funny so much as simply submit to the rides. First she becomes a victim of the Blowhole Theater. As her skirt is repeatedly lifted and her bloomers revealed, Tillie tries to lower her raised skirt. The film cuts repeatedly to the reactions of the laughing audience. Ultimately, Tillie and her escort fall down on the wobbly platform beneath their feet, exit, and respond by climbing the lurching Golden Stairs. Unlike Rube and Mandy, however, Tillie expresses joy in her repetitive surrender to the machines of pleasure, authorizing the spectator to react likewise to her submission to the movie machine of the theater. Tillie's good-natured laugh at her own loss of dignity makes her less a victim of voyeuristic humiliation than a tacit partner in her acquiescence to industrial mechanization as an oversized toy.

In fact, one movie reviewer so recognized the degree to which watching Dressler's extraordinary body resulted in becoming a fully physically engaged spectator that he worried about the actual deleterious effects her *feature-length* slapstick comedies might have on their audiences. In lavishing praise on the nonstop hilarity of *Tillie's Punctured Romance*, the *New York Daily Mail* reviewer said, "It is difficult to keep an audience in continuous laughter through six reels of film; facial muscles rebel and demand a rest."[22] Indeed, like Bean, Dressler's biographer, Victoria Sturtevant, recognizes that Dressler's slapstick success depended on the effect of an excessive corporeal body onscreen—like Arbuckle—moving in unexpected fashion so as to channel sensationalistic shock into comic violence, producing a "similarly depleting physical effect" on the spectators.[23] While the physical sensation of such movie spectatorship does not duplicate the physical experience of being on a thrill ride—even when watching Dressler *on* a thrill ride, it does produce a similar *physical effect* of pleasurable exhaustion or "depletion" that metonymically links the fully embodied movie spectator to the thrill rider.

If the slapstick of *Coney Island* attempts a similar effect, it operates within a different temporal framework as a twenty-minute short film. In *Tillie Wakes Up* the process of exhausting an audience with comedy (pleasurable laughter) occurs repeatedly: Tillie and J. Mortimer ride in succession the Human Whirlpool, the roulette wheel, the miniature railroad, and the Ferris wheel, so that comic violence stemming from the bodies in action perpetuates in a nonstop fashion over a longer period of time. The film, however, offers some respite and a broken rhythm by offering parallel scenes of narrative detail—the attractions' display of Tillie and J. Mortimer versus their spouses' dismayed reactions to the discovery of their absence. In this way the strict causal economy of the spouses' efforts to find the pair contrasts with the nonnarrative energies of the spectacle of Tillie and J. Mortimer. Ultimately, J. Mortimer and Tillie confront their spouses. J. Mortimer punches Henry before fleeing with Tillie on foot and then in a stolen automobile (another modern machine). Henry and Luella pursue them, and J. Mortimer drives the car into the ocean. Henry and Luella alert the lifeguards, and the lifeguards row out to rescue Tillie and J. Mortimer. Once they are rescued, Tillie and J. Mortimer are welcomed back into the open arms of their spouses, and they wink at each other.

In this instance the chase occurs not as the subject of the film across the grounds of the amusement park but merely as a coda to effect narrative closure and to reunite the four characters in one geographically continuous locale. Whereas chase films initially introduced the possibilities of action dispersed beyond the individual shot and allowed for a new geographic expansiveness unified by human action across topography, Tillie's chase serves a conservative narrative function. It reins in parallel action occurring across distinctively different spaces in order to reunite all the principal characters in an interlocking set of spaces and ultimately of them all together. The chase becomes the narrative's deus ex machina, a crudely motivated means for resolving the crisis introduced at the outset of the film. Its only climactic purpose is in relationship to what preceded it since it more importantly frees Tillie's and Mortimer's bodies from interaction with the machines of pleasure for display through action in the real world.

It may also serve as a kind of sequel to Tillie's plunge into the ocean at the end of *Tillie's Punctured Romance*, where Marie Dressler gets to display fantastic comic action with her body. In fact, King's assessment of that film's ending applies equally to *Tillie Wakes Up*: "What mattered most to [that film's director] Sennett was not closure, but climax—the 'ocean' as both setting and metaphor for a cumulative burst of frenetic action in which plot interest and development are finally swept away."[24] For King *Tillie's Punctured Romance* is important because it successfully extended slapstick humor to a feature-length film despite its indifference to organizing a coherent narrative. In *Tillie Wakes Up* the same impulse of alternating narrative and slapstick spectacle prevails with only the most minimal, slapdash resolution of the story.

But *Tillie Wakes Up* introduces a slapstick display of the body now interconnected with the pleasure machines of Coney Island. Tillie advances herself as a new kind of container for testing how mechanization unleashes the sexual repression of the body and the confinements of marriage. In this way the film further maps the satirical view of Victorian marriage offered by both *Jack Fat and Jim Slim* and *Coney Island*, and it contrasts repressive marriage to the cultural space of the amusement park as its antidote. The film, like the other Coney Island comedies, reproduces the cultural work of the amusement park as a social escape valve. The Coney Island comedies, however, specify the amusement park not just as a remedy for the ailments of industrial modernity but as a cure for the modern marriage.

SILENT FILMS OF THE 1920S AND THE AMUSEMENT PARK

Movies depicting the thrill of the amusement park did not end as the 1920s approached. After all, as Lucy Fischer points out, rural audiences continued to experience electrification only in urban or suburban settings until well into the 1930s, when the 1936 Rural Electrification Act finally encouraged electric distribution to rural American households.. But, as she notes, "By the 1920s, with electricity an established part of the American scene, the topic worked its way into the fabric of more extended and sophisticated cinematic narratives."[25] No longer a topic of novel excitement, the wonder of electricity only occasionally served as the focus for an entire film's scenario.[26] Likewise, the amusement park as a dazzling display of electrical illuminations and as a trope for the physical joy of industrial modernity became embedded in films with other purposes and themes. Silent films like *Number, Please?* (Rolin Films, dir. Fred C. Newmeyer and Hal Roach, 1920), *It* (Famous Players–Lasky, dir. Clarence G. Badger, 1927), *Sunrise* (Fox, dir. F. W. Murnau, 1927), Harold Lloyd's *Speedy* (Harold Lloyd, dir. Ted Wilde, 1928), *The Crowd* (MGM, dir. King Vidor, 1928), and *Lonesome* (Universal, dir. Pal Fejos, 1929, although it is partially a sound film) continued to display actors on amusement park attractions. In these films, however, Coney Island or its West Coast counterpart, Ocean Park in Los Angeles, became a backdrop for romance and courtship between sweethearts. The spectacle of bodies interacting with the park's technology became only one sequence or insert into the narrative rather than the backbone for the entire film, and the amusement park itself became a geographic counterpoint to the chaos, alienation, and geometric architecture of the modern industrial city.

These silent films most often depict working (and consuming) single women who enjoy the amusement park and embrace the industrial modern as itself the means for consumerism. *Speedy*, *It*, and *Lonesome* are all films whose female protagonists are narratively positioned as both sexually desirable and desiring, their sexualities frequently linked to their status as working girls. But they are not represented as Tillie is in relationship to the machines of industry and production in either work or leisure; instead, they participate in the amusement park and its technologies purely as acts of modern consumption. Their consumerism and the economic exchange they produce (they reward their suitors who "treat" them at the park with some display of physical intimacy) in relationship to the park's attractions is a matter of acquiring marital status, circumscribed by the narratives as romance on the innocent end of the spectrum and gold-digging on the cynical end. No longer is such unchaperoned courtship considered socially transgressive or a revolt against moral standards. Indeed, dating had become a heterosocial activity that was itself highly romanticized throughout these films and others of the 1920s. The films of this period transform a cycle of intertwining bodily thrills with pleasure machines by enmeshing the spectacular displays of the electrified amusement park and the slapstick automatism of the parkgoer's body in their exchange value as romantic comedy.

For example, *It* includes only a three-minute Coney Island sequence that frames Clara Bow's character, Betty Lou, with her beau in every shot. As a series of portraits of the couple, the two-shots establish their enjoyment of each other, flirtations, looks and smiles, and increasing physical intimacy. On a date with her department store boss, Mr. Waltham, salesgirl Betty Lou first introduces her upper-class boss to the hot dog in yet another example of the Coney Island hot dog serving as an icon of the amusement park as a whole (although the gluttony of *Rube and Mandy* is absent) and its associations with mass culture. The subsequent views of them on the Human Whirlpool and the Golden Stairs physically isolate them, showing them alone and separated from other parkgoers, and they laugh and stare at each other during the wild movements. But, since the camera never allows for a glimpse at their full bodies intertwined with the machinery, the sequence remains fixed on facial gestures and reactions and not on the relationships of the body to the mechanical.

In a logical narrative progression of courtship, the next shots depict them together sliding down a slide; Betty Lou sits in Mr. Waltham's lap, and an intertitle reads, "Hold me tight, Mr. Waltham." The follow-up, in which Betty Lou and Waltham fill the frame, depicts the two together laughing and arms flailing through not only this ride but a rolling barrel as well. As they exit the rolling barrel, an air jet blows Betty Lou's skirt up as the image fades to black. When the next shot fades in, the couple is arriving by car at Betty Lou's apartment, and it is the end of the date, one that efficiently developed the relationship from tentative smiles to flirtation to sexual closeness in a few minutes of screen time.

In *Speedy* a Coney Island sequence begins with what was by 1927 an old-fashioned postcard view of Luna Park. A long shot of the park's entrance displays the park as a civic monument, and the vantage point is high and distant, obviously not a point of view of the film's characters. It is instead that idealized viewing position touted by so many earlier films and post-cards establishing the amusement park as an urban spectacle. The film then offers a series of dissolves as time elapses: to the hero Speedy and his girlfriend Jane amid the crowd; to Speedy and Jane on an airplane ride; to Speedy and Jane on the Witching Waves; to another ride; to another postcard-long-shot view of Steeplechase Park; to Speedy and Jane on the steeplechase ride; to Speedy and Jane on shoot-the-chutes. The sequence ends with a cut to them getting out of their boat and approaching a hot dog stand on the Bowery. The film dispatches with the spectacle of bodies submitting to machinery in just a few minutes, as though this is a requisite feature of the park and movies about amusement parks but a mere formulaic establishing "nod" here.

Instead, what preoccupies most of the Coney Island sequence is the time that Speedy and Jane spend on the Bowery as a location pretext for several gags about Speedy and his new suit. The humor and plot here are all about Speedy's appearance and his role as a modern consumer. Even as the film returns Speedy and Jane to the crowd and the rides, they only momentarily participate in the attraction display of bodies intertwined with machinery— the human roulette wheel, the rotating barrel, the slide—before they resume their roles as consumers eating cotton candy, drinking colas, and purchasing corn on the cob.

The film dissolves to nighttime views of Luna Park, again conventional portraits of the electrified outlines of moving lights silhouetted against a dark sky like those more than twenty years earlier. But Speedy and Jane are now at another game concession, and this time they have lots of prizes on them. Again, the standard views of the amusement park as an urban spectacle function less to display the wonder of electrical illumination than to establish a time lapse from day to night and an ellipsis in the characters' ongoing pursuit of consumerist behavior. The spectacular view of the illuminated park gives way to Speedy and Jane filling the baby cradle he has won with all their prizes.

Coney Island here is neither an "escape valve" from a repressive marriage nor a mechanically induced means for bodily expression—although *Speedy* is still a slapstick film. It is not even an illustration of pleasurable leisure as an antidote to modern labor. It is a space in which documentary montage views of the park and rides serve as a backdrop for Speedy's and Jane's personality development as model family consumers. The exhibition of machinery and bodies occurs here but through a rapid montage that is more emblematic of time passing at the amusement park than of the corporeal spectacle of earlier amusement park films. In *Coney Island*, and even as early as *Rube and Mandy*, ice cream cones and hot dogs may have figured prominently as accents of the carnivalesque, reminders of the bodily. But in *Speedy*, food treats are not metonymns for gluttony or even gastronomic activity; they are rather gag elements for jokes about Speedy's new clothes. Coney Island is a set piece for building Harold Lloyd's standard persona as the boy with a can-do spirit associated with the pursuit of the American Dream and for rationalizing the marital union of the all-American boy and girl.

In fact, the scene that follows the Coney Island sequence cements this theme. Because Speedy has spent all his money, he, Jane, and their newly adopted dog catch a ride home in the back of a moving van. Inside the van they arrange the furniture into a parlor tableau and "play house." In this artificial domestic setting Speedy proposes marriage to Jane. The trajectory of the Coney Island trip thus narratively moves from courtship to "marriage" to the acquisition of the trappings of home—a cradle, dog, faux furniture, and even a hearth. Coney Island is no longer a space for escape from the confines of Victorian marriage but a place for modern, companionable courtship and consumerist training as a prelude to marriage and family.

Similarly, in *The Crowd* and in *Lonesome* Coney Island sequences contrast the monotony of the industrialized modern city and its alienated labor in order to function as the only fitting site for heterosexual romance that can result in marriage. Fischer summarizes the way Coney Island bridges this gap in *The Crowd*:

> The lackluster workaday universe is left behind and immediately replaced by the dazzling, electrically illuminated realm of the amusement park. . . . The couples enjoy numerous motor-driven rides: a rotating cylinder, a spinning disk, a carousel, and a "tunnel of love." As the tunnel ride draws to a close . . . a crowd outside can see which couples have been necking during their trip through the dark. At the end of the evening, John and Mary return home. . . . The rest of the film traces their subsequent marriage, parenthood, loss of a child, employment problems, economic struggles . . .[27]

For Fischer the weight of this sequence lies in "its association of the joys of urban life with electricity."[28] But her conclusion masks how minimally the spectacle of electrification operates as noteworthy in and of itself and how it serves an iconic purpose for setting up a montage of park-ride shots that trace a courtship in shorthand. Like *It*, *The Crowd* may economically narrativize heterosexual romance as a brief sequence of riding Coney Island attractions because the sexual connotations of rider relations are already well established.

Similarly, both *Lonesome* and *Sunrise* (*Sunrise*'s amusement park is entirely a studio set rather than an actual park) utilize amusement park sequences as social sites for romantic bonding during play. In the former film two alienated workers meet each other at Coney Island and develop a romantic attachment, playing out the kind of spontaneous love affair that social workers two decades earlier had decried. In the latter film a married couple rekindles the romance of their failed relationship at an amusement park. It is striking that in *Lonesome* the requisite montage of the nighttime illuminated skyline and the romantic pair on a series of mechanical rides gives way to a roller coaster ride that functions not to unite the pair but to separate them. The roller coaster ride provides a pivotal narrative turn since the couple's estrangement is a crisis that sets in motion the remainder of the film as the two search futilely for each other, and each returns home more alienated and alone than previously. The film's culmination is their reunion and ironic discovery that they are neighbors in the same apartment building. But if the ride itself does not fit comfortably into a new montage paradigm of couples achieving greater intimacy across a series of mechanical rides, it yet inserts a retrograde moment of pure attraction spectacle as it begins as a *Hale's Tours*-esque traveling point of view from the car of the coaster. Although it begins with the iconic image of the nighttime illuminated park, *Sunrise* dispenses altogether with the visual display of the couple on mechanical rides (probably because this was not actually a working amusement park but a studio set) and, extending the narrative space of the amusement parks in *It* and *Speedy*, features the couple instead at a series of game booths. Fischer speculates that because this couple is from the country, "perhaps the film wanted to avoid the condescending comic portrayals of 'country bumpkins' that had typified shorts like *Rube and Mandy at Coney Island* (1903)."[29] While Fischer suggests there is something inherently comic in the display of the human body overtaken by a mechanical thrill ride, what seems more relevant is that by the time of the late 1920s movies had already done away with the depiction of amusement park geography as a site for transforming the body through interaction with the mechanical modern.

Such a waning of interest in cinematically figuring the amusement park's amelioration of the shocks of modernity, its voyeuristic exuberance in bodies intertwined with machines, and its optically dazzling electrified spectacle mirrors the decline of amusement parks generally in this period as a mass playground. In fact, what is most interesting about *Speedy*'s rhetoric about modernity is not its amusement park sequence. It is instead that the notions of machinery and the body, thrill rides, travel, and modernist perception that were formerly associated with the amusement park now become transferred to the city as a whole.

If other films differentiated between the city and the amusement park, *Speedy* turns the city itself into an amusement park. The second half of the film has Speedy employed as a cab driver. First, he has problems with the automobile, and then he has problems with customers in a display of anti-machine and labor humor. A series of comic bits that allow for comic brawls between potential fares, however, gives way to the machine's transformation from a vehicle of productive labor into a machine of pure fun in Speedy's crazy traffic chases. Shot on location in New York City, the film follows Speedy (Harold Lloyd) as he weaves in and around trolleys and other autos and as he tries to outrun a motorcycle cop. Speedy picks up as a passenger the baseball celebrity Babe Ruth (who had just set his home run record the prior season), and the film cuts between Babe's horrified reaction to Speedy's driving to front views of approaching traffic and near misses to side views of accelerating speed. The sequence includes an extended phantom ride point of view from the front hood of the car as the auto runs wildly in traffic and narrowly misses pedestrians, other cars, and trucks. It demonstrates that the taxicab ride is itself a thrill ride across a city landscape now figured as an amusement park.

The taxi sequence establishes this motif for the film's climax, in which Speedy must "rescue" the horse-drawn, old-fashioned streetcar owned by Jane's father that traction company goons have stolen in order to take over her father's route. Speedy steals the trolley and, as he careens through the streets during his escape, the views are often from behind him in the driver's seat, showing New York City landmarks. Speedy's streetcar rescue and drive through town are the ultimate wild ride of the film, an amusement park thrill ride gone off the rails of the amusement park and transferred to the city proper as a new stand-in for everything the amusement park symbolized.

Throughout the 1930s, American films occasionally inscribed Coney Island as a familiar set piece for the temporal ellipsis of romantic courtship. For example, in *Mannequin* (MGM, dir. Frank Borzage, 1937), a tenement shop girl (played by Joan Crawford) goes out to Coney Island with her boyfriend-boss. Almost ten years after *It* portrayed a three-minute romantic interlude at Coney Island between a shop girl and her boss, this film abbreviates it even further, to just three shots—Luna Park's entrance at night, the illuminated skyline silhouette, and a *Hale's Tours*-esque shot of the couple shooting the chutes. Then the film cuts to a close-up of the romantic couple on a studio-set beach. Coney Island's purpose is fully readjusted from the comedy of physical interaction with machines to the glittering allure of nighttime seduction. The amusement park is no longer crucial for cinematic virtual travel and thrills. By the mid-1930s it had been reduced to one option among several for consumers of romantic courtship. In fact, when another tenement girl, Stella Dallas (Barbara Stanwyck), goes on a date with the company boss in the 1937 film *Stella Dallas* (Samuel Goldwyn, dir. King Vidor), she goes to the movies rather than to an amusement park. The movie theater, in this instance, serves as a more important narrative causal agent though not just for an ellipsis of romantic courtship but for demonstrating Stella's desire to mirror or mimic the Hollywood stars and upper-class romantic leads she sees on the screen.

The visceral engagement and fascination in physical spectacle for which amusement parks offered a privileged subject served a historically specific purpose of an earlier era when a conjoined celebration of speed, industrial power, and bodily kinetics meant kindling a national participation in technological modernity. This cinema's basis for pleasure lies not in the norms of passive spectatorship associated with the rise of Hollywood cinema but rather in its physical effect of *jouissance*, a decentered perceptual pleasure that occurs across the body. Doubling what the onscreen subjects themselves learned about the relationship of the body to the technological modern for producing pleasure, the Coney Island comedies historically offered lessons learned in the body about the body and modernist perception.

6

Conclusion

THE FUSION OF MOVIES
AND AMUSEMENT PARKS

> You're dead if you aim only for kids. Adults are only grown up kids,
> anyway.   —WALT DISNEY

ON JULY 17, 1955, DISNEYLAND OPENED IN ANAHEIM, CALIFORNIA.
The opening festivities, restricted to a few thousand Hollywood celebrities
and their families, were also broadcast as a two-hour live television program, "Dateline Disneyland," that was watched by ninety million people.[1]
The national marketing and response to the opening of an amusement park
illustrates not only that the old parks were being eclipsed by something new
but that the fusion of movies and amusement parks represented by Disneyland mattered even more in postwar America. Walt Disney learned his
lessons from the old parks and the movie business and applied them to
Disneyland.

By 1955 only a handful of old amusement parks remained. These parks,
originally located in suburbs that had easy train access to city centers, were
no longer remote outposts on the outskirts of towns. As cities grew around
and past them, the old amusement parks became increasingly associated
with inner city urban neighborhoods and their denizens. In the years after
World War II, as white middle-class citizens fled cities for new suburbs and

as suburbs overran the countryside, the old parks acquired new reputations as habitats for urban decay and haunts for urban criminals. They became sites of juvenile gang violence, illegal drug traffic, and racial conflicts. The paint peeled, facades fell into disrepair, and grime and dirt accumulated even while the parks still collected admissions. But these conditions killed off most of the remaining parks: Coney Island's Steeplechase closed in 1964, Chicago's Riverview in 1967, Baltimore's Glen Echo in 1968, Los Angeles's Pacific Ocean Park in 1969, Cleveland's Euclid Park in 1969, and New Jersey's Palisades Park in 1971.

Disneyland promised to be an antidote to the old parks that had fallen into disrepair and ruin. An expanding economy in the 1950s and the socio-spatial segmentation that fueled the suburbs as a white, middle-class residential and leisure refuge provided a basis for a new amusement park business intertwining broadcast television, amusement park rides, and American cinema. The new location for the new amusement park was on the outskirts of the new suburbs, where easy access to the burgeoning freeway system meant traveling to the park in an individual automobile, the icon of postwar car culture. (In later years Disney parks would come to depend on the commercial jet as the chief means of access to the parks.)[2]

Disneyland sanitized the electric park both literally and figuratively. Physically, Disneyland was an oasis of cleanliness, order, and efficiency.[3] There were no thrill rides that would cause shocks to one's system. There was no sexually risqué entertainment. There was no alcohol. There were no amusement zones for young men and women to develop sexual courtships by dancing together, swimming together, or drinking together. In fact, the rhetoric of the park was that this was a playground for family unity.[4] Walt Disney himself repeatedly called Disneyland "a family park where parents and children could have fun together." He made sure the opening broadcast reinforced this message: both onscreen hosts (Art Linkletter, Ronald Reagan, and Bob Cummings) and the many celebrities they interviewed repetitively introduced their children and testified to how much fun *their families* were having.

Of course, the original live broadcast of Disneyland's opening—rather than the filmed and edited views of the park that would predominate in succeeding years—was unlike *Coney Island* or *Tillie Wakes Up*.[5] There were limited views of rides in operation, of people giving themselves over to machinery, or even of people being amused by each other as part of the show. It depicted rebellion neither against social mores nor against marriage. Instead, the broadcast depended largely on a series of repetitive celebrity interviews. Postcard views of the park and individual attractions alternated with the sights serving as mere backdrops for "talking head" chatter about how much each family was enjoying each other's company. There was no spectacle of bodies on display—only testimony. Such a televisual style may be due more to the limitations of cumbersome television cameras that could not wander freely and required outdoor staging than to a desire to rely so heavily on the spoken word. But the limitations of television broadcast techniques served Disney's simple honed message. What is clear from the broadcast is that one element united the disparate geographical spaces, abrupt shifts in onscreen subjects, and even the gaffes of live broadcasting in an earlier era, and that was Walt Disney himself appearing regularly as an avuncular master of ceremonies, the entrepreneur who spoke directly to the camera as though he were a trusted family member.

As is well known, Disneyland depended on broadcast television not only for promotion but also for financing its construction. Disney struck a deal with the American Broadcasting Company (ABC): in exchange for its investment he would produce a one-hour television show for the new network looking to increase viewership. The reciprocity between Disney and ABC allowed Disney to use his television show (*Disneyland*) as a regular advertisement for the park, a strategy that became a model for entertainment industry synergy in the late twentieth century.[6] Unlike the old parks, Disneyland required neither postcards nor movie theaters to disseminate an idealized, ideological view of itself as a preeminent cultural symbol (although the park certainly sold postcard souvenirs): it had television and a weekly time slot that carried it to millions of American homes.

But more than simply cross-marketing both television and an amusement park, Disney reified the relationships between movies and amusement parks established by the earlier turn-of-the-century parks. The park that opened in 1955 had only a few of the attractions that became iconic Disneyland features over the next fifty years. Instead, Disney's five "lands" or sections—Main Street, U.S.A.; Frontierland; Adventureland; Fantasyland; and Tomorrowland—had architecture that resembled movie sets and plots. The reference point was less an indirect duplication of a world's fair or direct simulation of foreign exotic cultures and industrial modernity than Disney's repertoire of animated films, nature documentaries, and TV miniseries.[7] Frontierland resembled nothing more than the 1950s TV western set for *Davy Crockett*, had no thrill rides, and offered only musical variety shows on its steamboat and at its alcohol-free "saloon"—updated, cleaned-up versions of musical variety performances of fifty years earlier. Adventureland, which was not included in the opening live broadcast because of a gas leak in that part of the park, consisted only of the *Jungle Cruise* ride, a scripted mimicry of Disney animal documentaries that took riders on a scenic boat trip across a hodge-podge of Asia, Africa, and South America. Not too different from the *Tour du monde* at the 1900 Paris Exposition, Disney's "cruise" moved attendees through outdoor stationary scenery rather than placing panoramas before indoor stationary viewers and showcased native animal statues rather than live indigenous peoples. Even in spaces not specifically simulating previous Disney commodities—films and television episodes—Disneyland hybridized movies and old amusement park attractions for something that seemed new but that actually was the inheritance of how the old parks functioned. The park's entrance, Main Street, U.S.A., sported a working movie theater as a feature of its avenue: Disney's theater was a stand-in for both amusement park and downtown nickelodeons.

Most of the rides, however, were at Fantasyland, where all of the attractions replayed characters and themes from Disney animated films (*Alice in Wonderland* [1951]; *Peter Pan* [1953]; *The Adventures of Ichabod and Mr. Toad* [1949]; and *Snow White and the Seven Dwarfs* [1937]). *Mad Tea Party* was a Tickler or Tilt-a-Whirl that spun riders seated in large teacups. *Peter Pan's Flight* resembled numerous turn-of-the-century "dark rides" where one was seated in a conveyance that moved through darkened tunnels and passed a series of dioramas. Disney simply made the dioramas more elaborate and set them as scenes from his 1953 movie. *Mr. Toad's Wild Ride*, the most mechanically thrilling ride at the park, was a railroad variant of *Peter Pan's Flight* with *Mr. Toad*–themed dioramas and greater speed, sharp turns, sudden stops, and bumpy roadways. *Snow White's Adventures* and *Canal Boats of the World* similarly replayed Tunnel of Love and Old Mill rides through canals or darkened tunnels past scenery.

Inasmuch as all these attractions reproduced mechanical rides that were fifty years old, they were new only insofar as they became mid-twentieth-century phantasmagorias for popular movies. *Hale's Tours* may have flirted with fantasies about fictional characters and popular plots, and pyrodramas and disaster shows may have reproduced fantastic, epic visions; but Disney understood better than earlier amusement parks that being close to beloved fictional characters and inside one's favorite movies could form the backbone for an entire amusement park experience.

Nowhere was this more pointed than at Tomorrowland. Ostensibly an homage to technological utopianism and offspring of world's fairs, Tomorrowland opened with four attractions, three of which were direct descendants of turn-of-the-century illusion rides. (The only nonmovie attraction was Autopia, a kiddie-car ride on a mock freeway.) *Circarama* was a 360-degree wraparound movie where spectators watched panoramic views of western landmarks. *A Tour of the West* (1955–1960) seemingly realized the technological *and* touristic vision of the *Cinéorama* fifty-five years earlier. *Space Station X-1* was a panorama of aerial views of the United States with a viewing platform that slowly moved around the painting.

The jewel in the crown of Tomorrowland, however, was *Rocket to the Moon*, a *Hale's Tour*–style ride to outer space. *Rocket to the Moon* seated riders in a theater inside a mock rocket ship. As seats rocked and ambient sounds signaled liftoff, rocketeers could watch animation of the receding earth on a movie screen underneath the transparent floor and views of where they were headed on a movie screen directly in front of them. The ride took them around the moon and back home again. *Rocket to the Moon* may have been an heir to Coney Island's *Trip to the Moon*, but Disney reinvented its purpose. He may have returned *Hale's Tours* in all its glory to the amusement park, but he "repurposed" a ride that had more often emphasized picturesque travel and the social distinction of being a tourist in a new world understood as a playground for the West. *Rocket to the Moon* actually picked up where *When the Devil Drives* left off: it remade the fantasy of travel from visiting a destination that fulfilled the modern urbanite to the fantasy of being inside a movie.

More than the rides at Fantasyland, *Rocket to the Moon* harnessed the exhilarating sensations of kinesthesia and speed for the cinema. The moon trip that rocketeers experienced, after all, looked like science fiction movies of the 1950s, and the trip's "realism" depended entirely on its ability to make a movie look like a movie. In other words, as Disneyland and other parks have understood up to the present day in such *Hale's Tours*–esque rides as Disney World's *Star Tours* and Universal Studios' *Back to the Future: The Ride*, it is much easier to simulate reality when the reality being depicted is already a movie. It's not difficult to make a movie that looks like another movie. *Rocket to the Moon* may have been central to Tomorrowland because it played out fantasies and fears regarding the U.S. Cold War space race in the 1950s, but, more important, it sealed the deal that learning with the body at this park was the sublime fantasy of transcending mere movie spectatorship in order to "live inside the movies."[8]

In Disney's hands the new amusement park remade the cultural purpose of the old parks. If earlier parks used mechanical engagement to overthrow Victorian modes of repression and to unleash sexual independence, Disney replaced escape from sexual and decorous propriety with the infantilizing fantasy of freeing one's "inner child." Toward that end, surrendering to the pleasures of the rides meant finding one's identity through movie consumption—but enhanced consumption in which one reexperienced Disney animated films, nature documentaries, TV shows, and contemporary science fiction by momentarily living virtually inside the fictions.

Even Main Street, U.S.A., now represented the inverse of everything for which the old electric parks stood. The old parks' architecture, crowds, noise, continual motion, and, above all, electric lights dazzled consumers with an aestheticized sensation of industrial modernity and asked them to identify with metropolitanism. For the parkgoer entering Disneyland, Main Street, U.S.A., was a nostalgic vision of a mythical turn-of-the-century Main Street. Even its movie theater served this function: an old-fashioned storefront theater advertised *Steamboat Willie*, Walt Disney's first Mickey Mouse sound cartoon. The cartoon may be from 1928, but its name conjured up nostalgia for a movie-defined life that had passed and had been both technologically and industrially surpassed. As Disney critic Erika Doss observes, "The fantasy of Main Street was that it embodied what [people] wished small-town America could be, as opposed to the suburban strip mall reality they knew was waiting for them right outside Disneyland's parking lot."[9] Rather than looking forward to the future (despite the presence of Tomorrowland), Disneyland actually looked back to the world that the old parks were trying to overcome. It expressed nostalgia for one's own childhood at the individual level and for a mythical American homogeneous past at the collective level.

The purpose of the old amusement parks and their engagement of movies were very different from Disney's approach. The concepts of technological utopianism, giving one's body over to new machines for an affect of wonderment, and sharply differentiating between play or leisure and work helped to undergird the definition of a *national* collective identity at the moment when the United States was becoming a world power. The very definition of a *national* identity served to differentiate Americans from other cultures, to justify cultural superiority and state colonialism abroad, and to reconcile the influx of immigrants who were challenging traditional notions of who and what constituted an American. Across the country the parks helped to usher in and make sense of industrial modernity—its railroads, electricity, new patterns, and types of labor and leisure—across a wide-ranging, hetero-geneous population. Amusement parks contributed to the rise of the movies as a cultural institution even while the cinema and the amusement park both celebrated each other and worked with a common cultural purpose.

CODA: ADULTS AND SOON-TO-BE ADULTS ARE NOT "GROWN UP KIDS"

Even while Disneyland was ascending as the quintessential American amusement park, Pacific Ocean Park in Santa Monica—forty-one miles and "a stone's throw away" via freeway—was trying to compete with Disneyland. It was an updated version of the old Ocean Park that had begun in the 1890s and had been rebuilt several times. It was an old-style amusement park. However, in the late 1950s, P.O.P. (as it was known) often out-grossed Dis-neyland with its "pay one price" admission that allowed parkgoers unlimited access to most of its attractions. (Disneyland eventually had to follow suit in the latter 1960s.) But its urban location, reputation for harboring juve-nile delinquents and their criminal behavior, and sealed-off access to nearby freeways contributed to its demise in the late 1960s.

As a teenager I visited both parks when I spent the summer of 1964 in Los Angeles. They were not the first amusement parks I had attended—an old park still existed on the outskirts of my hometown—but they cemented my lifelong love for amusement parks while presenting a study in contrasts. Disneyland was clean, airy, open, brightly painted, and safe. Everything was visually unified in color, tone, and aesthetics. Invisible hands removed trash, kept concessions supplied and sanitary, and maintained order. No one worked, actual laborers were invisible, and there appeared to be only play and costumed characters who belonged to playful scenarios. These things in and of themselves—especially because my mother remarked on them repetitively—were a beauty to behold.

In contrast P.O.P. had narrow avenues that were often closed in and filled with shadows; paint everywhere was peeling; wooden structures looked dilapidated; trashcans overflowed; and the streets were dirty. P.O.P. pre-sented a cluttered view of signs, facades, and images from different eras all competing with one another. Park employees looked (to a fourteen-year-old girl, anyway) like roustabouts who leered with toothless smiles and moved machinery levers and controlled crowds with powerful bared forearms that featured lots of tattoos. Small clusters of dangerous-looking teenage boys loitered in alleyways, and I simply knew to keep far away from them. (No one loitered at Disneyland: one waited patiently for a turn at a ride. But no unsavory characters posed any threat.)

I visited Disneyland with my mother, sister, uncle, and cousins. It was a family outing, and it lived up to the advertisements I had watched on *Disneyland* since 1954. Disneyland was something one was supposed to desire. It took us hours in Los Angeles freeway stop-and-go traffic to get to Disneyland, and finally parking the car in Disney's distant parking lot so that we could take another car to the all-pedestrian park generated a lot of expectations. It was important for Disneyland to measure up to everything it had promised to be. But to an adolescent it was tame, and I was genuinely surprised that there were no exciting or scary rides. I was already too old to care about holding hands with Mickey Mouse. I craved more dangerous excitement.

P.O.P., however, came as a complete surprise. Being from out-of-state, I had never heard of it. I had no expectations. On the recommendation of an older cousin, I went with my younger sister simply for something to do one afternoon. We traveled by city bus a mere four miles from my uncle's house to Santa Monica, and, unaccompanied by any adults, two teenaged girls stayed until dark experiencing one thrill ride after another. Sure, I recall the dirt, the grime, the air of general disrepair, the unsavory characters. But what I remember more was an experience perhaps akin to what ruralites and urbanites, the working classes, knew at the turn of the last century—the exhilaration of "the imagination of disaster" and the thrill of subjecting one's body to mechanically induced deliriums. We experienced indoor dark rides, the more modern rocket ride and double Ferris wheel that had been added in the 1950s, but also a funhouse and Human Whirlpool that were from the turn of the century. We rode the 1926 wooden roller coaster that carried one out over the Pacific Ocean. I like to think that, like my turn-of-the-century counterparts, part of the excitement was the freedom from the rules and governance of those older and wiser. Although we were "good girls" and met no boys, struck up no new acquaintances, the opportunities to do so were also in and of themselves exciting, and even relays of sexual glances and strangers' looks were part of our newfound sense of liberation.

At the end of the day we took the bus home. At the end of the month we took the train back to the Midwest. I was more than fifty years removed from the girls who had inhabited the amusement parks all across the country in the first part of the twentieth century. But I shared more with them on a single day than I share with succeeding generations who make pilgrimages to Disneyland. Adults and those embarking on adulthood are not merely grown-up kids, as Disney would have it. His is a sanitized view in which children consumers transition seamlessly into childish adult consumers. It ignores all the sexual and social markers of identity that people acquire and that were the subjects of address for the old amusement parks.

DREAMLAND: THE LEGACY OF THE ELECTRIC PARK

Although Disney did transform and sanitize the amusement park, the result is also a mutated rejuvenation of the family, higher-class park from the turn of the century. After all, the turn-of-the-century amusement park had been a reference point in Walt Disney's boyhood. In his youth Disney visited Kansas City's Electric Park, not so very far from his boyhood home of Marceline, Missouri.[10] Someone so industriously nostalgic as he capitalized on such landmarks associated with a more youthful, innocent era. Disney also reinjected the modern postwar amusement park with the more contemporary scale, extravagance, and fantastic vision of more recent world's fairs—the Chicago Century of Progress Exposition of 1933 and the New York World's Fair of 1939–1940. (Disneyland and later Disney parks also capitalized on Disney's participation in the 1958 Exposition Universelle et Internationale de Bruxelles [Brussels] and the 1964 New York World's Fair, where Disney-designed pavilions for General Electric and for Pepsi-Cola/UNICEF were later dismantled and remade as Disney park attractions—the *Carousel of Progress* and *It's a Small World*.)[11] The reemergence of international expositions in the United States as fuel for national optimism and collective dreams at just the moment when the parks declined suggests that the parks' cultural function did not evaporate so much as find new outlets. Disney rechanneled these outlets back into the amusement park so that the dialogue between world's fairs and amusement parks that shaped the first generation of amusement parks continued to define amusement parks after World War II.

Disneyland was the standard bearer for all new amusement parks, as well for updating of old parks in the Cold War era. By 1980 there were about two dozen new super-parks or "theme" parks (in imitation of Disney's coherent fantasy approach).[12] A growing economy, increased leisure time, the construction of an interstate highway system, and the baby boom all contributed to the rise of new parks or remodeling of old parks as new automobile destination family entertainments in the 1960s and 1970s. In the retail age of fast food franchises and strip malls where national companies duplicated the same architecture and promised the same experience at different national geographic sites, companies like Great America and Six Flags similarly built suburban amusement parks "themed" through regional Americana or the variety of "cultures" that had historical sovereignty over Texas. To compete with Disneyland, Universal Studios built a park (1964) at its studio site in Los Angeles, although at first it was largely a riding tram backstage tour of its Universal City movie lot. Universal Studios, however, extended Disney's conceit of creating variety and thrill ride scenarios from its popular movies in order to put parkgoers virtually inside their favorite movies (e.g., *Jaws*, *King Kong*, *Back to the Future*, *Star Trek*). (In a further attempt to compete with Disney, Universal Studios opened a second movie-themed park in Orlando, Florida, in 1990.) It is not my purpose to analyze the role of these parks in late twentieth-century America but only to suggest that their continuities with the trolley parks were overshadowed by differences in ownership, economic control and marketing, relationships to transportation, and sociological makeup and purpose of park experiences.[13]

These parks have eliminated many of the defining features of the turn-of-the-century electric park—its entertainments and audiences who breached social and sexual mores, its more vulgar attractions of gambling and drinking, its enthusiasm for defining the exotic and the sensational, its excessive visual spectacle. Indeed, the very features that figured so prominently in old amusement parks have not been culturally eliminated but simply rerouted to the amusement parks' true American heir—the Las Vegas strip.[14] As Las Vegas critic William L. Fox says, "You go to Las Vegas precisely because you want to be overwhelmed by an excessive visual ordeal."[15] Fox argues that Las Vegas has reinvented itself by encompassing not only more and more spectacular live theatrical shows but exotic animal habitats, thrill rides, movie rides, simulations of exotic and fantasy locales, overwhelming electrified visual effects throughout the environment, and even rare art collections juxtaposed to displays of expensive commodity goods that serve as oddity museums—the very structural elements that defined the electric park experience. Las Vegas has become a themed tourist attraction, he says, where audiences are "treated as consumers of spectacle" and not as denizens of a specific desert environment.[16] It is Las Vegas spectacle itself, its visual rhetoric, and its signage that disguise that distinction. In new Las Vegas—where "reality is swamped" (Fox's term) by the absence of almost any way to keep track of time and space; the opulence associated with extraordinary wealth; hyperstimulating facades; the promise of overindulgence and transgressive behaviors; and the conflation of zoos, museums, and theaters with shopping malls—one is actually attending what Fox labels the "most aggressively branded" adult theme park in the world.[17] The Las Vegas strip is today's Coney Island, the flagship for a steadily growing number of imitators that serve as fantasy and sexual playgrounds for teaching Americans how to adjust to a postindustrial, post-9/11, postmodern society.

Those few old-time parks that have survived to compete with Las Vegas, Disneyland, and other modern theme parks have done so because they received new injections of capital, updated modern thrill rides (especially steel roller coasters), and new entertainment. But parks like Ohio's Cedar Point and Pittsburgh's Kennywood also pay homage to their past through historic plaques placed next to old buildings and rides, through National Historic Register status for individual attractions, as well as for the parks themselves (Kennywood received National Historic Register status in 1987), and even through reinventing their past appearance in a portion of the park (Kennywood opened "Lost Kennywood" in 1995). (In yet another instance Denver's Elitch Gardens simply shut down and rebuilt elsewhere as a modern theme park rivaling the brand-new ones.) One of many smaller parks that still exist, Santa Cruz's Boardwalk likewise touts its National Historic Register status and even includes a museum exhibit of its own history in its oldest building, the turn-of-the-century casino. But these memorials do not so much dramatize the continuing purpose of the trolley park as embed a visual, even spectacular, nostalgia for a past that no longer exists. Lakeside Park in Denver and Arnold's Park on Lake Okoboji in northwest Iowa might even be said to have "themed" themselves as nostalgia parks.

The synergy between movies and amusement parks has played quite differently in postwar parks where the fantasy of "living inside the movies" that structures Disney parks became mimicked by all others and especially by Universal Studios parks. Yet movie theaters themselves remain a staple of amusement park entertainment: theme parks now simply rely on newer cinema technologies—IMAX, 3D, and 360-degree projection—in movies that are still predominantly travelogues. In its reliance on movies and on mechanical (albeit now computer-driven) thrill rides, the modern theme park may represent a continuation of the technological utopianism associated with the electric park, but that utopianism is one element of an agenda of a distinctive era and serves a different purpose: these attractions are about Control and Nature. On the one hand they may benevolently control

Nature by "programming, directing, even sculpting" everything about the fantasy as a built environment (i.e., landscape, architecture, "animatronic" figures, timing and nature of parkgoer behavior).[18] On the other hand they reify society's successful defiance of Nature in rides whose rhetoric is that they are supernaturally big, expensive, and dangerous. Today's amusement parks thus consolidate a number of features beyond technological utopianism associated with post–Cold War corporate society—passive conformity, homogeneity, and instant gratification made possible through efficiency.

APPENDIX
• • • • • • • • • • • •

Directory of Amusement Parks in the United States Prior to 1915

This list remains partial and is based on trade industry directories (e.g., *Billboard, Street Railway Journal and Electric Railway Review*) and on local histories. For purposes of this list an "amusement park" is defined as such by the presence of at least a few mechanical rides. Picnic groves, nature preserves, and other designated "rural retreats" are not in and of themselves considered amusement parks until and if they incorporate multiple attractions. Where available, dates of operation, information about segregated parks, and ownership are provided. Where an exact opening or closing date is not known, a question mark has been substituted.

ALABAMA

Anniston, Lake Oxford Park (?–1950)
Birmingham, Blue Lake Park (1908–?): exclusively for African Americans
————, East Lake Park (1902–1917)
Mobile, Dixie Park (1908–?): exclusively for African Americans
————, Monroe Park: owned by the Mobile Light and Railway Company
Montgomery, Electric Park (1904–1909): owned by the Montgomery Street Railway Company
————, Washington Park (dates unknown): exclusively for African Americans; owned by the Montgomery Traction Company
Sheffield, Lincoln Park (dates unknown): exclusively for African Americans
Tuscumbia, Woodside Park (1907–?): exclusively for African Americans

ARKANSAS

Fort Smith, Electric Park (1905–1920): owned by the Fort Smith Light and Traction Company
Hot Springs, Washington Park
————, White City

————, Whittington (1894–1935) owned by the Hot Springs Street Railroad Company

Little Rock, Dreamland

————, Fairyland Park (1906–?)

————, Highland Park (1909–?): exclusively for African Americans

————, Ingersoll Park

————, Wonderland Park (1908–?)

Pine Bluff, Forest Park (1905–1912?): owned by Citizens' Light and Transit Company

Texarkana, Spring Lake (1909–?)

CALIFORNIA

Long Beach, The Pike (1902–1973): demolished in 1973

Los Angeles, Chutes Park (1905–1910)

————, Luna Park (1911–1914): formerly Chutes Park; owned by Frederick Ingersoll; sold in 1912 as a park exclusively for African Americans

————, Ocean Park or Venice Park (1905–1969)

Oakland, Idora Park (1904–1929): the park was torn down in 1929

Redondo Beach, Redondo Beach Park

Sacramento, Oak Park or Joyland: owned by Sacramento Electric Gas and Railway Company

San Diego, Wonderland Park (1913–1917)

————, Tent City or Coronado Beach (1900–1939)

San Francisco, The Chutes (1910–1911): destroyed by fire

————, Sutro Baths

San Jose, Luna Park (1910–1920): built by trolley car magnate Lewis E. Hanchett

Santa Cruz, Boardwalk (1907–present)

COLORADO

Denver, Elitch Pleasure Gardens (?–present)

————, Lakeside Park or White City (1909–present)

————, Luna Park (1908–1914): rebuilt on the site of Manhattan Beach

————, Manhattan Beach (?–1908): destroyed by fire

————, and Englewood, Tuileries Amusement Park (1906–1912)

Pueblo, Lake Minnequa Park (1904–1940)

Trinidad, Electric Park: owned by the Trinidad Electric Railroad Company

CONNECTICUT

Bridgeport, Steeplechase Island or Pleasure Beach (1906–1958)
————, Parlor Rock (?–1908)
Bristol, Lake Compounce (1895–present)
Middlebury, Quassy Park (1908–present)
New Haven (West Haven), White City or Savin Rock (1904–1993)
Torrington, Electric Park: owned by the Torrington and Winchester Street Railway Company
West Hartford, Luna Park (1906–1926)

DELAWARE

Wilmington, Brandywine Springs (1900–1923): owned by the People's Railway Company
————, Shellpot Park (1893?–1916): owned by the Wilmington and Philadelphia Traction Company

FLORIDA

Jacksonville, Dixieland Park (1906–1919)
————, Florida Ostrich Farm and Zoo (1912–?)
————, Lincoln Park: exclusively for African Americans; owned by Jacksonville Electric Company
Tampa, Ballast Point: owned by the Tampa Electric Company
————, Sulphur Springs

GEORGIA

Atlanta, Lakewood Park (?–1965)
————, Ponce de Leon Park (1903–1920): owned by the Georgia Railroad and Electric Company
————, White City Park (1907–?)
————, Wonderland Park
Augusta, Lake View Park: owned by the Augusta Railway and Electric Company
————, Monte Santa (1905–?)
Columbus, Wildwood Park: controlled by the Columbus Railroad Company
Macon, Crump's White City (1905–?)
Savannah, Lincoln Park: owned by the Savannah Electric Company; catered to African Americans

————, Thunderbolt (1904–1930): owned by the Savannah Electric Company; destroyed by fire

IDAHO

Boise, Riverside Park
————, White City (1907–1930s)

ILLINOIS

Aurora, Fox River or Riverview Park (1908–?)

Belleville, White City or Priester's Park (1908–?)

Cairo, White City

Centralia, White City (1907–?)

Champaign and Urbana, West End Park: owned by Champaign and Urbana Railway, Gas and Electric Company

Chicago, Chateau de Plaisance: owned by Leland Grant's Baseball and Amusement Association, an African American company

————, Chutes Park (1896–1907): owned by Paul Boynton

————, Forest Park (1908–1923): a 1922 fire destroyed much of the park

————, Luna Park (1907–1911): owned by James "Big Jim" O'Leary

————, Riverview Park (1904–1967)

————, Sans Souci (1899–1915): owned by the Chicago City Railway Company

————, White City (1905–1934)

Danville, Wonderland Park

Decatur, Dreamland (1905–1912)

DeKalb, Electric Park (1906–1912): owned by DeKalb, Sycamore and Inter-Urban Traction Company

East St. Louis, Lansdowne Park (1906–?)

Elgin, Trout Park (1909–1922)

Joliet, Dellwood Park (1907–1930): owned by Chicago and Joliet Electric Railway Company

Kankakee, Electric Park: owned by the Kankakee Electric Railway Company

Marion, Electric Park: owned by Coal Belt Electric Railway Company

Moline, Prospect Park (1909–?): owned by the Tri-City Railway and Light Company

Peoria, Al Fresco Park (1905–1925): destroyed by fire

Plainfield, Electric Park (1904–1932): owned by the Joliet, Plainfield and Aurora Railroad Company

Rockford, Harlem Park: owned by Rockford and Inter-Urban Railway Company

Rock Island, Black Hawk's Watch Tower (1890s–1927): owned by the Tri-City Railway and Light Company; purchased by the State of Illinois in 1927 and turned into a state park

Springfield, White City (1906–?)

————, Zoo Park

Waukegan, Electric Park: owned by the Waukegan, Fox Lake and Western Railway Company

INDIANA

Anderson, Mound's Park (1906–?): owned by the Indiana Union Traction Company

Bloomington, Wonderland

Eaton, Riverside Park (1903–?)

Evansville, Cook's Electric Park or Pleasure Park (1904–?)

————, Oak Summit (1904–?): owned by the Evansville and Southern Indiana Traction Company

Fort Wayne, Robison Park (1904–1919): owned by the Fort Wayne Electric Railway Company; the park went bankrupt in 1919

Gary, Lakewoods Park (1911–?)

Indianapolis, Broad Ripple Park or White City (1906–1908): owned by the Broad Ripple Rapid Transit Company; destroyed by fire

————, Fairview Park (1903–?): owned by Citizens Street Railway Company

————, Luna Park (1906–?): owned by Thompson and Dundy

————, Riverside Park (1904–1970); owned by Frederick Ingersoll and partners; in 1919 new owners instituted a "whites only" policy except for special Jim Crow Days

————, Wonderland (1906–1911): destroyed by fire

Michigan City, Washington Park (1905–?)

Muncie, Electric Park (1907–?)

————, West Side Park (1905–?)

Peru and Wabash, Boyd's Park (1905–?)

South Bend, Spring Brook Park or Playland (1905–?): owned by Chicago, South Bend and Northern Indiana Railway Company

Terre Haute, Lakeview or Fairland (1905–1909)
Vincennes, Lakewood Park (1906–1925)
Warsaw, Winona Lake (1903–?)

Iowa

Burlington, Electric Park (1906–?)
Cedar Rapids, Alamo Park (1906–1910): owned by the Cedar Rapids and Iowa City Railway and Light Company
Council Bluffs, Lake Manawa Park (?–1928): started by the Omaha and Council Bluffs Street Railway Company
Davenport, Suburban Island (1905–1918)
Des Moines, Ingersoll Park (1903–1912): owned by the Des Moines City Railway Company
—————, White City (1905–1911)
Dubuque, Union Park (1890s–1934): originally owned by Union Electric Company
Lake Okoboji and Arnold's Park, Arnold's Park (?–present)
Muscatine, Electric Park: owned by the Citizens Railway and Light Company
Sioux City, Riverside Park (1906–1920s): owned by the Sioux City Traction Company
Waterloo, Electric Park (1902–1933): built by the Waterloo and Cedar Falls Rapid Transit Railway

Kansas

Atchison, Forest Park: owned by the Atchison Railway, Light and Power Company
Coffeyville, Coffeyville Park
Fort Scott, Fern Lake Park (1906–?)
Hutchinson, Riverside Park (1901–1930)
—————, White City (1908–?)
Iola, Electric Park (1902–1918): owned by Frank V. Crouch
Kansas City, Carnival Park (1907–1909)
Topeka, Garfield Park
—————, Vinewood Park (1904–?): owned by Topeka Railway Company
Wichita, Wonderland Park (1905–1918)

APPENDIX

KENTUCKY

Ashland, Clyffeside: owned by the Ohio Valley Electric Railway
Lexington, Blue Grass Park (1910–?)
Louisville, Fountain Ferry (1905–1969)
————, Glenwood Park
————, River View Park (1902–?)
————, White City (1907–1921)
Ludlow, Lagoon Park (1895–1918)
Paducah, Wallace Park (1908–?): owned by Paducah Traction Company

LOUISIANA

New Orleans, Athletic Park or White City (1906–1912)
————, Scenic Park (1908–?)
————, Spanish Fort (1901–1928): operated by the New Orleans Railway and Light Company
————, West End Park (1901–1928): annexed to Spanish Fort in 1910
Shreveport, Gladstone Park (1909–?)

MAINE

Orchard Beach, Old Orchard Beach Park (1902–present)

MARYLAND

Baltimore, Bay Shore Park (1906–1947): built by the United Railways and Electric Company; for whites only
————, Carlin's Park (?–1950s)
————, Electric Park (1906–1915): for whites only
————, Glen Echo Park (1890s–1968): for whites only
————, Gwynn Oak Park (?–1972): owned by the United Railways and Electric Company; open to whites only
————, Hollywood Park (1910–?)
————, Lincoln Beach: exclusively for African Americans
————, Luna Park (1910–1911)
————, River View (1898–1929): owned by the United Railways and Electric Company; open to whites only with special Jim Crow Days for African Americans
————, Wonderland Park

Chesapeake Beach, Chesapeake Beach (1899–1972)

Prince George's County, Washington Park or Notley Hall (1901–1924): an African American park

Ocean City, Ocean City (1900–present)

Pen Mar, Pen Mar Park

Tolchester Beach, Tolchester Beach (1899?–1962)

MASSACHUSETTS

Boston, Paragon Park (1904–1985)

————, Wonderland or Revere Beach (1896–1996)

Brockton, Highland Park

Dedham, Westwood Park

Fitchburg, Whalom Park (1893–2000): built by the Fitchburg and Leominster Street Railway Company

Haverhill, Ingersoll Park

Holyoke, Mountain Park (?–1987): built by the Holyoke Street Railway Company

Lakeville, Lakeside Park: built by the Bay State Streetcar and Railway Company

Lawrence, Woodland Park

Lexington, Lexington Park: owned by Lexington and Boston Street Railway Company

Lowell, Lakeview Park

New Bedford/North Dartmouth, Lincoln Park (1894–1987): owned by the Dartmouth and Westport Street Railway Company

Newton, Norumbega (1897–1963)

Salem, Salem Willows (?–present): built by the Naumkeag Street Railway Company

Salisbury Beach, Salisbury Beach

Shrewsbury, White City (1905–1960): built by Horace Bigelow

Springfield, Riverside Park

Worcester, Pinehurst (1906–?)

————, Wonderland Park

MICHIGAN

Battle Creek, Gaguac Lake or Lakeside Park

Bay City, Winona Beach: owned by Bay City Traction and Electric Railway Company

Benton Harbor, House of David Amusement Park

Detroit, Electric Park (1906–1928): owned by the Arthur Gaulker family; condemned by the city of Detroit in 1927 and torn down in 1928

————, Riverview Park (1908–?)

————, Wolffs Amusement Park

Flint, Lakeside Park (1912–?)

Grand Rapids, Ingersoll Park

————, Ramona Park at Reed's Lake (1897–1955)

Houghton and Jacobsville, White City (1906–1919): owned by Houghton County Street Railway

Jackson, Vandercook's Lake or Hague's Park (dates unknown)

Kalamazoo, Casino Park (1904–1907): on the site of Lake View Park; torn down in 1907

————, Lake View Park (?–1904): started by the Citizens Street Railway Company; name changed to Casino Park in 1904

————, Oakwood Park (1907–1925): replaced Casino Park

Lansing, Waverly Park (?–1917): owned by the Michigan United Railway Company

Mt. Clemens, Mt. Clemens Park

Muskegon, Lake Michigan Park: owned by Muskegon Traction and Lighting Company

Port Huron, Kewahdin

Saginaw, Riverside (1894–1937): opened by the Saginaw Valley Traction Company

South Haven, Electric Park or South Haven Park

St. Joseph, Silver Beach (1910–1970): owned by Logan Drake and Louis Wallace

MINNESOTA

Duluth, White City (1906–?)

Lake Minnetonka, Big Island (1906–1911): operated by the Minneapolis and Suburban Railroad Company

Minneapolis, Forest Park

————, Twin City Wonderland (1905–1912)

St. Paul, Phalen Park

White Bear Lake and St. Paul, Wildwood (1899–1938): owned by Twin City Rail Transit Company

Mississippi

Columbus, Lake Park: owned by Columbus Railway, Light and Power Company

————, Washington Park: for African Americans; owned by Columbus Railway, Light & Power Company

Gulfport, Forest Park

Vicksburg, Suburban Park

Missouri

Excelsior Springs, Electric Park

Joplin, Lakeside Park: built by Southwest Missouri Electric Railway Company

————, Schifferdecker's Electric Park (1909–1912): built by brewer Charles Schifferdecker and leased to a local railway company

Kansas City, Electric Park (1907–1925): built and operated by Heim Brewery owners Mike and Ferdinand Heim; destroyed by fire

————, Fairmont Park (1897–1933): built by Arthur E. Stillwell, interurban railway magnate; destroyed by fire

————, Forest Park (1903–1912)

————, Lincoln Electric Park: exclusively for African Americans

St. Joseph, Lake Contrary Park (?–1964): owned by St. Joseph Railway, Light, Heat and Power Company; continuous flooding after World War II eventually destroyed the park

St. Louis, Forest Park Highlands (1896–1963): opened by the Home Brewery Company; destroyed by fire

————, Tranquilla Park

————, West End Heights

Springfield, Doling Lake Park (1907–1970s)

————, White City (1907–1912)

Montana

Butte, Columbia Gardens (1899–1972): built by copper magnate William A. Clarke, who was also a principal investor in the Butte Electric Railway Company

Great Falls, Electric Park

NEBRASKA

Lincoln, Capital Beach or Lincoln Beach
Omaha, Courtland Beach Park: owned by the Omaha and Council Bluffs Street Railway
————, Krug Park (1903–1940): started by Omaha brewer Fred Krug
————, Loop Park (1906–1906); destroyed by fire after being open only three weeks

NEVADA

Reno, Belle Isle

NEW HAMPSHIRE

Manchester, Pine Island Park: owned by Manchester Traction, Light and Power Company
Nashua, Lawndale Park
Salem, Canobie Lake Park (1902–present): started by the Massachusetts Northeast Street Railway Company

NEW JERSEY

Asbury Park, Asbury Park (?–1988)
Atlantic City, Steeplechase (1904–1986): started by George Tilyou
Bayonne, Melville Park (1905–?): built by Frank Melville
Burlington, Burlington Island (1900–1934): destroyed by fire in 1928 and 1934
Camden, Wood Lynne Park (1901–1912): owned by the Camden Suburban Railroad
Clementon, Clementon Park (1907–present)
Fort Lee, Palisades Park (1898–1971): built by the Bergen County Traction Company
Gloucester City, Washington Park (1895–1913): built by William J. Thompson; destroyed by fire
Lake Hopatcong, Bertrand Island
Long Branch, Ocean Park (1911–?)
Masonville, Rancocas Park (1912–?)
Newark, Electric Park (1903–1912)
————, Hillside Pleasure Park (1904–1927)

————, Olympic Park (1904–1965)

Pattenburg, Bellewood (1904–1916): built by the Lehigh Valley Railroad

Patterson, Fairyland (1905–1908)

————, Wildwood (?–present)

Pitman, Alcyon Park (?–1944)

Trenton, White City or Capitol (1907–?)

New York

Albany and Troy, Altro or Maple Beach Park (1907–?): the park was renamed Maple Beach in 1910

————, Electric Park or Lake Kinderhook

————, Renasselaer Park (?–1917)

Binghamton, White City

Brooklyn or New York City, Coney Island: Luna Park (1903–1944), Dreamland Park (1904–1911), Steeplechase Park (1897–1964)

Bronx or New York City, Clason Point

————, Fort George or Paradise Park (1895–1914)

Buffalo, Bellevue Park

————, Carnival Court or Athletic Park (1909–1920)

————, Erie Beach or Fort Erie

————, Luna Park (1904–1909); park was destroyed by fire and replaced by Carnival Court

————, Olcott Beach: owned by the International Railway Company

————, Sylvan Beach

Canarsie or New York City, Golden City (1907–1934): destroyed by fire

Elmira, Eldridge Park

————, Rorick's Glen Park: owned by Elmira Water, Light and Railroad Company

Glen Falls, Glen Island Park

Gloversville or Sacandaga, Sacandaga Park (1898–1930): owned by Fonda, Johnstown and Gloversville Railroad

Ithaca, Renwick Park (?–1915): owned by Ithaca Street Railway Company

Jamestown, Midway Park (1898?– present): built by the Jamestown and Lake Erie Railway

Jamestown and Celoron, Celoron Park or Chautauqua Lake (1893–1962): owned by Jamestown Street Railway Company

Middletown, Midway Park: owned by the Wallkill Transit Company

Newburgh, Orange Lake Park

Niagara Falls, Electric Park

North Beach or New York City (Queens), Gala Park (1894–1921): started by Steinway and Sons for their employees

Oneida, Carnival Park

Oriskany, Summit (1897–1927)

Peekskill, Electric Park

Rockaway Beach or New York City (Queens), Steeplechase Park or Rockaway Beach (1901–1928): started by Steeplechase Park magnate George Tilyou; absorbed into Rockaways' Playland

Rochester, Glen Haven or Dreamland Park (1899–present): started by the Glen Haven Railroad Company

————, Ontario Beach (?–1919): owned by the Rochester Railway Company

————, Seabreeze Park (?–present): owned by the Rochester and Suburban Railway Company

Rye, Oswego Lake

————, Rye Beach

Schenectady, Luna or Dolles Park (1904–1933)

Seneca Falls, Cayuga Lake Park: owned by Geneva, Waterloo, Seneca Falls and Cayuga Lake Traction Company

Staten Island or New York City, Happyland or South Beach (1906–1919): destroyed by fire

————, Midland Beach (1897–1920s)

Syracuse, Long Branch Park

————, White City (1906–1915)

Troy, White City

Utica, Little Coney Island: owned by Louis Hyman

————, Summit Park: owned by the Utica Mohawk Valley Railroad Company

————, Utica Park: owned by the Utica Mohawk Valley Railroad Company

NORTH CAROLINA

Charlotte, Electric Park

————, Lakewood Park (1910–1936): destroyed by tornado

Durham, Lakewood Park: owned by Durham Traction Company

Raleigh, Electric Park (1912–1915)

Оніо

Akron, Lakeside Park (?–1917): operated by Northern Ohio Traction and Light Company

————, Silver Lake Park (1894–1917)

Ashtabula, Woodland Beach Park (1902–?): owned by Pennsylvania and Ohio Railway Company

Canton, Meyer's Lake Park (?–1974): started by Northern Ohio Traction and Light Company

Cincinnati, Chester Park (dates unknown): owned by Cincinnati Traction Company

————, Coney Island (1896–1972)

Cleveland, Euclid Beach (1894–1969)

————, Luna Park (1905–1929): owned by Frederick Ingersoll

————, White City (1897–1907): destroyed by a windstorm

Columbus, Buckeye Lake Park

————, Indianola Park (1904–?)

————, Oletangy Park (1896–1937): started by the Columbus Railway and Light Company

Dayton, Fairview Park: owned by People's Railway Company

————, Lakeside Park (?–1967)

————, White City

Findlay, Riverside Park

Girard, Avon or Ferncliffe Park (1897–1920s)

Hamilton, Lindenwald Park

Kent, Brady Lake Park (?–1944)

Lima, Hover Park (1908–?)

————, McCullough Park

————, White City (1906–?)

Mansfield, Luna Park

Medina, Chippewa Lake Park (?–1978)

Mount Vernon, Hiawatha Park

Sandusky, Cedar Point (?–present)

Steubenville, Stanton Park (1906–1912): owned by Steubenville and East Liverpool Railway and Light Company

Toledo, Casino Beach Park or Lake Erie Park (1895–1910): destroyed by fire

————, White City (1907–?)

Youngstown, Idora Park or Terminal Park (1899–1984): started by Youngstown Park and Falls Street Railway Company

Zanesville, Moxahala Park (1906–?): owned by the Southeastern Ohio Railway, Light and Power Company

OKLAHOMA

Ardmore, Lorena Park (1909–1911)

Enid, Lakewood Electric Park (1907–?); owned by the Enid City Railway Company

Muskogee, Hyde Park (1907–?): owned by the Muskogee Electric Traction Company

Oklahoma City, Belle Isle Park (1910–1928): built by the Oklahoma Railway Company

————, Delmar Garden (1902–1911): built by John Sinopoulo; went out of business shortly after Oklahoma enacted Prohibition laws

Shawnee and Tecumseh, Benson Park (1907–1932): built by the Shawnee-Tecumseh Traction Company

Tulsa, Orcutt Park (1910–?)

————, Sand Springs Amusement Park (1911–mid-1930s)

OREGON

Portland, Council Crest Park (1911–1929)

————, The Oaks (1905–present): built by the Oregon Water Power and Navigation Company

PENNSYLVANIA

Allentown, Central Park: owned by the LeHigh Valley Transit Company

————, Dorney Park (1894–present): started by the Allentown and Reading Traction Company

Altoona, Lakemont Park (1894–present): started by the Altoona and Logan Valley Electric Railway Company

Bristol, Burlington Island Park (1900–1934): destroyed by fire

Butler, Alameda Park: owned by Butler Passenger Railway Company

Chalfont, Forest Park (?–1964)

Chambersburg, Dreamland (1906–?)

Clark's Summit, Electric Park

Conneaut Lake, Conneaut Lake Park (originally called Exposition Park) (1892–present)

Easton, Bushkill Park (1902–present): started by Northampton Traction Company

————, Island Park (dates unknown): closed due to frequent flooding

Ellwood City, Rock Point

Erie, Waldameer or Waldemere Park (?–present): built by the Buffalo and Lake Erie Traction Company

Franklin and Oil City, Monarch Park

Harrisburg, Paxtang Park (189?–1929): owned by the Central Pennsylvania Traction Company

Hazleton, Hazle Park (?–1956): started by the Lehigh Traction Company

Hershey, Hershey Park (?–present)

Hummel's Wharf, Rolling Green Park (1908–1971)

Johnstown, Luna Park

Lancaster, Rocky Springs Park (1901–1981): built by the Conestoga Transportation Company

Meadville, Exposition Park (1902–present)

Mt. Gretna, Mt. Gretna Park

New Castle, Cascade Park (1897–1934): owned by the New Castle Traction Company

Pen Mar, Pen Mar Park: started by the Western Maryland Railroad

Philadelphia, Beechwood Park (1907–1909)

————, Castle Rock Park (1899–1905): owned by Philadelphia and West Chester Traction Company

————, Chestnut Hill Park (1898–1912)

————, Point Breeze Park (1912–?)

————, Torresdale Park (?–1906)

————, White City (1898–1912): owned by the Philadelphia Rapid Transit Company

————, Willow Grove (1896–1976): owned by the Philadelphia Rapid Transit Company

————, Woodside Park (1897–1955): started by Fairmont Park Transportation Company

Pittsburgh, Coney Island (1906–1908)

————, Dream City (1906–1908)

————, Eldora Park

————, Kennywood Park (1898–present): originally built by the Monongahela Street Railway Company

—————, Luna or Ingersoll Park (1905–1909): one of the parks owned by Frederick Ingersoll; destroyed by fire

—————, Southern Park

—————, Westview Park (1906–1973): built by T. M. Harton; destroyed by fire

Pottstown, Saratoga Park: owned by Pottstown and Reading Street Railway Company

Pottsville, Tumbling Run: owned by Pottsville Union Traction Company

Reading, Carsonia Park (1896–1950): built by the United Traction Company

—————, Ingersoll Park

—————, Pendora Park

Rochester and New Brighton, Junction Park

Sayre, Keystone Park

Scranton, Luna Park (1907–1916); destroyed by fire

—————, Rocky Glen Park (1904–1987)

Shamokin, Edgewood or Indian Park: owned by Shamokin and Edgewood Electric Railway Company

Sharon, Roseville Park

Stonesboro, Lakeside Park

Tamaqun, Manila Grove: owned by the Eastern Pennsylvania Railways Company

Uniontown, Shady Grove

West Point, West Point Park (?–1987)

Wilkes–Barre, Luna Park

—————, Sans Souci (1902–1969)

York, Highland Park

RHODE ISLAND

Providence, Crescent Park (1901–1979)

—————, Vanity Fair (1907–1912)

—————, and Warwick, Rocky Point

SOUTH CAROLINA

Charleston, Isle of Palms

Spartanburg, Rock Cliff

South Dakota

Aberdeen, White City

Tennessee

Chattanooga, Olympia Park
Knoxville, Chilhowee Park
Memphis, Dixie Park: for African Americans only
————, East End Park
————, Fairyland
Nashville, Glendale Park (?–1932): owned by Nashville Railway and Light Company
————, Greenwood Park (1905–1949): owned by Preston Taylor; for African Americans only
————, White City

Texas

Amarillo, Glenwood Electric Park
Austin, Riverside Park
Dallas, Fair Park
————, Lake Cliff Park
El Paso, Washington Electric Park
Fort Worth, Lake Como Park
————, White City (1906–?)
Gainesville, Electric Park
Galveston, Chutes Park
————, Electric Park
Houston, Highland Park
————, San Jacinto Park
San Antonio, Exposition Park
————, White City
Temple, Midway Park: owned by Belton and Temple Traction Company

Utah

Farmington, Lagoon Park (1906–present)
Salt Lake City, Saltair Beach
————, Wandamere Park

Virginia

Alexandria, Luna Park (1906–1915): owned by Frederick Ingersoll
Charlottesville, Wonderland Park
Hampton, Bay Shore Beach (1898–1947): for African Americans only
————, Buckroe Beach (1897–1985)
Norfolk, Ocean View Park: owned by Norfolk and Ocean View Railway
————, Virginia Beach
————, White City (c. 1908–?)
Petersburg, Excelsior Park: for African Americans only
————, Ferndale Park
Richmond, Forest Hill Park (1910–?)
————, Idlewild Park (1906–?)

Washington

Bellingham, White City (1906–1919)
Seattle, Luna Park (1907–1914)
————, White City (1908–?)
Spokane, Natatorium (1909–1968): owned by Washington Water Power
Company

West Virginia

Chester, Rock Springs Park (1906–1970): started by The East Liverpool
Traction and Light Company (Ohio)
Charleston, Edgewood Park (1906–?)
————, Luna Park (1912–1923): destroyed by fire
Huntington, Camden Park (1903–present): started by Camden Interstate
Railway Company
Wheeling, Coney Island (?–1910)
————, Wheeling Park

Wisconsin

Milwaukee, Wonderland Park (1905–1916)
Oshkosh, Midway Park (1906–?)
————, White City or Electric Park (1906–1930s): owned by Eastern
Wisconsin Railway and Light Company
Racine, Joyland (1908–?)
Sheboygan, White City (1906–?): owned by Sheboygan Light, Power and
Railway Company

NOTES
·········

1. Introduction: Artificial Distractions

1. Rollin Lynde Hartt, "The Amusement Park," *Atlantic*, May 1907, 677.

2. David Nasaw argues that the amusement park did not endure, but I take exception to that claim. He may begin his book by lamenting, "They are all gone now," referring to amusement parks and early motion picture theaters alike. But clearly motion pictures themselves evolved and survived, as did amusement parks, which turned into theme parks. The two institutions may have lost some of the defining features and functions that characterized them in the early twentieth century, and that may be what Nasaw means. But, as institutions, both movies and amusement parks have endured. The delineation of their specific social purpose and structure at the beginning of the twentieth century, however, is the project of this volume. See David Nasaw, *Going Out: The Rise and Fall of Public Amusements* (Cambridge, MA: Harvard University Press, 1999), 1.

3. John Kasson, *Amusing the Million: Coney Island at the Turn-of-the-Century* (New York: Hill and Wang, 1978), 63.

4. "Coney Island Opens," *Billboard*, 20 May 1909, 17. For a detailed history of Coney Island see Rem Koolhaas, *Delirious New York: A Retroactive Manifesto for Manhattan* (New York: Oxford University Press, 1978), 21–65; Michael Immerso, *Coney Island: The People's Playground* (New Brunswick, NJ: Rutgers University Press, 2002).

5. Stan Barker, "Paradises Lost," *Chicago History* 22, no. 1 (March 1993): 28.

6. Columbus's population was approximately 150,000, and the *Billboard* reported regular Sunday attendance at Oletangy Park at 37,000 ("Park News," *Billboard*, 26 June 1909, 15).

7. Some ten thousand people passed through the gates of El Paso's Washington Electric Park on 4 July 1909 ("Park Notes," *Billboard*, 24 July 1909, 29).

8. A typical example is Elgin, Illinois (a town of about twenty-two thousand located in the Fox River Valley halfway between Chicago and Rockford): fifteen thousand people attended its amusement park's 1909 opening on Memorial Day weekend ("Elgin's New Resort," *Billboard*, 12 June 1909, 28).

9. This figure is my estimate, based on the *Billboard*'s park directories and coverage of the amusement park industry from 1906 to 1915. Historians Robert W. Rydell and Rob Kroes cite a figure of fifteen hundred parks in 1919, a reasonable industry estimate that already takes into account numerous park closures between 1915 and 1919. See Robert W. Rydell and Rob Kroes, *Buffalo Bill in Bologna: The Americanization of the World, 1869–1922* (Chicago: University of Chicago Press, 2005), 77.

10. A handful of American, English, and French companies made the silent movies, each just a few minutes in duration, and generally sold them outright at a rate by the number of feet. Thus, the exhibitor could show the print for weeks or until it broke or wore out.

11. "Hopkins' South Side Theatre," *Chicago Tribune*, 5 July 1896, 36.

12. Traveling lecturers, who had previously used magic lantern slides, began to incorporate motion pictures into their popular travel narratives. See Rick Altman, "From Lecturer's Prop to Industrial Product: The Early History of Travel Films," in *Virtual Voyages: Cinema and Travel*, ed. Jeffrey Ruoff (Durham, NC: Duke University Press, 2006), 61–78; Charles Musser and Carol S. Nelson, *High-Class Moving Pictures: Lyman H. Howe and the Forgotten Era of Traveling Exhibition, 1880–1920* (Princeton, NJ: Princeton University Press, 1991); Charles Musser, *Before the Nickelodeon: Edwin S. Porter and the Edison Manufacturing Company* (Berkeley: University of California Press, 1991).

13. The best-known extant example of this practice was actually the Mitchell and Kenyon Company, which filmed and exhibited local *actualités* in England. For a history of the company see Vanessa Thoulmin, *Electric Edwardians: The Films of Mitchell and Kenyon* (London: British Film Institute, 2008).

14. The best discussion of the impact of the Spanish-American War on early cinema appears in Charles Musser, *The Emergence of Cinema: The American Screen to 1907* (Berkeley: University of California Press, 1990), 225–261.

15. Ibid., 261.

16. For a year-by-year discussion of these developments see André Gaudreault, ed., *American Cinema, 1890–1909: Themes and Variations* (New Brunswick, NJ: Rutgers University Press, 2009), 1–178.

17. For a discussion of the origin of the nickelodeon in Pittsburgh see Michael Aronson, *Nickelodeon City: Pittsburgh at the Movies, 1905–1929* (Pittsburgh: University of Pittsburgh Press, 2008); for a thumbnail sketch on the nickelodeon see my essay, "1906: Movies and Spectacle," in Gaudreault, *American Cinema, 1890–1909*, 165–168. For more on the performance of a nickelodeon show, especially the sonic qualities of the nickelodeon experience, see Rick Altman, *Silent Film Sound* (New York City: Columbia University Press, 2005).

18. See my chapter on nickelodeon shows and audiences in Lauren Rabinovitz, *For the Love of Pleasure: Women, Movies, and Culture in Turn-of-the-Century Chicago* (New Brunswick, NJ: Rutgers University Press, 1998), 105–136.

19. Miriam Hansen, *Babel and Babylon: Spectatorship in American Silent Film* (Cambridge, MA: Harvard University Press, 1991), 90–118.

20. For case studies of the nickelodeon "boom" see, especially, Aronson, *Nickelodeon City*; Gregory Waller, *Main Street Amusements: Movies and Commercial Entertainment in a Southern City, 1896–1930* (Washington: Smithsonian Institution Press, 1995); and Douglas Gomery, *Shared Pleasures: A History of Movie Presentation in the United States* (Madison: University of Wisconsin Press, 1992), 18–33.

21. See Eileen Bowser, *The Transformation of the Cinema, 1907–15* (Berkeley: University of California Press, 1990), 6; Barton W. Curry, "The Nickel Madness," *Harper's Weekly*, 24 August 1907, 1246–1247.

22. Bowser, *The Transformation of the Cinema*, 6.

23. Ibid.

24. Bowser estimates that there were approximately eight thousand nickelodeons in the United States in 1908 (*The Transformation of the Cinema*, 4). Russell Merritt reports that there were ten thousand nickelodeons by 1910 (Russell Merritt, "Nickelodeon Theaters 1905–1914:

Building an Audience for the Movies," in *The American Film Industry*, ed. Tino Balio [Madison: University of Wisconsin Press, 1986], 86). Despite license-fee requirements in major cities, precise counts of nickelodeons are difficult since the storefronts often went in and out of business quite quickly.

25. Paul Kerr, *The Hollywood Film Industry* (London: British Film Institute, 1986), 188.

26. In some cities, where local theater ordinances required "bigger" amusements to pay higher licensing fees, theater owners might well limit the number of seats in order to qualify for a cheaper license—in many cities, including Chicago and New York City, the maximum was 299.

27. Hansen, *Babel and Babylon*, 30.

28. A partial list would include Fort Smith and Pine Bluff in Arkansas; San Diego, California; Tampa, Florida; Muscatine and Waterloo in Iowa; Shreveport, Louisiana; Battle Creek and Flint in Michigan; Vicksburg, Mississippi; Charlotte and Raleigh in North Carolina; Oklahoma City, Oklahoma; El Paso, Texas; and Charleston, West Virginia.

29. Louis I. Kaufman, "The Summer Season, Pittsburg [*sic*], PA," *Billboard*, 20 March 1909, 23.

30. David E. Nye, *Narratives and Spaces: Technology and the Construction of American Culture* (New York: Columbia University Press, 1997), 22.

31. J. J. Weaver, "Park Construction Maintenance and Amusements," *Billboard*, 18 March 1911, 20.

32. Donna DeBlasio, "The Immigrant and the Trolley Park in Youngstown, Ohio, 1899–1945," *Rethinking History* 5, no. 1 (2001): 77.

33. Aronson, *Nickelodeon City*, 14–15. Aronson also points out the availability of more expensive entertainment, including baseball park admission for twenty-five cents and higher-class vaudeville for prices of admission ranging from twenty-five cents to two dollars.

34. Anne Morey, "Early Film Exhibition in Wilmington, North Carolina," in *Hollywood in the Neighborhood: Historical Case Studies of Local Moviegoing*, ed. Kathryn Fuller-Seeley (Berkeley: University of California Press, 2008), 56.

35. Rydell and Kroes, *Buffalo Bill in Bologna*, 8.

36. David Mayer, *Stagestruck Filmmaker: D. W. Griffith and the American Theatre* (Iowa City: University of Iowa Press, 2009), 32.

37. Richard Abel, *Americanizing the Movies and "Movie-Mad" Audiences, 1910–1914* (Berkeley: University of California Press, 2006), 6.

38. There are excellent studies of these other modes of entertainment. See, e.g., Janet M. Davis, *The Circus Age: Culture and Society Under the American Big Top* (Chapel Hill: University of North Carolina Press, 2002); Joy S. Kasson, *Buffalo Bill's Wild West: Celebrity, Memory, and Popular History* (New York: Hill and Wang, 2001); Kristen Whissel, *Picturing American Modernity* (Durham, NC: Duke University Press, 2008), esp. chap. 2, "Placing Audiences on the Scene of History: Modern Warfare and the Battle Reenactment at the Turn of the Century" (63–116); David Mayer, *Stagestruck Filmmaker*.

39. Wolfgang Schivelbusch, *The Railway Journey: The Industrialization of Time and Space in the 19th Century*, trans. Anselm Hollo (New York: Urizen, 1977). Jonathan Crary's *Techniques of the Observer: On Vision and Modernity in the Nineteenth Century* (Cambridge, MA: MIT Press, 1992) and his *Suspensions of Perception: Attention, Spectacle, and Modern Culture* (Cambridge, MA: MIT Press, 2001) take the argument even further. Crary argues for a new

modern visual culture founded on the collapse of classical subject-object duality and on the admittance of sensory activity that severs perception from any necessary relationship to an exterior world. Rather, perception is relocated as fully embodied, thus paving the way for the historical emergence of autonomous vision understood as a *corporealization* of sensation. See also Lynne Kirby, *Parallel Tracks: The Railroad and Silent Cinema* (Durham, NC: Duke University Press, 1997).

40. Tom Gunning, "Tracing the Individual Body: Photography, Detectives, and Early Cinema," in *Cinema and the Invention of Modern Life*, ed. Leo Charney and Vanessa R. Schwartz (Berkeley: University of California Press, 1995), 15.

41. My position here on cinema's and the amusement park's service to modernity is one widely shared by scholars of early cinema, including Tom Gunning, Miriam Hansen, and Ben Singer, who were among the most outspoken advocates in the 1990s for a "modernity thesis" linking relationships among new technologies, the urban environment, and attendant perceptual "shocks" as fundamental to understanding cinema's cultural origins and development. See, for example, Ben Singer, *Melodrama and Modernity: Early Sensational Cinema and Its Contexts* (New York: Columbia University Press, 2001); Miriam Bratu Hansen, "The Mass Production of the Senses: Classical Cinema as Vernacular Modernism," *Modernism/Modernity* 6, no. 2 (1999): 59–77; Tom Gunning, "An Aesthetic of Astonishment: Early Film and the (In)Credulous Spectator," in *Viewing Positions: Ways of Seeing Film*, ed. Linda Williams (New Brunswick, NJ: Rutgers University Press, 1994), 114–133; Tom Gunning, "Modernity and Cinema: A Culture of Shocks and Flows," in *Cinema and Modernity*, ed. Murray Pomerance (New Brunswick, NJ: Rutgers University Press, 2006), 297–315. For an important selection of case studies that elaborate on this phenomenon see Charney and Schwartz, *Cinema and the Invention of Modern Life.*

The assumption about cinema's wholesale debt and responsiveness to technological modernity has become so thoroughly integrated into early cinema studies that recent serious studies about silent cinema now depend entirely on it; see, e.g., Whissel, *Picturing American Modernity*; Rob King, *The Fun Factory: The Keystone Film Company and the Emergency of Mass Culture* (Berkeley: University of California Press, 2008); Lucy Fischer, "'The Shock of the New': Electrification, Illumination, Urbanization, and the Cinema," in Pomerance, *Cinema and Modernity*, 19–37.

In fairness, however, a small minority of film scholars has critiqued this position less for understanding the historical specificity of the early twentieth century than for the application of the "modernity thesis" to cinema's long-term aesthetic and narrative development. While this is not the place to engage in further debate about the "modernity thesis" as an appropriate model for film scholarship of the early, transitional, or classical periods, I would refer the reader to Charlie Keil's summary of "the modernity thesis," the positions of its proponents, and his critique that summarizes the concerns of the like-minded group of film scholars following criticism put forward by David Bordwell; Charlie Keil, "'To Here from Modernity': Style, Historiography, and Transitional Cinema," in *American Cinema's Transitional Era: Audiences, Institutions, Practices*, ed. Charlie Keil and Shelley Stamp (Berkeley: University of California Press, 2004), 51–65.

42. Walter Benjamin, "On Some Motifs in Baudelaire," in *Illuminations: Essays and Reflections* (New York: Schocken Books, 1968), 155–200.

43. Walter Benjamin, *The Arcades Project*, trans. Howard Eiland and Kevin McLaughlin (Cambridge, MA: Harvard University Press, 2002); Georg Simmel, "The Metropolis and Mental Life," in *The Sociology of Georg Simmel* (New York: Free Press, 1950).

44. David E. Nye, "Electricity and Electrification," in *The Oxford Companion to United States History*, ed. Paul S. Boyer (New York: Oxford University Press, 2001), 220–222. See also David E. Nye, *Electrifying America: Social Meanings of a New Technology* (Cambridge, MA: MIT Press, 1990); Judith Adams, "The Promotion of New Technology Through Fun and Spectacle: Electricity at the World's Columbian Exposition," *Journal of American Culture* 18, no. 2 (1995): 45–55.

45. Urban households with electrical power reached more than an 80 percent saturation rate by 1932. Rural homes, however, lagged behind: only 11 percent of farm dwellings had electricity by 1932—a situation that resulted in the creation of the Rural Electrification Administration in 1935 in an effort to encourage rural domestic electrification.

46. Nye, "Electricity and Electrification," 221.

47. In addition, modernity at the individual consumer level also meant industrializing the kitchen and the home itself. What is lost in the philosophy about the "shocks of modernity" is the ways in which redefining the household as a site of consumption also incurred a cost of amplifying the labor and industrialized effects necessary to maintain the illusion of a new temporal and spatial division between labor and leisure that never existed as fully as has been argued. In short, modernizing the kitchen in this period may have transformed this domestic realm from a space of manufacturing one's food to a site of foodstuffs that originated from outside the household. But food preparation, as well as the labor necessary to maintain the new appliances and tools that stored, cooled, and cooked the food, required considerable work, work that was increasingly diminished in social importance and associated with female labor, whether that meant women householders or female servants. The kitchen is only the most attenuated example of how widespread discussion about the shocks of modernity tends to exclude the "shock of the new" in the domestic realm. For the definitive study of the impact of new technologies on the domestic realm see Ruth Cowan Schwartz, *More Work for Mother: The Ironies of Household Technology from the Open Hearth to the Microwave* (New York: Basic Books, 1985).

48. W. R. Rothacker, "The Coming Summer Season in Chicago," *Billboard*, 20 March 1909, 16.

49. Lucy Fischer, "'The Shock of the New,'" 23.

50. Iowa Secretary of State, *The Iowa Official Register*, vol. 20 (Des Moines: Iowa Secretary of State, 1905), 534–539.

51. Carolyn de la Peña, "Mechanized Southern Comfort: Touring the Technological South at *Krispy Kreme*," in *Dixie Emporium: Tourism, Foodways, and Consumer Culture in the American South*, ed. Anthony J. Stanonis (Athens: University of Georgia Press, 2008), 238.

52. Kasson, *Amusing the Million*, 6.

53. Nasaw, *Going Out*, 80–95.

54. This debate has been carried on for some time. Within the pages of *Cinema Journal* lively exchanges occurred in the mid-1990s about the nature and diversity of nickelodeons and their audiences, as well as how specific and generalizable were Manhattan's nickelodeon demographics by location, ethnicity, and class: Ben Singer, "Manhattan Nickelodeons: New Data on Audiences and Exhibitors," *Cinema Journal* 34, no. 3 (spring 1995): 5–35; Sumiko

Higashi, "Ben Singer's 'Manhattan Nickelodeons: New Data on Audiences and Exhibitors,'" *Cinema Journal* 35, no. 3 (spring 1996): 72–74; Ben Singer, "New York . . . Just Like I Pictured It: Ben Singer Responds," *Cinema Journal* 34, no. 3 (spring 1995): 104–128; Robert C. Allen, "Manhattan Myopia? or, Oh! Iowa!" *Cinema Journal* 35, no. 3 (spring 1996): 75–103; William Uricchio and Roberta E. Pearson, "Dialogue: Manhattan's Nickelodeons: New York? New York!" *Cinema Journal* 36, no. 4 (summer 1997): 98–102; Judith Thissen, "Oy Myopia! A Reaction from Judith Thissen on the Singer-Allen Controversy," *Cinema Journal* 36, no. 4 (summer 1997): 102–107; Ben Singer, "Manhattan Melodrama: A Response from Ben Singer," *Cinema Journal* 36, no. 4 (summer 1997): 107–112.

Robert Allen and Douglas Gomery in 1985 called for film historians to do individual, local histories of early cinema to offset the continuing emphasis on New York City; see their *Film History: Theory and Practice* (New York: McGraw-Hill, 1985). My own research on early cinema in Chicago (*For the Love of Pleasure*) was partially an effort to provide a counterpoint to the ways that studies of New York City early cinema dominated the field. In addition see J. A. Lindstrom, "Where Development Has Just Begun: Nickelodeon Location, Moving Picture Audiences, and Neighborhood Development in Chicago," in *American Cinema's Transitional Era: Audiences, Institutions, Practices*, ed. Charlie Keil and Shelley Stamp (Berkeley: University of California Press, 2004): 217–238; Abel, *Americanizing the Movies*; Waller, *Main Street Amusements*; Kathryn Fuller, *At the Picture Show: Small-Town Audiences and the Creation of Movie Fan Culture* (Charlottesville: University of Virginia Press, 2001); and Fuller-Seeley, *Hollywood in the Neighborhood*.

55. Waller, *Main Street Amusements*; Fuller, *At the Picture Show*; Abel, *Americanizing the Movies*.

56. Koolhaas, *Delirious New York*, 54–55.

57. Abel, *Americanizing the Movies*, 6.

58. Jane Addams, *The Spirit of Youth and the City Streets* (New York: Macmillan, 1910); Louise de Koven Bowen, *Five and Ten Cent Theaters: Two Investigations* (Chicago: Juvenile Protective Association, 1911); Sherman C. Kingsley, "The Penny Arcade and the Cheap Theatre," *Charities and the Common*, 8 June 1907, 295–297; Belle Lindner Israels, "The Way of the Girl," *Survey* 22 (3 July 1909): 386–497.

59. Addams, *The Spirit of Youth and the City Streets*, 15.

60. Louise De Koven Bowen, *Safeguards for City Youth at Work and at Play* (New York: Macmillan, 1914), 14.

61. Sherman C. Kingsley, as quoted in "Would Suppress Vicious Theaters," *Chicago Tribune*, 28 April 1907, 10.

62. For more detailed studies of the cultural anxieties over cinema and the subsequent regulation of theaters, censorship, and other consequences see Rabinovitz, *For the Love of Pleasure*, 105–136; Richard Abel, *The Red Rooster Scare: Making Cinema American* (Berkeley: University of California Press, 1999); and Lee Grieveson, *Policing Cinema: Movies and Censorship in Early-Twentieth-Century America* (Berkeley: University of California Press, 2004).

63. Hartt, "The Amusement Park," 670. A New England Congregationalist minister and journalist, Hartt was a regular contributor to the *Atlantic*; "The Amusement Park" was reprinted along with other *Atlantic* essays in *The People at Play* (Boston: Houghton Mifflin, 1909).

64. Richard Henry Edwards, *Christianity and Amusements* (New York: Association Press, 1915), 14.

2. Urban Wonderlands: The "Cracked Mirror" of Turn-of-the-Century Amusement Parks

1. F. C. McCarahan, "Chicago Amusements," *Billboard*, 10 August 1907, 7. Three and a half million people visited the fifty-acre site in 1906, and the following year Riverview claimed its Sunday attendance alone was greater than two hundred thousand each week.

2. A partial list includes Cleveland, Cincinnati, Denver, Indianapolis, West Hartford, Buffalo, Pittsburgh, Utica, Baltimore, Los Angeles, Schenectady, San Jose, and Seattle.

3. A partial list of White City amusement parks includes Denver, Duluth, Fort Worth, Shrewsbury, Atlanta, Syracuse, Toledo, Louisville, New Orleans, New Haven, Philadelphia, Trenton, Nashville, Boise, Norfolk, and Oshkosh.

4. A partial list of Wonderlands includes Boston, San Diego, Wichita, Minneapolis, Indianapolis, Charlottesville, and Milwaukee. Besides Coney Island's Dreamland there were Dreamlands in Little Rock, Decatur, and Rochester, New York. Fairylands existed in Patterson, Little Rock, and Memphis. There were Joylands in Racine and Sacramento.

5. For example Krug Park (1903–1940) in Omaha, Ingersoll Park (1905–1909) in Pittsburgh, and Doling Park (1907–1970s) in Springfield, Missouri.

6. For example, "Electric Parks" were in Detroit, Kansas City, Baltimore, Oshkosh, Charlotte, Muskogee, San Antonio, and Waterloo, Iowa.

7. Andrew W. Kahrl, "The Slightest Semblance of Unruliness: Steamboat Excursions, Pleasure Resorts and the Emergence of Segregation Culture on the Potomac River," *Journal of American History* 94, no. 4 (March 2008): 1116.

8. Lakewood's "whites only" season ran from May 10 until September 4; its African American season ran from September 6 until October 15. White City began an African American season in October 1908. In the *Billboard*'s "Park List" that ran in each issue, parks identified themselves as "This park is for colored people exclusively" or indicated a separate season for African Americans.

9. John F. Kasson, "Workers Seek Leisure Time and Space," in *Major Problems in American Popular Culture*, ed. Kathleen Franz and Susan Smulyan (New York: Wadsworth, 2011), 140.

10. David Nasaw, *Going Out: The Rise and Fall of Public Amusements* (New York: Basic Books, 1993), 91–92.

11. Kenneth L. Kusmer, *A Ghetto Takes Shape: Black Cleveland, 1897–1930* (Urbana: University of Illinois Press, 1976), 58.

12. Donna DeBlasio, "The Immigrant and the Trolley Park in Youngstown, Ohio, 1899–1945," *Rethinking History* 5, no. 1 (2001): 82.

13. For more on Washington, D.C., African Americans who preferred to attend River View Park on Jim Crow Days rather than the black-owned African American Washington Park, see Kahrl, "The Slightest Semblance of Unruliness," 1109.

14. Unidentified oral history informant quoted in Kusmer, *A Ghetto Takes Shape*, 58.

15. A partial list of my own making based on annual directories in the *Billboard* (1907–1915) and descriptions of company assets in the *Street Railway Journal* (1906–1912) includes Blue Lake Park (1908–?) in Birmingham, Alabama; Dixie Park (1908–?) in Mobile, Alabama; Washington Park (dates unknown) in Montgomery, Alabama; Lincoln Park (dates unknown) in Sheffield, Alabama; Woodside Park (1907–?) in Tuscumbia, Alabama; Highland Park (1909–?) in Little Rock, Arkansas; Luna Park (from 1912–1914 only) in Los Angeles;

Lincoln Park (dates unknown) in Jacksonville, Florida; Lincoln Park (dates unknown) in Savannah, Georgia; Chateau de Plaisance in Chicago (dates unknown, and it is unclear if this park actually had mechanical amusements); Lincoln Beach (dates unknown) in Baltimore; Washington Park (dates unknown) in Columbus, Mississippi; Lincoln Electric Park (dates unknown) in Kansas City, Missouri; Dixie Park (dates unknown) in Memphis, Tennessee; Greenwood Park (1905–1949) in Nashville; Bay Shore Beach Park (1906–1947) in Hampton, Virginia; Excelsior Park (dates unknown) in Petersburg, Virginia; Washington Park or Notley Hall (1901–1924) outside Washington, D.C.

16. Many, however, were short-lived, generally because of poor management or periodic financial panics that made business entrepreneurship a roller coaster ride in and of itself during this period.

17. Frederic Thompson, "Amusing the Million," *Everybody's Magazine*, September 1908, 385.

18. William Judkins Hewitt, "The Amusement Park," *Billboard*, 25 July 1907, 45.

19. Rollin Lynde Hartt, "The Amusement Park," *Atlantic*, May 1907, 667.

20. Robert W. Rydell and Rob Kroes, *Buffalo Bill in Bologna: The Americanization of the World, 1869–1922* (Chicago: University of Chicago Press, 2005), 74.

21. For a history of Cedar Point see Hugo John Hildebrandt, "Cedar Point: A Park in Progress," *Journal of Popular Culture* 15 (summer 1981): 87–107.

22. Rem Koolhaas, *Delirious New York: A Retroactive Manifesto for Manhattan* (New York: Oxford University Press, 1978), 27.

23. John Kasson, *Amusing the Million: Coney Island at the Turn of the Century* (New York: Hill and Wang, 1978), 82.

24. For a description of typical urban conveyance stories of disaster and an analysis of their significance for the cinematic imagination see Ben Singer, "Modernity, Hyperstimulus, and the Rise of Popular Sensationalism," in *Cinema and the Invention of Modern Life*, ed. Leo Charney and Vanessa Schwartz (Berkeley: University of California Press, 1995), 72–99.

25. The basic psychology and function of the mechanical thrill ride has not been surpassed, only updated, by more modern machinery in today's theme parks.

26. Guy Wetmore Carryl, "Marvelous Coney Island," *Munsey's Magazine*, September 1901, 811–812.

27. Tom Gunning, "The Cinema of Attraction: Early Film, Its Spectator, and the Avant-Garde," *Wide Angle* 8, nos. 3–4 (1986): 63–70; repr. in *Early Cinema: Space, Frame, Narrative*, ed. Thomas Elsaesser (London: British Film Institute, 1990), 56–62. For an excellent summary of the phrase "cinema of attractions" and its evolutionary development by Gunning, André Gaudreault, and others see Wanda Strauven, "Introduction to an Attractive Concept," in *The Cinema of Attractions Reloaded*, ed. Wanda Strauven (Amsterdam: Amsterdam University Press, 2007), 11–30.

28. Mary Ann Doane, "Technology's Body," in *A Feminist Reader in Early Cinema*, ed. Jennifer M. Bean and Diane Negra (Durham, NC: Duke University Press, 2002), 535.

29. Tony Bennett, "A Thousand and One Troubles: Blackpool Pleasure Beach," *Formations of Pleasure*, ed. Tony Bennett et al. (London: Routledge, 1983), 147–148.

30. Kathy Peiss, *Cheap Amusements: Working Women and Leisure in Turn-of-the-Century New York* (Philadelphia: Temple University Press, 1986), 134–135.

31. John Sloan, quoted in Kasson, *Amusing the Million*, 91.

32. Peiss, *Cheap Amusements*, 101–102.

33. See, for example, Peiss, *Cheap Amusements*, 148–153; Lauren Rabinovitz, *For the Love of Pleasure: Women, Movies, and Culture in Turn-of-the-Century Chicago* (New Brunswick, NJ: Rutgers University Press, 1998), 105–136; Shelley Stamp, *Movie-Struck Girls: Women and Motion Picture Culture After the Nickelodeon* (Princeton, NJ: Princeton University Press, 2000), 10–40.

34. Belle Lindner Israels, "The Way of the Girl," *Survey* 22 (3 July 1909): 486–497.

35. O. Henry, "Brickdust Row," in *The Trimmed Lamp* (New York: S. S. McClure, 1907), 89–101. O. Henry sets another story at Coney Island in which he describes the park through the eyes of a young Irish worker; see "The Greater Coney," in *Sixes and Sevens* (New York: Doubleday, Page, 1903), 220–226.

36. Jane Addams, quoted in Kasson, *Amusing the Million*, 100. Reformers especially worried about those whom they deemed more naturally and fully innocent—women and children.

37. Richard Henry Edwards, *Christianity and Amusements* (New York: Association Press, 1915), 100, 20.

38. "Third Annual Convention of the Iowa Street and Interurban Railway Association," *Street Railway Journal* 27 (28 April 1906): 667.

39. "The Second Quarterly Meeting of the Street Railway Association of the State of New York," *Street Railway Journal* 27 (7 April 1906): 562.

40. Olympic Park publicity brochure, quoted in Judith A. Adams, *The American Amusement Park Industry: A History of Technology and Thrills* (Boston: Twayne, 1991), 69.

41. DeBlasio, "The Immigrant and the Trolley Park in Youngstown, Ohio," 84.

42. "Remember Alamo Park?" *Cedar Rapids Gazette*, 27 June 1999, 34; Alamo Park clippings file, Linn County Historical Society, Cedar Rapids, Iowa.

43. "Conducting Pleasure Parks," *Street Railway Journal* 27 (5 May 1906): 693.

44. David Nasaw, *Going Out*, 46.

45. E. V. Morrison, "Moving Pictures and the Open-Air Season," *Billboard*, 23 March 1912, 27.

46. Kahrl, "The Slightest Semblance of Unruliness," 1109–1110.

47. Ibid.

48. See, for example, Robert Wilson Neal, "New York's City of Play," *World To-Day* 11, no. 2 (August 1906): 818–826; Lindsay Denison, "The Biggest Playground in the World," *Munsey's Magazine*, August 1905, 556–566; Day Allen Wiley, "The Open Air Amusement Park," *Theatre Magazine*, July 1909, 18–19.

49. For a good summary of amusement park criticism leveled at Coney Island see Kasson, *Amusing the Million*, 95–105.

50. James Huneker, *New Cosmopolis: A Book of Images. Intimate New York* (New York: Charles Scribner's Sons, 1915), 154.

51. Part of a nationwide craze regarding the novelty of aerial flight, famous aviators like "[John] Frisbie, the Man-Bird" executed especially daring stunts; "Frisbie, the Man-Bird" advertisement, *Billboard*, 12 March 1910, 125. Because there were a number of instances when aerial stuntmen died or were severely injured in front of the crowds, park managers seem to have been moved by the high mortality rate to switch their allegiance after 1910 to automobile stunt shows.

52. These names represent just a cross section of dancing girl attractions advertised in the

Billboard in the 1910 season; "Chicago Parks Open," *Billboard*, 7 May 1910, 29; "Chester Park Opens," *Billboard*, 21 May 1910, 17; "New York Park News," *Billboard*, 11 June 1910, 32; "Amusement Parks," *Billboard*, 30 July 1910, 28; "Princess Olga" advertisement, *Billboard*, 13 August 1910, 16.

53. Harry Bonnell, "Coney Island Events," *Billboard*, 29 July 1907, 16.

54. Mary C. Higginbotham, "In Genuine Cowgirl Fashion: Nan Aspinwall Gable Lambell and the Image of the Cowgirl in Wild West Entertainment, 1880–1930," master's thesis, University of Nebraska, 1996, 27.

55. Nan Aspinwall Gable Scrapbooks, Aspinwall Family Collection MS3513, series 3, Manuscript Collections, Nebraska State Historical Society, Lincoln. All subsequent information about Nan Aspinwall Gable is based on her scrapbook from this period. The scrapbook contains programs, undated newspaper clippings, handbills, and photographs.

56. Fatimah Tobing Rony, *The Third Eye: Race, Cinema, and Ethnographic Spectacle* (Durham, NC: Duke University Press, 1996), 21–44; Alison Griffiths, *Wondrous Difference: Cinema, Anthropology, and Turn-of-the-Century Visual Culture* (New York: Columbia University Press, 2002), 44–85.

57. Griffiths, *Wondrous Difference*, 64–68.

58. Their stops included Coney Island's Dreamland and Los Angeles's Chutes Park (1905–1906), Oshkosh Wisconsin's White City (1906), Chicago's Riverview and San Souci Parks (1906–1907), Detroit's Electric Park (1907), and Ohio's Cedar Point (1907) and Oletangy Park (1907); "Pat-Chats," *Billboard*, 17 March 1906, n.p.; "Chicago's Great Amusement Parks," *Billboard*, 8 September 1906, 19. See also "Igorrote Village" display advertisement, *Billboard*, 31 August 1907, 33.

59. "Phenomenal Success of Chicago's Riverview," *Billboard*, 1 December 1906, 28–29.

60. "Big Town Amusements," *Billboard*, 25 June 1910, 31.

61. "Igorottes May Now be Citizens," *Los Angeles Times*, 12 August 1906, 7.

62. "Fun for the Darkies," *New York Times*, 2 June 1895, 16.

63. Karen Sotiropoulos, *Staging Race: Black Performers in Turn of the Century America* (Cambridge, MA: Harvard University Press, 2006), 22–23.

64. "Fun for the Darkies," 16.

65. "Metropolitan Parks," *Billboard*, 25 June 1910, 32.

66. Albert A. Hopkins, quoted in Nick Yablon, "'A Picture Painted in Fire': Pain's Reenactments of *The Last Days of Pompeii*, 1879–1914," in *Antiquity Recovered: The Legacy of Pompeii and Herculaneum*, ed. Jon Seydl and Victoria Gardner-Coates (Los Angeles: Getty Publications, 2006), 184.

67. Ibid.

68. White City advertisement, *Billboard*, 12 March 1910, 32.

69. "The Big Show at Revere," *Billboard*, 6 August 1910, 17. In addition see "Amusement Parks," *Billboard*, 18 June 1910, for its claim: "*The Monitor and the Merrimac*, with its marine warfare, is as ever, the big attraction of the park [Riverview in Chicago], and never seems to wane in popularity" (1).

70. "Jackson Park Prosperous," *Billboard*, 6 August 1910, 17. The dates of Hague Park's opening and closing are unknown.

71. Koolhaas, *Delirious New York*, 42.

72. Connie J. Zeigler, "Indianapolis Amusement Parks, 1903–1911: Landscapes on the Edge," master's thesis, Indiana University, Bloomington, 2007, 41.

73. The *New York Times* described *Battle in the Clouds* at its Coney Island opening:

> The scene represents a war between the inhabitants of the City of Science . . . and an attacking party from the planet Mars. . . . The scene opens with the city en fete to celebrate the opening of communication with Mars. A strange craft suddenly appears from the direction of the war-like planet, and the inhabitants of the earth are thrown into confusion. After a scene of considerable rejoicing, the Martians declare war, and the remainder of the spectacle shows what a contest in the clouds will be like half a century hence. The battle affords an opportunity for Mr. Pain to produce many of his most famous pyrotechnic displays. During the intermissions several acrobats perform in the arena, and there are ballet dances on a large scale. ("Airships a Feature in Pain's New Show," *New York Times*, 30 June 1909, 7)

 For the Riverview Park show see "Chicago Parks," *Billboard*, 16 July 1910, 28.

74. Scott A. Newman, "Jazz Age Chicago: Urban Leisure from 1893 to 1945," http://chicago.urban-history.org/ven/pks/w_city.shtml (accessed 25 August 2011).

75. Lynn Kathleen Sally, *Fighting the Flames: The Spectacular Performance of Fire at Coney Island* (New York: Routledge, 2006), 1.

76. Koolhaas, *Delirious New York*, 42.

77. David Mayer, "*The Last Days of Pompeii*: James Pain," in *Playing Out the Empire: "Ben Hur" and Other Toga Plays and Films, 1883–1908*, ed. David Mayer (Oxford: Clarendon Press, 1994), 91–92.

78. Ibid. For at least one report on injuries sustained during a *Pain's Fire Works* performance at Manhattan Beach see "Too Much like Real War," *New York Times*, 25 June, 1893, 8: the newspaper reported that the previous evening Pain's show, *The Storming of Vicksburg*, caused serious injury to six men and boys when their clothes caught on fire from exploding powder.

79. Mayer, "*The Last Days of Pompeii*," 92.

80. Ibid., 93–94.

81. Ibid., 94. Pain's Manhattan Beach pyrotechnic spectacles included *The Bombardment of Alexandria*, *The Storming of Pekin*, *The Graeco-Turkish War*, *The Siege of Sebastapol*, and *The Burning of Moscow*; see Michael Immerso, *Coney Island: The People's Playground* (New Brunswick, NJ: Rutgers University Press, 2002), 34. In 1907 *Pain's Fire Works* moved to a newer arena in next-door Brighton Beach Park, where the company continued to offer such pyrodramas as *The Destruction of Jerusalem*, *Sheridan's Ride*, and *Battle in the Clouds*; ibid., 76.

82. Zeigler, "Indianapolis Amusement Parks," 69.

83. Advertisement, *Indianapolis Star*, 8 July 1907, (quoted in Zeigler, "Indianapolis Amusement Parks," 69).

84. Yablon, "'A Picture Painted in Fire,'" 190.

85. "A Drama in Pyrotechnics: Last Days of Pompeii Enacted at Manhattan Beach," *New York Times*, 12 June 1885, 2.

86. *History of Coney Island* (New York: Burroughs, 1904), n.p.

87. Lynde Hartt, "The Amusement Park," 673.

88. The Lagoon Park manager reported, "The realism of the shows is well attested by the crowds that stand as though enthralled by recollection of the days of war and the wild cheering into which they break as after each conflict 'Old Glory' emerges triumphant" ("Reproductions of Famous Naval Battles at Ludlow [KY] Lagoon," *Billboard*, 20 August 1910, 28).

89. Ibid.

90. Kristen Whissel, *Picturing American Modernity: Traffic, Technology, and the Silent Cinema* (Durham, NC: Duke University Press, 2008), 81–82.

91. Ibid., 72.

92. "White City's Big Feature," *Billboard*, 12 May 1906, 36.

93. Margaret Malamud, "The Greatest Show on Earth: Roman Entertainments in Turn-of-the-Century New York," *Journal of Popular Culture* 35, no. 3 (2001): 56.

94. A very small partial list of films includes *Fire Rescue Scene* (Edison, 1894), *A Morning Alarm* (Edison, 1896), *The Burning Stable* (Edison, 1896), *Fighting the Fire* (Edison, 1896), *Firemen Rescuing Men and Women* (Edison, 1899), *Buffalo Fire Department* (American Mutoscope and Biograph, 1899), *Burning of Durland's Riding Academy* (Edison, 1902), *Life of an American Fireman* (Edison, 1903), *New York Fire Department Returning* (American Mutoscope and Biograph, 1903), *Annual Parade, New York Fire Department* (Edison, 1904), and *The Great Baltimore Fire* (American Mutoscope and Biograph, 1904).

95. Koolhaas, *Delirious New York*, 48.

96. Newman, "Jazz Age Chicago."

97. "Airships a Feature in Pain's New Show," *New York Times*, 30 June 1909, 7.

98. "The Amusement Park Situation," *Billboard*, 5 February 1910, 14.

99. Mayer, "The Last Days of Pompeii," 94.

100. "Frisco Park in Ruins," *Billboard*, 3 June 1911, 6.

101. "Fire at Columbus Park," *Billboard*, 10 June 1911, 11.

102. These eight fires occurred at Electric Park in Kansas City (21 June 1911); Riverview in Chicago (30 June 1911); Kennywood Park, Pittsburgh (12 August 1911); Combination Park in Medford, Massachusetts (12 August 1911); Dixieland Park in Jacksonville (15 August 1911); Wonderland Park in Indianapolis (27 August 1911); Steeplechase Park at Coney Island (7 September 1911); and Chicago's White City (29 September 1911). See "Disastrous Park Fires," *Billboard*, 26 August 1911, 4–5; "Fire at Dixieland Park," *Billboard*, 26 August 1911, 30; "Amusement Park Burns," *Billboard*, 9 September 1911, 30; "Steeplechase Conflagration," *Billboard*, 16 September 1911, 30; and "Fire at Chicago Park," *Billboard*, 7 October 1911, 6.

103. "Fire at Boston Park," *Billboard*, 2 December 1911, 6; "Luna Park Burns," *Billboard*, 16 December 1911, 6; "Fire at Luna Park," *Billboard*, 23 December 1911, 6. At the beginning of the 1912 summer season the *Billboard* took note of the frequency of fires in 1911; see R. S. Uzzell, "Lessons from Last Year's Park Business," *Billboard*, 23 March 1912, 17.

104. "Fire Visits Ingersoll Park," *Billboard*, 12 May 1906, 36.

105. Although in Buffalo, the land was sold, and another amusement park was built on that site in 1910; "Presages Prosperity," *Billboard*, 5 March 1910, 28.

106. "Luna Park Destroyed," *Billboard*, 16 July 1910, 28; "Managers of Luna Park Will Begin Reconstruction at Once," *Billboard*, 23 July 1910, 10.

107. "Park Incinerated," *Billboard*, 23 June 1906, 24.

108. In another example Wichita's Wonderland Park (1905–1918) was located on Ackerman Island in the Arkansas River near the city's downtown. While the park initially closed in 1918 when local "blue laws" banned Sunday shows at the park's three theaters, rebuilding became moot when the city enacted flood control measures on the river and submerged the island.

109. "Amusement Park News," *Billboard*, 8 July 1911, 20.

110. In an even more inopportune calamity Denver's *Monitor and Merrimac* amphitheater at Elitch Gardens collapsed on 16 June 1910, putting that attraction out of business; see "Park Building Collapses," *Billboard*, 25 June 1910, 33.

111. For a sweeping discussion of the exportation of American popular culture in this period and its "Americanization" effect see Rydell and Kroes, *Buffalo Bill in Bologna*.

112. Ibid., 167.

113. "Hall of Fame Inductees: Frederick Ingersoll," International Association of Amusement Parks and Attractions, www.iaapa.org/aboutus/hof/hofbios.asp (accessed 22 January 2011); Marilyn Pitz, "Luna Park's Luminary: Entrepreneur/Roller Coaster Designer Deserves His Due," *Pittsburgh Post-Gazette*, 1 September 2008, www.post-gazette.com/pg/08245/908516-42.stm (accessed 25 August 2011).

3. Thrill Ride Cinema: *Hale's Tours and Scenes of the World*

1. Raymond Fielding, "Hale's Tours: Ultrarealism in the Pre-1910 Motion Picture," in *Before Griffith*, ed. John L. Fell (Berkeley: University of California Press, 1983), 120.

2. Tom Gunning, "The World as Object Lesson: Cinema Audiences, Visual Culture, and the St. Louis World's Fair, 1904," *Film History* 6 (1994): 440; for further description of *Hale's Fire Fighters* at the exposition also see Lynn Kathleen Sally, *Fighting the Flames: The Spectacular Performance of Fire at Coney Island* (New York: Routledge, 2006), 51–54.

3. Stephan Oettermann, *The Panorama: History of a Mass Medium*, trans. Deborah Lucas Schneider (New York: Zone Books, 1997), 22.

4. Ibid., 20.

5. Alison Griffiths, "'Shivers Down Your Spine': Panoramas and the Origins of the Cinematic Re-enactment," *Screen* 44 (spring 2003): 3. Griffiths, as well as film scholar William Uricchio and art historian Angela Miller, has noted the panorama's importance as a precursor to the aesthetics of the cinematic image and to cinema's spectatorial possibility of the "immersive view." See Alison Griffiths, *Shivers Down Your Spine: Cinema, Museums, and the Immersive View* (New York: Columbia University Press, 2008), 37–78; Angela Miller, "The Panorama, the Cinema, and the Emergence of the Spectacular," *Wide Angle* 18, no. 2 (April 1996): 34–69; and William Uricchio, "Panoramic Visions: Stasis, Movement, and the Redefinition of the Panorama," in *The Birth of Film Genres*, ed. Leonardo Quaresima, Alessandra Raengo, and Laura Vichi (Udine, Italy: University of Udine, 1999), 125–133.

6. Griffiths, "'Shivers Down Your Spine,'" 24.

7. *The Battle of Gettysburg* enjoyed long runs in purpose-built rotunda buildings in downtown Chicago, New York City, and Boston; see Griffiths, "'Shivers Down Your Spine,'" 20. This panorama is today at Gettysburg National Military Park, Gettysburg, Pennsylvania. For a discussion of the Mississippi River panoramas (none of which are extant) see

John McDermott, *The Lost Panoramas of the Mississippi* (Chicago: University of Chicago Press, 1958).

8. The other single Civil War panorama that is extant today is *The Battle of Atlanta* (1887), housed at the Atlanta Cyclorama. The guided (and scripted) interpretation by a live narrator at today's installation emphasizes the Confederacy's victimization at the hands of the Union army and the Civil War itself as a battle over the economic resources of southern cities like Atlanta. The original panorama, however, was commissioned and executed to depict the heroism of the Union army. This is information gleaned from my November 2004 visit to the Atlanta Cyclorama.

9. Ralph Hyde, *Panoramania! The Art and Entertainment of the "All-Embracing" View* (London: Trefoil Publications, 1988), 135.

10. James P. Boyd, *The Paris Exposition of 1900: A Vivid Descriptive View and Elaborate Scenic Presentation of the Site, Plan, and Exhibits* (Philadelphia: P. W. Ziegler, 1900), 535–536, Special Collections, World's Fairs Collection, Smithsonian Institution Library, Washington, D.C.

11. Charles Musser actually credits the ill-fated *Cinéorama* as Hale's inspiration but also speculates that the *Cinéorama* never opened publicly at all; see Charles Musser, *The Emergence of Cinema: The American Screen to 1907* (Berkeley: University of California Press, 1994), 429.

12. "Exposition Sideshows: Majority of Those at Paris Are Disappointing," *New York Times*, 9 September 1900, 16. This reviewer's comment about "expectoration" also hints at his disdain for the actors as not only bored performers but as less-than-civilized.

13. For an excellent extended summary of *A Trip to the Moon* see Michael Immerso, *Coney Island: The People's Playground* (New Brunswick, NJ: Rutgers University Press, 2002), 61.

14. Albert Bigelow Paine, "The New Coney Island," *Century Magazine*, August 1904, 535.

15. Oettermann, *The Panorama*, 12.

16. Hyde, *Panoramania!* 37. Both Griffiths and Kristen Whissel further discuss how the battle reenactment itself functioned to make distant "bloody" events close and patriotic in order to forge an American national identity at the close of the nineteenth century (although Whissel focuses exclusively on the early reenactment film). See Griffiths, "'Shivers Down Your Spine'"; and Kristen Whissel, *Picturing American Modernity: Traffic, Technology, and the Silent Cinema* (Durham, NC: Duke University Press, 2008), 63–116.

17. Fielding, "Hale's Tours," 119.

18. Ibid., 120. When the government issued a patent for the mechanical apparatus, the patent assigned ownership to Hale, Gifford, and Keefe. For descriptions of the 1904 patent (no. 767,281) and a subsequent refinement of the pleasure-railway system (patent no. 800,100) see *The Official Gazette of the United States Patent Office* 111 (Washington, D.C.: U.S. Government Publications, August 1904): 1577; and 118 (Washington, D.C.: U.S. Government Publications, September 1905): 788–789.

19. *Billboard*, 27 January 1906, 20.

20. For more on the involvement of Zukor and other fledgling movie moguls in *Hale's Tours* see Fielding, "Hale's Tours," 122–123.

21. Ibid.

22. "Coney Island on the Outside," *Billboard*, 26 May 1906, 30. In addition two variants of *Hale's Tours* simultaneously opened just outside Coney Island: *Hurst's Touring New York*, an illu-

sion ride like *Hale's Tours* except that it was set in an automobile (on Surf Avenue), and the touring car illusion ride *New York to 'Frisco* (in the Bowery).

23. Warren A. Patrick, "The Chicago Park Season Epitomized and Reviewed," *Billboard*, 22 September 1906, 9. Chicago's Sans Souci Park also had *Palace Touring Cars*, an imitation of *Hale's Tours* railway illusion. *Cessna's Sightseeing Auto Tours* was installed in a downtown storefront at 129 S. Clark Street, two blocks from the *Hale's Tours* storefront installation.

24. "Parks," *Billboard*, 3 February 1906, 20; "Parks," *Billboard*, 9 June 1906, 24. The list of parks that reported *Hale's Tours* among their top-grossing concessions is extensive: Luna Park in Baltimore; Ponce de Leon in Atlanta; Riverview and White City in Chicago; Alamo in Cedar Rapids, Iowa; Vinewood in Topeka; Minneapolis's Wonderland and Forest Park; St. Paul's Wildwood; Duluth's White City; Lakewood in Durham, North Carolina; Cincinnati's Coney Island; Willow Grove in Philadelphia; Luna Parks in Johnstown and Scranton; and Wonderland in Milwaukee. See also "Duluth's New Summer Park," *Billboard*, 28 July 1906, 28; and "Riverview," *Billboard*, 1 December 1906, 28.

25. Hale and Gifford advertisement, *Billboard*, 17 February 1906, 19.

26. Ibid.

27. Fielding, "Hale's Tours," 123.

28. While the gentleman could simply be the owner of the establishment, his posture and position make it seem more likely that he functions as the lecturer; untitled photograph, EXEBD 61544, Bill Douglass Collection, Bill Douglass Centre, University of Exeter, Exeter, England.

29. See, for example, the following display advertisements: "Hale Tour Films, Selig Polyscope 'Latest Films,'" *Views and Films Index*, 20 April 1907, 5; "Hale Tour Runs," *Biograph Bulletin*, no. 73, 30 June 1906, repr. in *Biograph Bulletins, 1896–1908*, ed. Kemp R. Niver (Los Angeles: Artisan Press, 1971), 250–252.

30. For a longer discussion of phantom rides see Christian Hayes, "Phantom Rides," *BFI Screen Online: The Definitive Guide to Britain's Film and TV History*, 2008, www.screenonline.org.uk/film/id/1193042/ (accessed 8 September 2011).

31. "Hale Tour Runs," *Biograph Bulletin*, no. 73, 30 June 1906, 250. In addition a generally overlooked element is that the American Mutoscope Company, later renamed American Mutoscope and Biograph, was principally financed by New York railroad companies. See Paul Spehr, "Politics, Steam and Scopes: Marketing the Biograph," in *Networks of Entertainment: Early Film Distribution, 1895–1915*, ed. Frank Kessler and Nanna Verhoeff (Eastleigh, UK: John Libbey, 2007), 147–156.

32. *Billboard*, 3 February 1906, 20.

33. The sales figure is from Fielding, "Hale's Tours," 128.

34. Christian Hayes, "Phantom Carriages: Reconstructing Hale's Tours and the Virtual Travel Experience," unpublished essay, 2008.

35. Kristin Thompson, *Exporting Entertainment: America in the World Film Market, 1907–1934* (London: British Film Institute, 1985), 30–31.

36. These films are all available at the British Film Institute National Archive, London.

37. Hale's Tours of the World Postcard, Bill Douglass Collection, Bill Douglass Centre, University of Exeter.

38. *The Official Gazette of the United States Patent Office* 126 (Washington, D.C.: U.S. Government Publications, January-February 1907): 3292.

39. *Hale's Tours* advertisement, *Billboard*, 18 May 1907, 29.

40. *Official Gazette of the United States Patent Office* 126: 3292.

41. Trolley Car Tours advertisement, *Billboard*, 26 March 1906, 39.

42. *Billboard*, 27 January 1906, 23.

43. Ibid.

44. Patent no. 874,169, *The Official Gazette of the United States Patent Office* 131: 1846.

45. *White & Langever's Steamboat Tours of the World* advertisement, *Billboard*, 22 September 1906, 44. See also patent no. 828,791, *The Official Gazette of the United States Patent Office* 121 (Washington, D.C.: U.S. Government Publications, July-August 1906): 2246–2247.

46. *Hruby & Plummer's Tours and Scenes of the World* advertisement, *Billboard*, 3 March 1906, 25.

47. Patent no. 838,137, *The Official Gazette of the United States Patent Office* 126 (December 1906): 1832–1833.

48. *A Trip to California* advertisement, *Billboard*, 31 March 1906, 31; and 26 May 1906, 31.

49. E. C. Thomas, "Vancouver, B.C. Started with 'Hale's Tours,'" *Moving Picture World*, 15 July 1916, 373.

50. Noël Burch, *Life to Those Shadows*, trans. Ben Brewster (Berkeley: University of California Press, 1990), 39.

51. Thomas, "Vancouver, B.C. Started With 'Hale's Tours,'" 373.

52. Lynne Kirby, *Parallel Tracks: The Railroad and Silent Cinema* (Durham, NC: Duke University Press, 1997), 57.

53. Whissel, *Picturing American Modernity*, 124–127.

54. Fielding, "Hale's Tours," 123.

55. Barbara Maria Stafford, *Good Looking: Essays on the Virtue of Images* (Cambridge, MA: MIT Press, 1997), 212.

56. "Dreamland and the Beautiful Is Pearl of Coney Island," *Billboard*, 9 June 1906, 6.

57. Edison Manufacturing Company advertisement, *New York Clipper*, 28 April 1906.

58. Fielding, "Hale's Tours," 128.

59. Adolph Zukor, quoted in ibid.

60. Like *The Great Train Robbery* (1903), *The Hold-Up of the Rocky Mountain Express* was likely an adaptation of a popular stage melodrama. A stage play of the same name by George Klimt and Frank Gazzolo circulated in the first decade of the century, and, even if this film was a loose reworking of the play, it capitalized on the play's popularity to garner audiences.

61. For further discussion of "how the real world could be pressed into service as a site for the fictional" in phantom train films in the period of 1903 to 1906 immediately preceding *Hale's Tours*, see Charles Musser, "The Travel Genre in 1903–1904," *Iris* 2 (1984): 47–59, repr. in *Early Cinema: Space, Frame, Narrative*, ed. Thomas Elsaesser (London: British Film Institute, 1990), 123–132; Charlie Keil, "Steel Engines and Cardboard Rockets: The Status of Fiction and Nonfiction in Early Cinema," in *F is for Phony: Fake Documentary and Truth's Undoing*, ed. Alexandra Juhasz and Jesse Lerner (Minneapolis: University of Minnesota Press, 2006), 39–49.

62. My gratitude to the anonymous manuscript reviewer who pointed out that the two earlier, quite popular, Méliès films featured the same trick.

63. In his discussion of *The Great Train Robbery*, Charles Musser speculates that sound effects

may have been used during those portions of the story that depart from the viewer-as-passenger point of view, such as the bang of a revolver being fired in the holdup films or musical effects. In addition, even when he is discussing the visual dynamics of the film's landmark concluding close-up, he notes that it heightened realism because realism itself was associated not with greater pictorial naturalism but with increased identification and emotional involvement in the drama. See Charles Musser, *Before the Nickelodeon: Edwin S. Porter and the Edison Manufacturing Company* (Berkeley: University of California Press, 1991), 265.

4. The Miniature and the Giant: Postcards and Early Cinema

1. The bibliography on the interrelationships among cinema and other arts is extensive. See, for example: Rick Altman, *Silent Film Sound* (New York: Columbia University Press, 2005) on the relationships between early cinema and magic lantern shows. On cinema's relationships to commercial panoramas see Angela Miller, "The Panorama, the Cinema, and the Emergence of the Spectacular," *Wide Angle* 18, no. 2 (April 1996): 34–69; William Uricchio, "Panoramic Visions: Stasis, Movement, and the Redefinition of the Panorama," in *The Birth of Film Genres*, ed. Leonardo Quaresima, Alessandra Raengo, and Laura Vichi (Udine, Italy: University of Udine, 1999), 125–133; Alison Griffiths, *Shivers Down Your Spine: Cinema, Museums, and the Immersive View* (New York: Columbia University Press, 2008). For the relationships between early cinema and contemporary painting see Nancy Mowll Mathews, ed., *Moving Pictures: American Art and Early Film, 1880–1910* (New York: Hudson Hills Press, 2005). See Alison Griffiths, *Wondrous Difference: Cinema, Anthropology, and Turn-of-the-Century Culture* (New York: Columbia University Press, 2002) on the relationships between early cinema and living displays at museums and world's fairs. On the relationships between theater and cinema see David Mayer, *Stagestruck Filmmaker: D. W. Griffith and the American Theatre* (Iowa City: University of Iowa Press, 2009); William Uricchio and Roberta E. Pearson, *Reframing Culture: The Case of the Vitagraph Quality Films* (Princeton, NJ: Princeton University Press, 1993); and Linda Williams, *Playing the Race Card: Melodramas of Black and White from Uncle Tom to O. J. Simpson* (Princeton, NJ: Princeton University Press, 2002).

2. Elizabeth Edwards and Janice Hart, eds., *Photographs, Objects, Histories: On the Materiality of Images* (New York: Routledge, 2004), 1.

3. See Jonathan Crary, *Techniques of the Observer: On Vision and Modernity in the Nineteenth Century* (Cambridge, MA: MIT Press, 1992); and Jonathan Crary, *Suspensions of Perception: Attention, Spectacle, and Modern Culture* (Cambridge, MA: MIT Press, 2001).

4. David Prochaska and Jordana Mendelson, introduction to *Postcards: Ephemeral Histories of Modernity* (University Park: Pennsylvania State University Press, 2010), 2.

5. Susan Stewart, *On Longing: Narratives of the Miniature, the Gigantic, the Souvenir, the Collection* (Durham, NC: Duke University Press, 1993), 137–138.

6. Edwards and Hart, *Photographs, Objects, Histories*, 3.

7. Tom Gunning, "An Aesthetic of Astonishment: Early Film and the (In)Credulous Spectator," in *Viewing Positions: Ways of Seeing Film*, ed. Linda Williams (New Brunswick, NJ: Rutgers

University Press, 1994), 129.

8. Although there were earlier cards bearing a message or advertisement and sent through the mail, commercially printed souvenir cards of appealing views began only in 1893.

9. All postcard quotations are from actual postmarked cards in my personal collection.

10. This move initiated what is today known as the "divided back era" of postcards, the period between 1907 and 1915. Cards in circulation prior to 1907 had "undivided backs." In 1915, postcard companies began to frame the pictorial image with white margins, thus marking what is known as the "white border" period. Then, in 1930, postcard companies changed their paper stock to one with a higher rag content that gave the impression of being linen or some type of cloth. Cards of this type, produced primarily until World War II, are known as postcards from "the linen era." These material features are the predominant means for dating both postmarked and unpostmarked postcards. Since a postcard view might be sold for several years, such material properties are the best approximate indications of when a postcard was produced. Throughout this book, illustrations of postcards rely on dates either of actual postmarks (when the card was mailed) or of the dating system just explained.

11. Steven Dotterer and Galen Cranz, "The Picture Postcard: Its Role and Development in American Urbanization," *Journal of American Culture* 5, no. 1 (1982): 44.

12. Ibid.

13. *Dry Goods Reporter*, quoted in George and Dorothy Miller, *Picture Postcards in the United States, 1893–1918* (New York: Clarkson N. Potter, 1976), 22.

14. John Walker Harrington, "Postal Carditis and Some Allied Manias," *American Magazine*, March 1906, 562.

15. "The Pernicious Picture Postcard," *Atlantic*, August 1906, 287–288.

16. Naomi Schor, "*Cartes Postales*: Representing Paris 1900," *Critical Inquiry* 18 (winter 1992): 211.

17. Ibid.; see also Samuel D. Price, "What to Do with Your Post Cards," *Ladies' Home Journal*, March 1913, 98.

18. Ellen Garvey, *The Adman in the Parlor: Magazines and the Gendering of Consumer Culture, 1880s to 1910s* (New York: Oxford University Press, 1996), 26.

19. Ibid., 28, 43.

20. Walker Percy, "The Loss of the Creature," in *Message in the Bottle: How Queer Man Is, How Queer Language Is, and What One Has to Do with the Other* (New York: Farrar, Straus and Giroux, 1975), 45–63.

21. Postcards and movies of amusement parks represent only a small fraction of the subjects available in both media. But they mattered as subjects from the outset of each medium. See, for example, *Shooting the Chutes* (Edison, 1896); *Shooting the Chutes* (American Mutoscope and Biograph, 1897); and *Aerial Slide at Coney Island* (American Mutoscope and Biograph, 1897).

22. Leo Marx, *The Machine in the Garden: Technology and the Pastoral Ideal in America* (New York: Oxford University Press, 1964).

23. See, e.g., *Shoot the Chutes Series* (Edison, 1899); *Shooting the Chutes* (American Mutoscope and Biograph, 1902) at a Boston park; *Shooting the Chutes, Luna Park* (American Mutoscope and Biograph, 1903); *Shooting the Chutes at Luna Park, Coney Island* (American Mutoscope and Biograph, 1903); and *Racing Chutes at Dreamland* (American Mutoscope and Biograph,

1904).

24. Examples of these films include *Around the Flip-Flap Railroad* (American Mutoscope and Biograph, 1900), *Merry-Go-Round* (Edison, 1898), *Baby Merry-Go-Round* (American Mutoscope and Biograph, 1897), *Razzle Dazzle* (Edison, 1903), and *Steeplechase, Coney Island* (American Mutoscope and Biograph, 1897).

25. Commercially made individual portraits of parkgoers were rare despite the popularity of portrait postcards. Portrait postcards were heir to popular cabinet cards, photographs mounted on small rectangular cards that since the 1880s had been a commercial staple for memorializing individual and family portraits, as well for distributing likenesses of popular celebrities. Perhaps because many amusement parks sported photographers' studios where park patrons could themselves pose for and purchase their own likenesses on postcards or cabinet cards, amusement parks actually sold few views of individual "generic" models posed at park attractions. When they did, postcards either featured individuals directly facing the camera in casual, relaxed, informal poses or paired in male-female romantic courtship and often with humorous captions that lightheartedly presumed amusement park space as a setting for modern courtships.

26. John Kasson, *Amusing the Million: Coney Island at the Turn of the Century* (New York: Hill and Wang, 1978), 45–49.

27. Interestingly enough, when Walter Benjamin commented briefly on the amusement park in his notebooks, he saw the parks chiefly as extensions of expositions for the ways they made participation in the masses a distraction of pure reactions, a condition or subjective state he believed made these masses prey to industrial as well as political propaganda. Was Benjamin relying on memories of his own experiences or on photographs, most notably picture postcards? Certainly, the latter category heralded the crowd as a joyful, celebratory experience. See Walter Benjamin, *The Arcades Project*, trans. Howard Eiland and Kevin McLaughlin (Cambridge, MA: Harvard University Press, 1999), 18.

28. See my argument regarding this, as set in a gendered relay of looking relations, in *For the Love of Pleasure: Women, Movies, and Culture in Turn-of-the-Century Chicago* (New Brunswick, NJ: Rutgers University Press, 1998), 30–36.

29. In his Edison phonograph cylinder *Uncle Josh's Trip to Coney Island* (1896), Uncle Josh arrives at Coney Island by streetcar. In fact, he makes much of the trip since the joke was on him when he was financially duped by the streetcar conductor. What he records of the rest of his trip is his visit to *Streets of Cairo* and watching the dancing girls.

30. Charles Musser, *The Emergence of Cinema: The American Screen to 1907* (Berkeley: University of California Press, 1990), 350.

31. Jonathan Auerbach, *Body Shots: Early Cinema's Incarnations* (Berkeley: University of California Press, 2007), 60–61.

32. Ibid.

33. Charles Musser says the shot was removed after the first prints were made perhaps because "the playfulness appears too dangerous and bad for the school's image" (Charles Musser, *Before the Nickelodeon: Edwin S. Porter and the Edison Manufacturing Company* [Berkeley: University of California Press, 1991], 321).

34. In another version of this film, now available commercially in digital format, Miss Knapp gets tricked and thrown into the ocean early in the film before the girls ride the amusement

park rides. The film then moves through the mechanical ride sequences and "ends" midshot with the girls riding a swing. This odd, illogical order leaves the impression that the film is "incomplete," a fact noted by the British Film Institute online database, whose film summary matches this version (http://ftvdb.bfi.org.uk/sift/title/28535?view=synopsis). This version is only eight minutes long, shorter than either the LOC or MOMA versions.

35. Kristen Whissel, *Picturing American Modernity: Traffic, Technology, and the Silent Cinema* (Durham, NC: Duke University Press, 2008), 120.

36. Other films shot by Porter include *Circular Panorama of the Base of the Electric Tower Ending Looking Down the Mall, Circular Panorama of the Electric Tower, Circular Panorama of the Esplanade and Forecourt, Circular Panorama of the Esplanade with the Electric Tower in the Background, Circular Panorama of the Electric Tower and Pond, Circular Panorama of the Midway, Panoramic View of an Electric Tower from a Balloon,* and *Panoramic View of the Temple of Music and Esplanade.*

37. Whissel, *Picturing American Modernity*, 138.

38. David E. Nye, *Narratives and Spaces: Technology and the Construction of American Culture* (New York: Columbia University Press, 1997), 122.

39. Ibid., 124.

40. See Whissel, *Picturing American Modernity*, 117–159; Tom Gunning, "The World as Object Lesson: Cinema Audiences, Visual Culture, and the St. Louis World's Fair, 1904," *Film History* 6 (1994): 422–444; and Lucy Fischer, "'The Shock of the New': Electrification, Illumination, Urbanization, and the Cinema," in *Cinema and Modernity*, ed. Murray Pomerance (New Brunswick, NJ: Rutgers University Press, 2006), 19–37.

41. Fischer, "'The Shock of the New,'" 23.

5. Coney Island Comedies: Slapstick at the Amusement Park and the Movies

1. Donald Crafton, "Pie and Chase: Gag, Spectacle and Narrative in Slapstick Comedy," in *Classical Hollywood Comedy*, ed. Kristine Brunovska Karnick and Henry Jenkins (New York: Routledge, 1995), 108.

2. Tom Gunning, "Crazy Machines in the Garden of Forking Paths: Mischief Gags and the Origins of American Film Comedy," in *Classical Hollywood Comedy*, ed. Kristine Brunovska Karnick and Henry Jenkins (New York: Routledge, 1995), 99.

3. Rob King, *The Fun Factory: The Keystone Film Company and the Emergence of Mass Culture* (Berkeley: University of California Press, 2008), 180–209, 181.

4. John F. Kasson, *Amusing the Million: Coney Island at the Turn of the Century* (New York: Hill and Wang, 1978), 82.

5. King, *The Fun Factory*, 193.

6. Ibid., 196.

7. Jennifer Bean, "Early Cinema and the Philosophies of Laughter, or, Marie Dressler's Feature-Length Female Body," unpublished paper presented at "Women & the Silent Screen," Santa Cruz, California, 2 November 2001, 1. While it is not my project to lay out concepts of humor, the joke, or even the cognitive and psychological reasons that people laugh, it is necessary to note in passing that the laughing spectator is one fully conscious of the bodily plea-

sures of the cinematic experience (pleasures also available in such "bodily oriented genres" as pornography, action adventure, horror, and melodrama). For further discussion of bodily oriented genres see Linda Williams, "Film Bodies: Gender, Genre, Excess," in *Film Theory and Criticism*, ed. Leo Braudy and Marshall Cohen, 7th ed. (New York: Oxford University Press, 2009), 649–657.

8.   King, *The Fun Factory*, 198.

9.   "Fatty Arbuckle," Paramount Pictures Corporation advertisement, *Moving Picture World*, 7 April 1917, 31; "*Jack Fat and Jim Slim at Coney Island*," *Moving Picture World*, 17 December 1910, 1428; "*The Cook*," *Moving Picture World*, 14 September 1918, 1609; "*Cohen at Coney Island*," *Moving Picture World*, 9 October 1909, 489.

10. "*Jack Fat and Jim Slim at Coney Island*," *Moving Picture World*, 1 December 1910, 1416.

11. Francesco Casetti, *Inside the Gaze: The Fiction Film and Its Spectator*, trans. Nell Andrew and Charles O'Brien (Bloomington: Indiana University Press, 1998), 8–9.

12. See Crafton, "Pie and Chase"; Gunning, "Crazy Machines in the Gardens of Forking Paths"; and Charlie Keil, *Early American Cinema in Transition: Story, Style, and Filmmaking, 1907–1913* (Madison: University of Wisconsin Press, 2001), 47–49, 86–87.

13. "*Jack Fat and Jim Slim at Coney Island*," *Moving Picture World*, 17 December 1910, 1428.

14. Ibid.

15. Ibid.

16. Jonathan Auerbach, *Body Shots: Early Cinema's Incarnations* (Berkeley: University of California Press, 2007), 93.

17. Tony Bennett, "A Thousand and One Troubles: Blackpool Pleasure Beach," in *Formations of Pleasure*, ed. Tony Bennett et al. (London: Routledge, 1983), 147–148.

18. Gunning, "Crazy Machines in the Garden of Forking Paths," 99.

19. Bean, "Early Cinema and the Philosophies of Laughter," 4. Dressler's initial run as "Tillie" was in the stage comedy *Tillie's Nightmare* (1910), where she became famous for her "virtuoso grotesqueries" that were the focal point of the show and flouted conventions of feminine appearance and deportment. See King, *The Fun Factory*, 119–120. (Coincidentally, Marie Dressler worked for a short time selling hot dogs at Coney Island in the 1890s.)

20. Bean, "Early Cinema and the Philosophies of Laughter," 4.

21. For a discussion of this alternation in *Tillie's Punctured Romance* see King, *The Fun Factory*, 124–127.

22. Quoted in Victoria Sturtevant, *A Great Big Girl like Me: The Films of Marie Dressler* (Champaign: University of Illinois Press, 2009), 25.

23. Ibid.

24. King, *The Fun Factory*, 133.

25. Lucy Fischer, "'The Shock of the New': Electrification, Illumination, Urbanization, and the Cinema," in *Cinema and Modernity*, ed. Murray Pomerance (New Brunswick, NJ: Rutgers University Press, 2006), 25.

26. Fischer cites Buster Keaton's 1922 *The Electric House* (First National Pictures) as one such instance; ibid.

27. Ibid., 28.

28. Ibid.

29. Ibid., 34.

6. Conclusion: The Fusion of Movies and Amusement Parks

1. In 1955 there were thirty-nine million TV sets in the United States, which approximated 65 percent of all American households. Today, only the Super Bowl draws more than ninety million viewers in a country with more than 285 million television sets. By all counts the opening of Disneyland drew a viewing audience that is still a record.

2. For a discussion of the interrelationships among commercial air travel, airports, automobiles, and Disney parks see Michael Sorkin, "See You in Disneyland," in *Variations on a Theme Park: The New American City and the End of Public Space*, ed. Michael Sorkin (New York: Hill and Wang, 1992), 205–232.

3. Disney critics regularly comment on the cleanliness and efficiency of the parks, made even more so by the "invisibility" of the labor that services the parks because of a vast underground system of rooms, mechanical systems, tunnels, staging areas, and elevators that allow workers to move around largely unseen by the park customers. See, for example, Paul J. C. Friedlander, "Disney World Goes Underground," *New York Times*, 28 March 1971, sec. X, 37; David M. Johnson, "Disney World as Structure and Symbol: Re-Creation of the American Experience," *Journal of Popular Culture* 15 (summer 1981): 158–159; The Project on Disney, "Working at the Rat," *Inside the Mouse: Work and Play at Disney World* (Durham, NC: Duke University Press, 1995), 110–162.

4. The literature on Walt Disney, his company, and the development of Disney amusement parks as "themed" parks is voluminous. For an overview see Steven Watts, *The Magic Kingdom: Walt Disney and the American Way of Life* (Columbia: University of Missouri Press, 2001); for discussion of the design and development of Disney parks see Karal Ann Marling, ed., *Designing Disney's Theme Parks: The Architecture of Reassurance* (Flammarion: Paris, 1997). Disney critics unanimously agree that Disneyland's influence on the postwar park is that it made amusement parks "clean, wholesome, attractive, safe and family-oriented" (Hugo John Hildebrandt, "Cedar Point: A Park in Progress," *Journal of Popular Culture* 15 [summer 1981]: 98).

5. "Dateline Disneyland," *Walt Disney Treasures—Disneyland USA (1955)* [DVD] (Los Angeles: Walt Disney Video, 2001). All references to the live broadcast of "Dateline Disneyland" are from the 1955 broadcast available on this DVD.

6. The television show changed its name to *Walt Disney Presents* in 1958. In 1960 the show was retitled *Walt Disney's Wonderful World of Color*, and in 1969 it became *The Wonderful World of Disney*. For an excellent history of the television show see: J. P. Telotte, *Disney TV* (Detroit: Wayne State University Press, 2004).

7. Disney had been producing "True Life Adventure" live-action, nature documentaries since 1948, as an effort to diversify into the education market. He debuted a five-episode series of Davy Crockett shows on his TV show, beginning on 15 December 1954.

8. For a more detailed discussion on this phenomenon see my essay "More Than the Movies, a History of Somatic Culture Through *Hale's Tours*, IMAX, and Motion Simulation Rides," in *Memory Bytes: History, Technology, and Digital Culture*, ed. Lauren Rabinovitz and Abraham Geil (Durham, NC: Duke University Press, 2004), 99–125, esp. 116–121.

9. Erika Doss, "Making Imagination Safe in the 1950s: Disneyland's Fantasy Art and Architecture," in *Designing Disney's Theme Parks: The Architecture of Reassurance*, ed. Karal Ann Marling (Flammarion: Paris, 1997), 181.

10. Neil Gabler, *Walt Disney: The Triumph of the American Imagination* (New York: Knopf, 2006), 92, 484.

11. Watts, *The Magic Kingdom*, 414–418.

12. Hildebrandt, "Cedar Point," 99.

13. An interesting discussion of the cultural significance of Disneyland and Marriott's Great America for late twentieth-century American culture occurs in Elizabeth Walker Mechling and Jay Mechling, "The Sale of Two Cities: A Semiotic Comparison of Disneyland with Marriott's Great America," *Journal of Popular Culture* 15 (summer 1981): 168–179. This essay stands in stark contrast to Russel B. Nye's assertion in the same volume that the new theme parks represent continuity with the past: Russel B. Nye, "Eight Ways of Looking at an Amusement Park," *Journal of Popular Culture* 15 (summer 1981): 63–75.

14. For an interesting comparison between Coney Island and Las Vegas that considers the kinship between the two—especially as racialized spaces—see Sharon Zukin et al., "From Coney Island to Las Vegas in the Urban Imaginary: Discursive Practices of Growth and Decline," *Urban Affairs Review* 33 (May 1998): 627–654.

15. William L. Fox, *In the Desert of Desire: Las Vegas and the Culture of Spectacle* (Las Vegas: University of Nevada Press, 2005), 49.

16. Ibid., 97.

17. Ibid., 23, xii.

18. Mechling and Mechling, "The Sale of Two Cities," 176.

FILMS CITED

The Adventures of Ichabod and Mr. Toad (Walt Disney, 1949)
Aerial Slide at Coney Island (American Mutoscope and Biograph, 1897)
Alice in Wonderland (Walt Disney, 1951)
Annual Parade, New York Fire Department (Edison, 1904)
Arab Act, Luna Park (American Mutoscope and Biograph, 1903)
Around the Flip-Flap Railroad (American Mutoscope and Biograph, 1900)
Arrival at Falls View Station (American Mutoscope and Biograph, 1901)
Ascent and Descent of the Dolomite Towers (Charles Urban, 1907)
At Coney Island (Keystone, dir. Mack Sennett, 1912)
Baby Merry-Go-Round (American Mutoscope, 1897)
Bamboo Slide (American Mutoscope and Biograph, 1903)
The Battle of Manila Bay (American Vitagraph, 1898)
Bird's Eye View of San Francisco, Cal., from a Balloon (Edison, 1902)
Boarding School Girls (Edison, 1905)
Buffalo Fire Department (American Mutoscope and Biograph, 1899)
Burning of Durland's Riding Academy (Edison, 1902)
The Burning Stable (Edison, 1896)
Circular Panorama of the Base of the Electric Tower Ending Looking Down the Mall (Edison, 1901)
Circular Panorama of the Electric Tower (Edison, 1901)
Circular Panorama of the Electric Tower and Pond (Edison, 1901)
Circular Panorama of the Esplanade and Forecourt (Edison, 1901)
Circular Panorama of the Esplanade with the Electric Tower in the Background (Edison, 1901)
Circular Panorama of the Midway (Edison, 1901)
Cohen at Coney Island (American Vitagraph, 1909)
Cohen's Dream of Coney Island (Vitagraph, 1909)
Coney Island (Comique, dir. Fatty Arbuckle, 1917); a.k.a. *Fatty at Coney Island*
Coney Island at Night (Edison, 1905)

The Cook (Comique, dir. Fatty Arbuckle, 1918)

The Crowd (MGM, dir. King Vidor, 1928)

The Deadwood Sleeper (American Mutoscope and Biograph, 1905)

Double Ring Act, Luna Park (American Mutoscope and Biograph, 1903)

Dream of a Rarebit Fiend (Edison, 1906)

Fighting the Fire (Edison, 1896)

Fighting the Flames, Dreamland (American Mutoscope and Biograph, 1904)

Fire and Flames at Luna Park, Coney Island (Edison, 1904)

Fire Rescue Scene (Edison, 1894)

Firemen Rescuing Men and Women (Edison, 1900)

Frazer Canyon (American Mutoscope and Biograph, 1899)

The Gap, Entrance to the Rocky Mountains (American Mutoscope and Biograph, 1899)

Gone to Coney Island (Thanhauser, 1910)

Grand Hotel to Big Indian (American Mutoscope and Biograph, 1906)

The Great Baltimore Fire (American Mutoscope and Biograph, 1904)

The Great Train Robbery (Edison, 1903)

Haverstraw Tunnel (American Mutoscope and Biograph, 1897)

Hold-Up of the Rocky Mountain Express (American Mutoscope and Biograph, 1906)

Into the Heart of the Catskills (American Mutoscope and Biograph, 1906)

It (Famous Players–Lasky, dir. Clarence G. Badger, 1927)

Jack Fat and Jim Slim at Coney Island (Vitagraph, 1910)

Life of an American Fireman (Edison, 1903)

Lonesome (Universal, dir. Pal Fejos, 1929)

Lower Rapids, Niagara (American Mutoscope and Biograph, 1896)

Mannequin (MGM, dir. Frank Borzage, 1937)

Merry-Go-Round (Edison, 1898)

A Morning Alarm (Edison, 1896)

New York Fire Department Returning (American Mutoscope and Biograph, 1903)

New York to Brooklyn via Brooklyn Bridge, No. 1 (Edison, 1899)

Number, Please? (Rolin Films, dir. Hal Roach and Fred Newmeyer, 1920)

104th Street Curve, New York, Elevated Railway (Edison, 1899)

Pan-American Exposition by Night (Edison, 1901)

Panorama of Esplanade by Night (Edison, 1901)

Panoramic View of Electric Tower from a Balloon (Edison 1901)

Panoramic View of the Temple of Music and Esplanade (Edison, 1901)

Peter Pan (Walt Disney, 1953)

Phantom Ride from Chamonix to Vallorcine (Éclair, 1910)

Princess Rajah Dance (American Mutoscope and Biograph, 1904)

Le Raid Paris-Monte Carlo en deux heures [*From Paris to Monte Carlo*] (Star Films, 1905)

Racing Chutes at Dreamland (American Mutoscope and Biograph, 1904)

Raising Old Glory over Morro Castle (Edison, 1899)

Razzle Dazzle (Edison 1903)

A Reckless Romeo (Comique, dir. Fatty Arbuckle, 1917)

Ride on the Gothard Railway (Warwick, 1910)

A Ride Through the Ardennes (Hepworth, 1906)

Rube and Mandy at Coney Island (Edison, 1903)

Shoot the Chutes Series (Edison, 1899)

Shooting the Chutes (Edison, 1896)

Shooting the Chutes (American Mutoscope and Biograph, 1897)

Shooting the Chutes, Luna Park (American Mutoscope and Biograph, 1903)

Snow White and the Seven Dwarfs (Walt Disney, 1937)

Soldiers at Play (Selig Polyscope, 1898)

Speedy (Harold Lloyd, dir. Ted Wilde, 1928)

Steamboat Willie (Walt Disney, 1928)

Steeplechase, Coney Island (American Mutoscope and Biograph, 1897)

Stella Dallas (Samuel Goldwyn, dir. King Vidor, 1937)

A Submarine Pirate (Triangle, 1915)

Sunrise (Fox, dir. F. W. Murnau, 1927)

Tillie Wakes Up (Peerless, 1917)

Tillie's Punctured Romance (Keystone, dir. Mack Sennett, 1914)

Tour of the West (Walt Disney, 1955)

A Trip Around the Pan American Exposition (Edison, 1901)

A Trip Down Mt. Tamalpais (Miles Brothers, 1906)

Trip in a Balloon (manufacturer and date unknown)

A Trip on the Catskill Mt. Railway (American Mutoscope and Biograph, 1906)

A Trip on the Metropolitan Railway from Baker St. to Uxbridge and Aylesbury (unknown mfg., 1910)

A Trip Through British Borneo (Charles Urban, 1907)

Trip Through the Black Hills (Selig Polyscope, 1907)

Turkish Dance, Ella Lola (Edison, 1898)
Ute Pass from a Freight Train (Selig Polyscope, 1906)
Voyage à travers l'impossible [*The Impossible Voyage*] (Star Films, 1904)
What Happened in the Tunnel (Edison, 1903)
When the Devil Drives (Charles Urban, 1907)

SELECTED BIBLIOGRAPHY

Abel, Richard. *Americanizing the Movies and "Movie-Mad" Audiences, 1910–1914*. Berkeley: University of California Press, 2006.

———. *The Red Rooster Scare: Making Cinema American*. Berkeley: University of California Press, 1999.

Adams, Judith. *The American Amusement Park Industry: A History of Technology and Thrills*. Boston: Twayne, 1991.

———. "The Promotion of New Technology Through Fun and Spectacle: Electricity at the World's Columbian Exposition." *Journal of American Culture* 18, no. 2 (1995): 45–55.

Addams, Jane. *The Spirit of Youth and City Streets*. New York: Macmillan, 1909.

Altman, Rick. "From Lecturer's Prop to Industrial Product: The Early History of Travel Films." In *Virtual Voyages: Cinema and Travel*, ed. Jeffrey Ruoff, 61–78. Durham, NC: Duke University Press, 2006).

———. *Silent Film Sound*. New York City: Columbia University Press, 2005.

Aronson, Michael. *Nickelodeon City: Pittsburgh at the Movies, 1905–1929*. Pittsburgh: University of Pittsburgh Press, 2008.

Auerbach, Jonathan. *Body Shots: Early Cinema's Incarnations*. Berkeley: University of California Press, 2007.

Barker, Stan. "Paradises Lost." *Chicago History* 22, no. 1 (March 1993): 26–49.

Bean, Jennifer M., and Diane Negra, eds. *A Feminist Reader in Early Cinema*. Durham, NC: Duke University Press, 2002.

Benjamin, Walter. *The Arcades Project*. Trans. Howard Eiland and Kevin McLaughlin. Cambridge, MA: Harvard University Press, 1999.

Bennett, Tony. "A Thousand and One Troubles: Blackpool Pleasure Beach." In *Formations of Pleasure*, ed. Tony Bennett et al., 138–155 London: Routledge, 1983.

Bowser, Eileen. *The Transformation of the Cinema, 1907–15*. Berkeley: University of California Press, 1994.

Burch, Noël. *Life to Those Shadows*. Trans. Ben Brewster. Berkeley: University of California Press, 1990.

Casetti, Francesco. *Inside the Gaze: The Fiction Film and Its Spectator*. Trans. Nell Andrew and Charles O'Brien. Bloomington: Indiana University Press, 1998.

Charney, Leo, and Vanessa R. Schwartz, eds. *Cinema and the Invention of Modern Life*. Berkeley: University of California Press, 1995.

Crary, Jonathan. *Suspensions of Perception: Attention, Spectacle, and Modern Culture*. Cambridge, MA: MIT Press, 2001.

———. *Techniques of the Observer: On Vision and Modernity in the Nineteenth Century*. Cambridge, MA: MIT Press, 1992.

Curry, Barton W. "The Nickel Madness." *Harper's Weekly*, 24 August 1907, 1246–1247.

Davis, Janet M. *The Circus Age: Culture and Society Under the American Big Top*. Chapel Hill: University of North Carolina Press, 2002.

DeBlasio, Donna. "The Immigrant and the Trolley Park in Youngstown, Ohio, 1899–1945." *Rethinking History* 5, no. 1 (2001): 75–91.

De Koven Bowen, Louise. *Safeguards for City Youth at Work and at Play*. New York: Macmillan, 1914.

Dotterrer, Steven, and Galen Cranz. "The Picture Postcard: Its Role and Development in American Urbanization," *Journal of American Culture* 5, no. 1 (1982): 44–50.

Edwards, Elizabeth, and Janice Hart, eds. *Photographs, Objects, Histories: On the Materiality of Images*. New York: Routledge, 2004.

Edwards, Richard Henry. *Christianity and Amusements*. New York: Association Press, 1915.

Fielding, Raymond. "Hale's Tours: Ultrarealism in the Pre-1910 Motion Picture." In *Before Griffith*, ed. John L. Fell, 116–130. Berkeley: University of California Press, 1983.

Fox, William L. *In the Desert of Desire: Las Vegas and the Culture of Spectacle*. Las Vegas: University of Nevada Press, 2005.

Fuller-Seeley, Kathryn, ed. *Hollywood in the Neighborhood: Historical Case Studies of Local Moviegoing*. Berkeley: University of California Press, 2008.

Garvey, Ellen. *The Adman in the Parlor: Magazines and the Gendering of Consumer Culture, 1880s to 1910s*. New York: Oxford University Press, 1996.

Gaudreault, André, ed. *American Cinema, 1890–1909: Themes and Variations*. New Brunswick, NJ: Rutgers University Press, 2009.

Gomery, Douglas. *Shared Pleasures: A History of Movie Presentation in the United States*. Madison: University of Wisconsin Press, 1992.

Grieveson, Lee. *Policing Cinema: Movies and Censorship in Early-Twentieth-Century America*. Berkeley: University of California Press, 2004.

Griffiths, Alison. *Shivers Down Your Spine: Cinema, Museums, and the Immersive View*. New York: Columbia University Press, 2008.

——. "'Shivers Down Your Spine': Panoramas and the Origins of the Cinematic Re-enactment." *Screen* 44 (spring 2003): 1–37.

——. *Wondrous Difference: Cinema, Anthropology, and Turn-of-the-Century Culture*. New York: Columbia University Press, 2002.

Gunning, Tom. "An Aesthetic of Astonishment: Early Film and the (In)Credulous Spectator." In *Viewing Positions: Ways of Seeing Film*, ed. Linda Williams, 114–133. New Brunswick, NJ: Rutgers University Press, 1994.

——. "The Cinema of Attraction: Early Film, Its Spectator, and the Avant-Garde." *Wide Angle* 8, nos. 3–4 (1986): 63–70. Repr. as "The Cinema of Attractions" in *Early Cinema: Space, Frame, Narrative*, ed. Thomas Elsaesser, 56–62. London: British Film Institute, 1990.

——. "The World as Object Lesson: Cinema Audiences, Visual Culture, and the St. Louis World's Fair, 1904." *Film History* 6 (1994): 422–444.

Hansen, Miriam. *Babel and Babylon: Spectatorship in American Silent Film*. Cambridge, MA: Harvard University Press, 1991.

Hansen, Miriam Bratu. "The Mass Production of the Senses: Classical Cinema as Vernacular Modernism." *Modernism/Modernity* 6, no. 2 (1999): 59–77.

Harrington, John Walker. "Postal Carditis and Some Allied Manias." *American Magazine*, March 1906.

Hartt, Rollin Lynde. "The Amusement Park," *Atlantic*, May 1907, 667–675.

——. *The People's Playground: Excursions in the Humor and Philosophy of Popular Amusements*. Boston: Houghton Mifflin, 1909.

Higginbotham, Mary C. "In Genuine Cowgirl Fashion: Nan Aspinwall Gable Lambell and the Image of the Cowgirl in Wild West Entertainment, 1880–1930." Master's thesis, University of Nebraska, 1996.

Hildebrandt, Hugo John. "Cedar Point: A Park in Progress." *Journal of Popular Culture* 15 (summer 1981): 87–107.

Huneker, James. *New Cosmopolis: A Book of Images. Intimate New York*. New York: Charles Scribner's Sons, 1915.

Hyde, Ralph. *Panoramania! The Art and Entertainment of the 'All-Embracing' View*. London: Trefoil, 1988.

Immerso, Michael. *Coney Island: The People's Playground*. New Brunswick, NJ: Rutgers University Press, 2002.

Israels, Belle Lindner. "The Way of the Girl." *Survey* 22 (3 July 1909): 486–497.

Kahrl, Andrew W. "The Slightest Semblance of Unruliness: Steamboat Excursions, Pleasure Resorts, and the Emergence of Segregation Culture on the Potomac River." *Journal of American History* 94, no. 4 (March 2008): 1108–1136.

Karnick, Kristine Brunovska, and Henry Jenkins, eds. *Classical Hollywood Comedy*. New York: Routledge, 1995.

Kasson, John F. *Amusing the Million: Coney Island at the Turn of the Century*. New York: Hill and Wang, 1978.

——. "Workers Seek Leisure Time and Space." *Major Problems in American Popular Culture*, ed. Kathleen Franz and Susan Smulyan, 137–143. New York: Wadsworth, 2011.

Kasson, Joy S. *Buffalo Bill's Wild West: Celebrity, Memory, and Popular History*. New York: Hill and Wang, 2001.

Keil, Charlie. *Early American Cinema in Transition: Story, Style, and Filmmaking, 1907–1913*. Madison: University of Wisconsin Press, 2001.

——. "Steel Engines and Cardboard Rockets: The Status of Fiction and Nonfiction in Early Cinema." In *F Is for Phony: Fake Documentary and Truth's Undoing*, ed. Alexandra Juhasz and Jesse Lerner, 39–49. Minneapolis: University of Minnesota Press, 2006.

Keil, Charlie, and Shelley Stamp, eds. *American Cinema's Transitional Era: Audiences, Institutions, Practices*. Berkeley: University of California Press, 2004.

Kessler, Frank, and Nanna Verhoeff, eds. *Networks of Entertainment: Early Film Distribution, 1895–1915*. Eastleigh, UK: John Libbey, 2007.

King, Rob. *The Fun Factory: The Keystone Film Company and the Emergence of Mass Culture*. Berkeley: University of California Press, 2008.

Kirby, Lynn. *Parallel Tracks: The Railroad and Silent Cinema*. Durham, NC: Duke University Press, 1997.

Koolhaas, Rem. *Delirious New York: A Retroactive Manifesto for Manhattan*. New York: Oxford University Press, 1978.

Malamud, Margaret. "The Greatest Show on Earth: Roman Entertainments in Turn-of-the-Century New York." *Journal of Popular Culture* 35, no. 3 (2001): 43–58.

Marling, Karal Ann, ed. *Designing Disney's Theme Parks: The Architecture of Reassurance*. Paris: Flammarion, 1997.

Marx, Leo. *The Machine in the Garden: Technology and the Pastoral Ideal in America*. New York: Oxford University Press, 1964.

Mathews, Nancy Mowll, ed. *Moving Pictures: American Art and Early Film, 1880–1910*. New York: Hudson Hills Press, 2005.

Mayer, David. "*The Last Days of Pompeii*: James Pain." In *Playing Out the Empire: "Ben Hur" and Other Toga Plays and Films, 1883–1908*, ed. David Mayer, 90–103. Oxford: Clarendon Press, 1994.

——. *Stagestruck Filmmaker: D. W. Griffith and the American Theatre*. Iowa City: University of Iowa Press, 2009.

McDermott, John. *The Lost Panoramas of the Mississippi*. Chicago: University of Chicago Press, 1958.

Merritt, Russell. "Nickelodeon Theaters, 1905–1914: Building an Audience for the Movies." In *The American Film Industry*, ed. Tino Balio, 83–102. Madison: University of Wisconsin Press, 1986.

Miller, Angela. "The Panorama, the Cinema, and the Emergence of the Spectacular." *Wide Angle* 18, no. 2 (April 1996): 34–69.

Miller, George, and Dorothy Miller. *Picture Postcards in the United States, 1893–1918*. New York: Clarkson N. Potter, 1976.

Musser, Charles. *Before the Nickelodeon: Edwin S. Porter and the Edison Manufacturing Company*. Berkeley: University of California Press, 1991.

——. *The Emergence of Cinema: The American Screen to 1907*. Berkeley: University of California Press, 1990.

——. "The Travel Genre in 1903–1904." *Iris* 2 (1984): 47–59. Repr. in *Early Cinema: Space, Frame, Narrative*, ed. Thomas Elsaesser, 123–132. London: British Film Institute: 1990.

Musser, Charles, and Carol S. Nelson. *High-Class Moving Pictures: Lyman H. Howe and the Forgotten Era of Traveling Exhibition, 1880–1920*. Princeton, NJ: Princeton University Press, 1991.

Nasaw, David. *Going Out: The Rise and Fall of Public Amusements*. Cambridge, MA: Harvard University Press, 1999.

Nye, David E. *Electrifying America: Social Meanings of a New Technology*. Cambridge, MA: MIT Press, 1990.

——. *Narratives and Spaces: Technology and the Construction of American Culture*. New York: Columbia University Press, 1997.

Oettermann, Stephan. *The Panorama: History of a Mass Medium*. Trans. Deborah Lucas Schneider. New York: Zone Books, 1997.

Peiss, Kathy. *Cheap Amusements: Working Women and Leisure in Turn-of-the-Century New York*. Philadelphia: Temple University Press, 1986.

Percy, Walker. "The Loss of the Creature." In *Message in the Bottle: How Queer Man Is, How Queer Language Is, and What One Has to Do with the Other*, 45–63. New York: Farrar, Straus and Giroux, 1975.

Pomerance, Murray, ed. *Cinema and Modernity*. New Brunswick, NJ: Rutgers University Press, 2006.

Price, Samuel D. "What to Do with Your Post Cards." *Ladies Home Journal*, March 1913.

Prochaska, David, and Jordana Mendelson, eds. *Postcards: Ephemeral Histories of Modernity*. University Park: Pennsylvania State University Press, 2010.

Rabinovitz, Lauren. *For the Love of Pleasure: Women, Movies, and Culture in Turn-of-the-Century Chicago*. New Brunswick, NJ: Rutgers University Press, 1998.

——. "More Than the Movies, a History of Somatic Culture Through *Hale's Tours*, IMAX, and Motion Simulation Rides." In *Memory Bytes: History, Technology, and Digital Culture*, ed. Lauren Rabinovitz and Abraham Geil, 99–125. Durham, NC: Duke University Press, 2004.

Ruoff, Jeffrey, ed. *Virtual Voyages: Cinema and Travel*. Durham, NC: Duke University Press, 2006.

Rydell, Robert W., and Rob Kroes. *Buffalo Bill in Bologna: The Americanization of the World, 1869–1922*. Chicago: University of Chicago Press, 2005.

Sally, Lynn Kathleen. *Fighting the Flames: The Spectacular Performance of Fire at Coney Island*. New York: Routledge, 2006.

Schivelbusch, Wolfgang. *The Railway Journey: The Industrialization of Time and Space in the 19th Century*. Trans. Anselm Hollo. New York: Urizen, 1977.

Schor, Naomi. "*Cartes Postales*: Representing Paris 1900." *Critical Inquiry* 18 (winter 1992): 188–244.

Singer, Ben. *Melodrama and Modernity: Early Sensational Cinema and Its Contexts*. New York: Columbia University Press, 2001.

Sorkin, Michael. "See You in Disneyland." In *Variations on a Theme Park: The New American City and the End of Public Space*, ed. Michael Sorkin, 205–232. New York: Hill and Wang, 1992.

Sotiropoulos, Karen. *Staging Race: Black Performers in Turn of the Century America*. Cambridge, MA: Harvard University Press, 2006.

Stafford, Barbara Maria. *Good Looking: Essays on the Virtue of Images*. Cambridge, MA: The MIT Press, 1997.

Stamp, Shelley. *Movie-Struck Girls: Women and Motion Picture Culture After the Nickelodeon*. Princeton, NJ: Princeton University Press, 2000.

Stewart, Susan. *On Longing: Narratives of the Miniature, the Gigantic, the Souvenir, the Collection*. Durham, NC: Duke University Press, 1993.

Strauven, Wanda, ed. *The Cinema of Attractions Reloaded*. Amsterdam: Amsterdam University Press, 2007.

Sturtevant, Victoria. *A Great Big Girl like Me: The Films of Marie Dressler*. Champaign: University of Illinois Press, 2009.

Thompson, Kristin. *Exporting Entertainment: America in the World Film Market, 1907–1934*. London: British Film Institute, 1985.

Thoulmin, Vanessa. *Electric Edwardians: The Films of Mitchell and Kenyon*. London: British Film Institute, 2008.

Tobing Rony, Fatimah. *The Third Eye: Race, Cinema, and Ethnographic Spectacle*. Durham, NC: Duke University Press, 1996.

Uricchio, William. "Panoramic Visions: Stasis, Movement, and the Redefinition of the Panorama." In *The Birth of Film Genres*, ed. Leonardo Quaresima, Alessandra Raengo, and Laura Vichi, 125–133. Udine, Italy: University of Udine, 1999.

Uricchio, William, and Roberta E. Pearson. *Reframing Culture: The Case of the Vitagraph Quality Films*. Princeton, NJ: Princeton University Press, 1993.

Waller, Gregory. *Main Street Amusements: Movies and Commercial Entertainment in a Southern City, 1896–1930*. Washington: Smithsonian Institution Press, 1995.

Watts, Steven. *The Magic Kingdom: Walt Disney and the American Way of Life*. Columbia: University of Missouri Press, 2001.

Whissel, Kristen. *Picturing American Modernity: Traffic, Technology, and the Silent Cinema*. Durham, NC: Duke University Press, 2008.

Williams, Linda. *Playing the Race Card: Melodramas of Black and White from Uncle Tom to O. J. Simpson*. Princeton, NJ: Princeton University Press, 2002.

Yablon, Nick. "'A Picture Painted in Fire': Pain's Reenactments of *The Last Days of Pompeii*, 1879–1914." In *Antiquity Recovered: The Legacy of Pompeii and Herculaneum*, ed. Victoria C. Gardner Coates and Jon L. Seydl, 189–206. Los Angeles: Getty Publications, 2006.

INDEX
· · · · · · · · ·

FILM AND CULTURE
∙∙∙∙∙∙∙∙∙∙∙∙∙∙∙∙∙∙∙∙∙∙∙∙∙∙∙

A SERIES OF COLUMBIA UNIVERSITY PRESS
EDITED BY JOHN BELTON

Shivers Down Your Spine: Cinema, Museums, and the Immersive View
    ALISON GRIFFITHS
Weimar Cinema: An Essential Guide to Classic Films of the Era
    NOAH ISENBERG
African Film and Literature: Adapting Violence to the Screen
    LINDIWE DOVEY
Film, A Sound Art
    MICHEL CHION
Film Studies: An Introduction
    ED SIKOV
Hollywood Lighting from the Silent Era to Film Noir
    PATRICK KEATING
Levinas and the Cinema of Redemption: Time, Ethics, and the Feminine
    SAM B. GIRGUS
Counter-Archive: Film, the Everyday, and Albert Kahn's Archives de la Planète
    PAULA AMAD
Indie: An American Film Culture
    MICHAEL Z. NEWMAN
Pretty: Film and the Decorative Image
    ROSALIND GALT
Film and Stereotype: A Challenge for Cinema and Theory
    JÖRG SCHWEINITZ
Chinese Women's Cinema: Transnational Contexts
    EDITED BY LINGZHEN WANG
Hideous Progeny: Disability, Eugenics, and Classic Horror Cinema
    ANGELA M. SMITH
Hollywood's Copyright Wars: From Edison to the Internet
    PETER DECHERNEY